THE COUNTERREVOLUTION

THE COUNTERREVOLUTION

How Our Government Went to War
Against Its Own Citizens

Bernard E. Harcourt

BASIC BOOKS
New York

Basic Books
Hachette Book Group
1290 Avenue of the Americas, New York, NY 10104
www.basicbooks.com

Printed in the United States of America
First Edition: February 2018

Published by Basic Books, an imprint of Perseus Books, LLC, a subsidiary of Hachette Book Group, Inc. The Basic Books name and logo is a trademark of the Hachette Book Group.

The publisher is not responsible for websites (or their content) that are not owned by the publisher.

Print book interior design by Timm Bryson, em em design, LLC.

Library of Congress Cataloging-in-Publication Data
Names: Harcourt, Bernard E., 1963- author.
Title: The counterrevolution : how our government went to war against its
    own citizens / Bernard E. Harcourt.
Description: New York : Basic Books, [2018] | Includes bibliographical
    references and index.
Identifiers: LCCN 2017038849 (print) | LCCN 2017054652 (ebook) | ISBN
    9781541697270 (ebook) | ISBN 9781541697287 (hardcover)
Subjects: LCSH: Electronic surveillance—United States. | Counter-
    insurgency—United States. | Civil-military relations—United States.
Classification: LCC TK7882.E2 (ebook) | LCC TK7882.E2 .H365 2018
    (print) | DDC 323.44/820973—dc23
LC record available at https://lccn.loc.gov/2017038849

ISBNs: 978-1-5416-9728-7 (hardcover), 978-1-5416-9727-0 (ebook)
LSC-C

10 9 8 7 6 5 4 3 2 1

"Subjects should be warned not to be subjugated more than is strictly necessary."

—William of Ockham,
A Short Discourse on Tyrannical Government
(circa 1340)

In memory of Sheldon S. Wolin

CONTENTS

PART IV
From Counterinsurgency to The Counterrevolution

THE BIRTH OF THE COUNTERREVOLUTION

O N December 9, 2014, California senator Dianne Fein-
stein made public a 547-page report by the Senate Select Committee on Intelligence documenting the widespread use of torture by the
United States after 9/11. The Senate report revealed far more intensive
applications of torture than had previously been known. One prisoner
was waterboarded "at least 183 times." At one point, within less than 24
hours, he was subjected to "more than 65 applications of water" during
4 waterboarding sessions.[1]

Another prisoner was subject to torture for almost 20 straight days
"on a near 24-hour-per-day basis." During the period, he was waterboarded 2 to 4 times a day "with multiple iterations of the watering
cycle during each application." During one waterboarding session,
the prisoner became "completely unresponsive, with bubbles rising
through his open, full mouth," and "remained unresponsive until medical intervention, when he regained consciousness and expelled 'copi-
ous amounts of liquid.'" During the same period, that prisoner was
also subjected "in varying combinations, 24 hours a day" to "walling,

attention grasps, slapping, facial hold, stress positions, cramped confinement, white noise, and sleep deprivation." When he was left alone, it was either in a stress position, on the waterboard, or locked in coffin-size boxes. In fact, during the period, he "spent a total of 266 hours (11 days, 2 hours) in the large (coffin-size) confinement box and 29 hours in a small confinement box, which had a width of 21 inches, a depth of 2.5 feet, and a height of 2.5 feet." His interrogators told him that "the only way he would leave the facility was in the coffin-shaped confinement box."[2]

In addition to exposing the scope of these known torture techniques, the Senate report also revealed the previously undisclosed use of mock executions, ice-water baths, "rectal rehydration" (defined as "rectal feeding without documented medical necessity"), and "threats to harm the children of a detainee, threats to sexually abuse the mother of a detainee, and a threat to 'cut [a detainee's] mother's throat.'" The Senate report uncovered the true nature of seemingly restrained techniques. The use of sleep deprivation, for instance, involved "keeping detainees awake for up to 180 hours, usually standing or in stress positions, at times with their hands shackled above their heads." The report documented at least one fatality: "A detainee who had been held partially nude and chained to a concrete floor died from suspected hypothermia at the facility." (The late journalist Anthony Lewis documented another death, according to an autopsy report, by "asphyxia due to smothering and chest compression.") The report also revealed orchestrated efforts to cover up the extent of the torture, making full documentation impossible. In one case, for instance, a review of the catalogue of videotapes "found that recordings of a 21-hour period [of interrogation], which included two waterboarding sessions, were missing."[3] Still today, the full extent of the use of torture by American personnel is unknown.

Only a few hours before the release of the Senate torture report, the Bureau of Investigative Journalism reported that the United States had launched a Predator drone strike in the Shabwa province of Yemen.

Yemen was not then, and is not now, a conventional war zone for the United States, like Afghanistan or Iraq. Yet the US military operation involved, in addition to the drone strike, at least forty US Special Forces. The attack was apparently intended to rescue two hostages, but they were killed in the operation. In total, thirteen persons were killed— eight reported to be civilians, one a ten-year-old child. One villager told Reuters that five of his sons were killed. According to a local elder, "Some of the villagers were awakened by the explosions, they looked out of their windows, and the Americans shot them dead. [American and Yemeni soldiers] shot anyone who was close to the house that the hostages were in and raided at least four homes."[4]

The first armed drone reached Afghanistan on October 7, 2001, a few weeks after the World Trade Center attacks. Soon thereafter, President George W. Bush signed an executive order directing the creation of a secret list of "high-value targets"—known colloquially as the "kill list"—and authorized the CIA to kill anyone on the list without further instructions or presidential approval. Drone use proliferated greatly after President Barack Obama took office in January 2009. Between January 20, 2009, and December 31, 2015, the Obama administration reportedly launched 473 strikes *outside* areas of active hostility.[5] As of June 2017, the Bureau of Investigative Journalism had documented the accidental drone deaths of between 739 and 1,407 civilians, of which 240 to 308 were children, in Pakistan (since 2004), Afghanistan (since 2015), Yemen (since 2002), and Somalia (since 2007).[6] As the philosopher Grégoire Chamayou wrote at the time, the drone became "one of the emblems of Barack Obama's presidency, the instrument of his official antiterrorist doctrine, 'kill rather than capture': replace torture and Guantánamo with targeted assassination and the Predator drone."[7]

At the same time as the drone strike in the Shabwa province, the press also reported that the US Foreign Intelligence Surveillance Court (FISC) had issued a classified order reauthorizing the Section 215 program of the USA PATRIOT Act for another ninety days. Section 215, passed by Congress following 9/11, provides for the bulk collection of telephony metadata held by American telecommunications companies. Under the program, the National Security Agency (NSA) amassed the telephone records of millions upon millions of American customers on a daily basis.[8] In the words of a federal judge, Section 215 "enables the Government to store and analyze phone metadata of every telephone user in the United States." That judge—appointed to the bench by President George W. Bush—called the NSA technology "almost Orwellian."[9]

Section 215 was running alongside a number of other NSA programs for the massive bulk-collection and analysis of personal data of Americans and others, with ominous names such as PRISM, BOUNDLESS INFORMANT, BULLRUN, MYSTIC, UPSTREAM, and so on. The PRISM program, launched in 2007, gave the NSA direct access to the servers of Google, Facebook, Microsoft, Yahoo, Paltalk, YouTube, Skype, AOL, Apple, and more. In conjunction with other programs, such as XKeyscore, PRISM allowed NSA agents and contractors to extract any person's e-mail contacts, user activities, webmail, and all their metadata; using other programs and tools, like the DNI Presenter, the agency could, according to the investigative reporting of Glenn Greenwald, "read the content of stored emails," "read the content of Facebook chats or private messages," and "learn the IP addresses of every person who visits any website the analyst specifies." According to the *Washington Post*, already in 2010 the NSA was intercepting and storing 1.7 billion communications per day.[10]

While the FISC was reauthorizing domestic surveillance, the New York City Police Department (NYPD) was secretly targeting American Muslims in their investigations of domestic political activity. From at least 2010 to 2015, the NYPD directed 95 percent of its covert surveillance on American Muslim individuals or political activities associated with Islam.[11] In doing so, the NYPD was continuing a decade-long history of monitoring American Muslims in and around the city.

Shortly after 9/11, the NYPD created a massive undercover surveillance operation that targeted American Muslim mosques, businesses, and community groups throughout New York City and the surrounding area. The NYPD had what it called "mosque crawlers" monitoring sermons and prayer services, infiltrating the faithful, and gleaning as much intelligence as possible from more than one hundred mosques, Muslim businesses, and student groups—without prior evidence of wrongdoing. The NYPD surveilled Muslim American citizens to determine where they lived, worked, ate, and prayed. It requested the NYC Taxi & Limousine Commission to run a report on every Pakistani taxi driver in New York City. It even sent an undercover operative on a whitewater rafting trip with Muslim students from City College of New York to listen to their conversations and conduct undercover surveillance.[12]

By 2007, the NYPD intelligence unit had created what they called "secret Demographics Unit reports" of Newark, New Jersey (sixty pages long), of Suffolk County (seventy pages), and of Nassau County (ninety-six pages), among other locations, with multiple maps of neighborhoods, indexed and coded for mosques, madrassahs, and Muslim population density. These Demographics Unit reports mapped all the Islamic institutions, with photographs of the buildings and comprehensive profiles and notes, as well as intelligence reports on Muslim businesses detailing their addresses, telephone numbers, photographs, ethnicity, and "information of note" entries.[13]

And at the same time as the release of the Senate torture report, the drone strike in the Shabwa province, the reauthorization of NSA's domestic surveillance, and NYPD's targeting of American Muslims, a second wave of protests against police shootings erupted in Ferguson, Missouri—the site of the fatal police shooting of eighteen-year-old Michael Brown on August 9, 2014. The renewed protests were fueled in part by the decision of the grand jury in Staten Island, New York, to refuse to indict NYPD officer Daniel Pantaleo in the choking death of Eric Garner. It was during those many waves of protests—in Ferguson and elsewhere around the country—that we witnessed the full militarization of police forces in the United States, now equipped with M4 rifles, sniper scopes, camouflage gear and helmets, tanks and mine-resistant ambush-protected vehicles, and grenade launchers from the wars in Iraq and Afghanistan.

Heavily weaponized police officers in fully armored vehicles faced-off mostly peaceful and unarmed civilian protesters. A new militarized police force was deployed on Main Street USA, and images like these flooded our news feeds and social media.

––––––––––

Waterboarding and coffin-sized confinement boxes. Drone strikes outside conventional war zones—alongside indefinite detention at Guantánamo Bay and special military commissions. Total NSA surveillance. The secret infiltration of American mosques and Muslim student groups—without any evidence of wrongdoing. A hypermilitarized police force on American streets.

Some observers view these incidents as isolated, improvised, or unrelated excesses, or even as necessary but temporary deviations from our core American values during times of global terrorism and domestic turmoil post-9/11. Other commentators suggest that they constitute a new "state of exception"—a provisional radical mode of governing outside the rule of law.

But far from exceptional or aberrant or isolated—or temporary—these measures exemplify a new way that we, in the United States, govern ourselves abroad and at home: a new model of government inspired by the theory and practice of counterinsurgency warfare. These episodes are not spasmodic moments of temporary excess. They are not brief departures from the rule of law. Rather, these measures fit together like pieces of a jigsaw puzzle in a far broader and more momentous historical and political transformation: *not from the rule of law to a state of*

Police advance on unarmed protester in Ferguson, Missouri, on August 11, 2014. (Photo by Scott Olson/Getty Images, reproduced by permission.)

Police take up position at protest in Ferguson, Missouri, on August 12, 2014. (Photo by Scott Olson/Getty Images, reproduced by permission.)

exception, but from a model of governing based on large-scale battlefield warfare to one modeled on tactical counterinsurgency strategies.

The central tenet of counterinsurgency theory is that populations—originally colonial populations, but now *all* populations, including our own—are made up of a small active minority of insurgents, a small group of those opposed to the insurgency, and a large passive majority that can be swayed one way or the other. The principal objective of counterinsurgency is to gain the allegiance of that passive majority. And its defining feature is that counterinsurgency is not just a military strategy, but more importantly a political technique. Warfare, it turns out, is political.

On the basis of these tenets, counterinsurgency theorists developed and refined over several decades three core strategies. First, *obtain total information*: every communication, all personal data, all metadata of everyone in the population must be collected and analyzed. Not just the active minority, but everyone in the population. Total information awareness is necessary to distinguish between friend and foe, and then to cull the dangerous minority from the docile majority. Second, *eradicate the active minority*: once the dangerous minority has been identified, it must be separated from the general population and eliminated by any means possible—it must be isolated, contained, and ultimately eradicated. Third, *gain the allegiance of the general population*: everything must be done to win the hearts and minds of the passive majority. It is their allegiance and loyalty, and passivity in the end, that matter most.

Counterinsurgency warfare has become our new governing paradigm in the United States, both abroad and at home. It has come to dominate our political imagination. It drives our foreign affairs and now our domestic policy as well.

But it was not always that way. For most of the twentieth century, we governed ourselves differently in the United States: our political imagination was dominated by the massive battlefields of the Marne, of Verdun, by the *Blitzkrieg* and the fire-bombing of Dresden—and by the use of the atomic bomb. It was an imagination of large-scale war, with waves of human bodies and columns of tanks, military campaigns, battlefields, fronts, theaters of war. And alongside those vast military engagements, President Franklin D. Roosevelt launched an equally massive economic and political campaign—the New Deal. J. Edgar Hoover declared a large-scale War on Crime. Lyndon B. Johnson, in an effort to create the Great Society, inaugurated a society-wide War on Poverty. Richard Nixon and Ronald Reagan initiated a massive War on Drugs. Others, President Bill Clinton among them, reinvigorated a vast law-and-order assault that would give rise to what we now call "mass incarceration": by the turn of the twenty-first century, a full 1 percent of the adult population was behind bars in the United States, about seven million or more people were under correctional supervision, and seventy-nine million had criminal records—collectively amounting to one of the broadest public initiatives in American history with a devastating human toll, all organized around the model of large-scale battlefield warfare.

Yet the transition from large-scale battlefield warfare to anticolonial struggles and the Cold War in the 1950s, and to the war against terrorism since 9/11, has brought about a historic transformation in our political imagination and in the way that we govern ourselves. In contrast to the earlier sweeping military paradigm, we now engage in surgical microstrategies of counterinsurgency abroad and at home. This style of warfare—the very opposite of large-scale battlefield wars like World War I or II—involves total surveillance, surgical operations, targeted strikes to eliminate small enclaves, psychological tactics, and political techniques to gain the trust of the people. The primary target is no longer a regular army, so much as it is the entire population. It involves a new way of thinking about politics, about strategy, and about victory. Counterinsurgency warfare foregrounds the political, or more precisely, fuses the military and political in a way earlier models of warfare had not. And it produces a *counterinsurgency warfare model of politics*—a new political way of thinking and governing that has come to dominate America's military, then its foreign affairs, and now its domestic policy.

Long in the making, this historic transformation accelerated after 9/11. Over the past decades, the change has come about in three major waves.

First, *militarily*. In Vietnam and then in Iraq and Afghanistan, US military strategy shifted from a conventional model of large-scale battlefield war to unconventional forms of counterinsurgency warfare. As a result, war began to be fought differently. New techniques were developed to control anticolonial rebels and to repress anti-imperialist, often Communist revolutions. They were refined during the 1950s and 1960s in the colonies by Western powers, especially Britain, France, and the United States. And since 9/11, they have been deployed aggressively in the US wars in Iraq and Afghanistan. First, the NSA surveillance programs and the tortured interrogations provided total intelligence in order to distinguish between an insurgent minority and the passive general population in Iraq and Afghanistan. Second, drone strikes, special operations, targeted assassinations, and indefinite detention— as well as the most brutal forms of torture—served to terrorize and eliminate the active minority. And third, the US military attempted to win the hearts and minds of the masses through minimal humanitarian interventions, including building infrastructure and handing out goods; curating digital media (such as YouTube videos by moderate imams) and targeting them to individuals identified as being more susceptible to radicalization; and deploying armed drones that communicated the unique power of the United States to control territory.[14]

Second, *in foreign affairs*. As the counterinsurgency paradigm took hold militarily, US foreign policy began to shift to accommodate and embrace the core strategies of unconventional warfare—turning to total information awareness, targeted eradication of radical groups, and psychological pacification of the general populations abroad, even *outside* the confines of particular wartime conflicts. Drone strikes proliferated outside of war zones—in Pakistan, Yemen, and Somalia—and with them, complicated international negotiations over airspace and the use and location of military bases. NSA total information awareness went global, and digital propaganda campaigns extended across the globe. Counterinsurgency strategies, and especially counterinsurgency *needs,* gradually began to dominate foreign policy. To be sure, the international implications differed at different times. During the administration of President George W. Bush, foreign relations were deeply affected, for instance, by the rendition of suspects to cooperating countries; under President Barack Obama, by joint special operations and drone strikes within accommodating countries, as well as the sharing of intelligence with allies; and under President Donald Trump, by immigration bans, the construction of a wall on the southern border, and an actual or threatened withdrawal from multilateral agreements and organizations. But in truth, these differences are just variations on a counterinsurgency model of foreign affairs.

Third, *at home.* With the militarized policing of African American protesters, the monitoring of American mosques and targeting of American Muslims, and the demonization of Mexican Americans and Hispanics, the counterinsurgency has been domesticated. Big and small cities across America amassed counterinsurgency military equipment and know-how, and increasingly deploy these strategies in routine encounters—not only to fight terrorism, but also as an integral part of their day-to-day policing. At least one state, North Dakota, has already passed legislation authorizing the use of armed drones by law-enforcement agencies; in another state, Texas, a local police department deployed a robot bomb—in effect, an armed drone—to assassinate a criminal suspect. Counterinsurgency strategies are beginning to permeate the routine policing of democratic protest. Muslims and persons with Arab surnames are increasingly suspected and treated like high-value targets—along with antipolice protesters, minority youth, and undocumented residents. Programs like PRISM, Section 215, and others now provide the US government access to Americans' personal data. Total surveillance has been turned on the American people.

It is we, Americans, who have become the target of our government's counterinsurgency strategies. The three core strategies now shape the way that the United States, and increasingly the broader Euro-American West, governs: total NSA surveillance of domestic communications, relentless targeting of suspected minorities, and the continuous effort to win the allegiance of the passive masses. From domestic antiterrorism law enforcement to ordinary street policing, from schools to prisons, from our computers and smart TVs to the phones in our pockets, a new way of seeing, thinking, and governing has taken hold at home—and it is founded on a counterinsurgency war paradigm.

The result is radical. We are now witnessing the triumph of a counterinsurgency model of government on American soil *in the absence of an insurgency, or uprising, or revolution.* The perfected logic of counterinsurgency now applies regardless of whether there is a domestic insurrection. We now face a counterinsurgency without insurgency. A counterrevolution without revolution. The pure form of counterrevolution, without a revolution, as a simple modality of governing at home—what could be called "The Counterrevolution."

Counterinsurgency practices were already being deployed domestically in the sixties. In the United States, the FBI's treatment of the Black Panthers under J. Edgar Hoover took precisely the form of counterinsurgency tactics at exactly the same time that those strategies were being developed in Vietnam.[15] As James Baldwin correctly diagnosed decades ago, "the Panthers . . . became the native Vietcong, the ghetto became the village in which the Vietcong were hidden, and in the ensuing search-and-destroy operations, everyone in the village became suspect."[16] Elsewhere as well. In Britain, for instance, the government brought home counterinsurgency strategies it had developed and refined in Palestine and Malaya to combat the Irish Republican Army and police the homeland.

But since 9/11, the counterinsurgency strategies first developed and tested abroad and occasionally used at home have been deployed across the United States in an unprecedented and pervasive manner.

The tactics have been refined, legalized, and systematized. New digital technologies have made possible techniques of surveillance and drone warfare that were simply unimaginable forty years ago. Generations of American soldiers have been steeped in counterinsurgency training and are now back home. The strategies and methods have come to permeate the political imagination.

Even more importantly, what is truly novel and unique today is that the counterinsurgency paradigm has been untethered from its foundation. It is now a form of governing, domestically, *without* any insurrection or uprising to suppress. Yes, there are a handful of deeply unstable individuals who gravitate toward radical Islamic discourse (as well as toward white supremacy and radical Christian discourse) and wreak terrible damage—alongside a daily drumbeat of more ordinary multiple-victim shooting attacks in the United States. (In 2015, there was on average more than one shooting per day in the US that left four or more people dead or wounded.)[17] But there is simply no veritable insurgency at home.

This is a difference in kind, not just in degree, and it produces a dangerous self-fulfilling prophecy. The Counterrevolution creates, out of whole cloth, the specter of a radical insurgency in this country that can then be embraced by unstable individuals—such as the San Bernadino shooter or the Chelsea bomber—and through which *we* can then imagine *them* as an active minority. In effect, The Counterrevolution produces the illusion of an insurgency—an illusion that then radically transforms our public imagination and our perception and treatment of minority communities. It generates a narrative of insurrection that turns whole groups and neighborhoods—of American Muslims or Mexicans, of African Americans, of Hispanics, of peaceful protesters— into suspected insurgents. In the process, entire families, blocks, and neighborhoods that could benefit from public services are transformed into counterinsurgency military targets.

The United States has turned the techniques of counterinsurgency on its own people. The torture, indefinite detention, and drone strikes are a vital part of how we got to this point, but it would be a mistake to stop there. Those strategies form just the basis of a much larger historical transformation that has fundamentally altered the way that we govern ourselves abroad and at home.

This book traces the arc of that transformation: from the development and refinement of counterinsurgency practices in the 1950s and 1960s, to its deployment in Iraq and Afghanistan after 9/11, to its domestication and use on American soil, and finally to the ultimate stage of a domesticated counterinsurgency model of governing in the very absence of any domestic insurrection—The Counterrevolution.

The Counterrevolution was well in place before the election of President Donald Trump, but his election, if anything, sealed the historical transformation. Despite Donald Trump's campaign endorsements of waterboarding, of the indefinite detention of American suspects at Guantánamo, of a travel ban on Muslims, and of renewed surveillance of American mosques, Trump won the Electoral College with over sixty-two million votes, reflecting that a vast number of Americans are perfectly comfortable or actively embrace the domestication of counterinsurgency.

In his first months in office, President Trump filled his cabinet with counterinsurgency warriors, appointing tried-and-true practitioners to the highest security positions: retired Army lieutenant general H. R. McMaster as national security adviser, retired four-star Marine general James Mattis as secretary of defense, and retired four-star Marine general John F. Kelly first as secretary of homeland security and then as chief of staff at the White House. All three have extensive counterinsurgency backgrounds, and practiced and refined those strategies in Iraq. Also in his first months, Donald Trump signed executive orders that targeted Muslims (what became known as the "Muslim ban"), Mexicans (through his enhanced enforcement and deportation of undocumented residents and executive order to build "the wall"), police protesters (by lifting federal consent decrees with local police departments and encouraging new antiprotest legislation at the state level), and the LGBTQ community (by singlehandedly undoing progress on workplace antidiscrimination and then banning military service).

All these executive actions combined to confirm the historical transformation: counterinsurgency strategies at home, despite the lack of an insurgency on American soil. Trump even referred to his administration's enforcement efforts against undocumented residents in the United States as "a military operation," reflecting the embrace of a domestic counterinsurgency mentality.[18] A few months later, even more pointedly, Trump urged Americans to adopt counterinsurgency strategies used by the United States in its colonies to suppress insurgents in the Philippines in the early twentieth century. Trump directly referenced American modern warfare on its own territory, tweeting on August 17, 2017, that we should "Study what General Pershing of the United States did to terrorists when caught. There was no more Radical Islamic Terror for 35 years!" More than ever, a distinct minority of the American population—Muslims, African Americans, Mexicans, and political protesters—is being turned into a putative active insurgency that needs to be isolated and extracted from the passive masses.

American history is replete with the false demonization of interior enemies, from the Red Scare, to the Japanese internment camps, to the juvenile "superpredators" of the 1990s. It is crucial that we not repeat that dark history, that we avoid turning Muslims, peaceful protesters, and other minorities into our new internal enemies. It is vital that we come to grips with this new mode of governing and recognize its unique dangers, that we see the increasingly widespread domestication of counterinsurgency strategies and the new technologies of digital surveillance, drones, and hypermilitarized police for what they are: a counterrevolution without a revolution. We are facing something radical, new, and dangerous. It has been long in the making, historically. It is time to identify and expose it.

In my previous book, *Exposed: Desire and Disobedience in the Digital Age*, I explored the ways in which our own desire to take selfies, post snapchats, check Facebook, tweet, and stream videos on Netflix unwittingly feed the total surveillance machinery of the NSA, Google, Amazon, Microsoft, Facebook, and so on. I argued that we have become an "expository society" where we increasingly exhibit ourselves online, and in the process, freely give away our most personal and private data. No longer an Orwellian or a panoptic society characterized by a powerful central government forcibly surveilling its citizens from on high, ours is fueled by our own pleasures, proclivities, joys, and narcissism. And even when we try to resist these temptations, we have practically no choice but to use the Internet and shed our digital traces.

I had not fully grasped, though, the relation of our new expository society to the other brutal practices of the counterinsurgency war on terrorism—to drone strikes, indefinite detention, or our new hypermilitarized police force at home. But as the fog lifts from 9/11, the full picture becomes clear. The expository society is merely the first prong of The Counterrevolution. And only by tying together our digital exposure with our new mode of counterinsurgency governance can we begin to grasp the whole architecture of our contemporary political condition. And only by grasping the full implications of this new mode of governing—The Counterrevolution—will we be able to effectively resist it and overcome.

PART I

THE RISE OF MODERN WARFARE

The historical transition from World War II to the anticolonial struggles and the Cold War brought about a fundamental shift in the way that the United States and its Western allies waged war. Two new models of warfare emerged in the late 1940s and 1950s, and began to reshape US military strategy: nuclear warfare and unconventional warfare. Though polar opposites in terms of their respective scopes, both were developed in large part at the nerve center of US military strategy, the RAND Corporation. Formed in 1948 as an outgrowth of the research wing for the US Air Force, RAND worked closely with the Pentagon and intelligence agencies to craft these new warfare paradigms.[1]

At one end of the spectrum, the United States developed nuclear-weapon capability and strategy, as did some of its Western allies. There emerged a whole field of military planning that brought together game theory and systems analysis, and produced a warfare logic very much at odds with conventional war strategy. Nuclear-weapon strategists invented theories of "massive retaliation" and "mutually assured destruction"—military paradigms that were dramatically different from earlier forms of engagement and far greater in scale than conventional warfare. American nuclear strategy focused on the superpower rivalry with the Soviet Union and presumed a global conflict of extraordinary proportions.

At the other end of the spectrum, there emerged a very different model localized especially in the colonies—a far more surgical, special-operations approach targeting small revolutionary insurgencies and what were mostly Communist uprisings. Variously called "unconventional," "antiguerrilla" or "counterguerrilla," "irregular," "sublimited," "counterrevolutionary," or simply "modern" warfare, this burgeoning domain of military strategy flourished during France's wars in Indochina and Algeria, Britain's wars in Malaya and Palestine, and America's war in Vietnam. It too was nourished by the RAND Corporation, which was one of the first to see the potential of what the French commander Roger Trinquier called "modern warfare" or the "French view of counterinsurgency." It offered, in the words of one of its leading students, the historian Peter Paret, a vital counterweight "at the opposite end of the spectrum from rockets and the hydrogen bomb."[2]

Like nuclear-weapon strategy, the counterinsurgency model grew out of a combination of strategic game theory and systems theorizing; but unlike nuclear strategy, which was primarily a response to the Soviet Union, it developed more in response to another formidable game theorist, Mao Zedong. The formative moment for counterinsurgency theory was not the nuclear confrontation that characterized the Cuban Missile Crisis, but the earlier Chinese Civil War that led to Mao's victory in 1949—essentially, when Mao turned guerrilla tactics into a revolutionary war that overthrew a political regime. The central methods and practices of counterinsurgency warfare were honed in response to Mao's strategies and the ensuing anticolonial struggles in Southeast Asia, the Middle East, and North Africa that imitated Mao's approach.[3] Those struggles for independence were the breeding soil for the development and perfection of unconventional warfare.

By the turn of the twentieth century, when President George W. Bush would declare a "War on Terror" following 9/11, counterinsurgency warfare was well-developed and mature.[4] And with the spectacular rise of US general David Petraeus, counterinsurgency theory gained dominance in US military strategy. Today, given the geopolitics of the twenty-first century, modern warfare has replaced the military paradigm of large-scale battlefield warfare of the earlier century.

Counterinsurgency warfare has been one of the most consequential innovations of the post–World War II period, in terms of our contemporary politics. In hindsight, it is Mao, rather than the USSR, who was the more momentous and long-lasting foe. Mao is the one who turned warfare into politics—or, more precisely, who showed us how modern warfare could become a form of governing. Perhaps only in retrospect, post-9/11, can we truly understand the full implications of early counterinsurgency theory.

———————————————

1

COUNTERINSURGENCY IS POLITICAL

THE COUNTERINSURGENCY MODEL CAN BE TRACED BACK through several different genealogies. One leads to British colonial rule in India and Southeast Asia, to the insurgencies there, and to the eventual British redeployment and modernization of counterinsurgency strategies in Northern Ireland and Britain at the height of the Irish Republican Army's independence struggles. This first genealogy draws heavily on the writings of the British counterinsurgency theorist Sir Robert Thompson, the chief architect of Great Britain's antiguerrilla strategies in Malaya from 1948 to 1959. Another genealogy traces back to the American colonial experience in the Philippines at the beginning of the twentieth century. Others lead back to Trotsky and Lenin in Russia, to Lawrence of Arabia during the Arab Revolt, or even to the Spanish uprising against Napoleon—all mentioned, at least briefly, in General Petraeus's counterinsurgency field manual. Alternative genealogies reach back to the political theories of Montesquieu or John Stuart Mill, while some go even further to antiquity and to the works of Polybius, Herodotus, and Tacitus.[1]

But the most direct antecedent of counterinsurgency warfare as embraced by the United States after 9/11 was the French military response in the late 1950s and 1960s to the anticolonial wars in Indochina and Algeria. This genealogy passes through three important figures—the historian Peter Paret and the French commanders David Galula and Roger Trinquier—and, through them, it traces back to Mao Zedong. It is Mao's idea of the political nature of counterinsurgency that would prove so influential in the United States. Mao politicized warfare in a manner that would come back to haunt us today. The French connection also laid the seeds of a tension between brutality and legality that would plague counterinsurgency practices to the present—at least, until the United States discovered, or rediscovered, a way to resolve the tension by legalizing the brutality.

In the late 1950s, Peter Paret, then a young PhD student in military history studying at the University of London under the supervision of Sir Michael Howard (one of Britain's greatest military historians), became interested in the new French military tactics that were being developed and deployed in response to what had become known as "*la guerre révolutionnaire.*" Paret would eventually become a formidable historian best known for his research on Carl von Clausewitz. A professor at the School of Historical Studies at the Institute of Advanced Study at Princeton, he became particularly renowned in strategic-studies circles as the editor of the second edition of *Makers of Modern Strategy from Machiavelli to the Nuclear Age*, which remains a classic textbook for teaching the history of military strategy. But as a young scholar, Paret was one of the first people in the United States to discover, translate, and popularize the French doctrine of counterinsurgency warfare.

Paret practically coined the term "revolutionary warfare" for Americans in the early 1960s. He was introduced to the central tenets of insurgent revolutionary warfare, in his words, "during a stay in France in 1958." He first wrote about it in a 1959 article titled "The French Army and *La Guerre Révolutionnaire*," published in the *Journal of the Royal United Service Institution*. From those early writings, Paret developed a fascination for the new military approach, and, as a frequent contributor to the Princeton Studies in World Politics, often highlighted the emerging strategies and debates surrounding counterinsurgency theory and practice.[2]

In his book *French Revolutionary Warfare from Indochina to Algeria: The Analysis of a Political and Military Doctrine*, published in 1964, Paret examined both the tenets of revolutionary insurgency that anticolonial revolutionaries were developing in Indochina and North Africa, as well as the emerging doctrine of *counter*revolutionary war that French commanders were refining on the ground. In Paret's view—a view shared by many scholars and practitioners at the time—the revolutionary strategies had their source in the writings and practices of Mao Zedong. Most of the French pioneers of counterrevolutionary methods had turned to Mao to get their bearings, and did so very early—for instance, in 1952 already, General Lionel-Max Chassin published *La conquête de la Chine par Mao Tsé-Toung (1945–1949)*, which would lay the groundwork for modern warfare theory.[3]

A founding principle of revolutionary insurgency—what Paret referred to as "the principal lesson" that Mao taught—was that "an inferior force could outpoint a modern army so long as it succeeded in gaining at least the tacit support of the population in the contested area."[4] The core idea was that the military battle was less decisive than the political struggle over the loyalty and allegiance of the masses: the war is fought over the population or, in Mao's words, "The army cannot exist without the people."[5]

As a result of this interdependence, the insurgents had to treat the general population well to gain its support. On this basis Mao formulated early on, in 1928, his "Eight Points of Attention" for army personnel:

1. Talk to people politely.
2. Observe fair dealing in all business transactions.
3. Return everything borrowed from the people.
4. Pay for anything damaged.

5. Do not beat or scold the people.

6. Do not damage crops.

7. Do not molest women.

8. Do not ill-treat prisoners-of-war.[6]

Two other principles were central to Mao's revolutionary doctrine: first, the importance of having a unified political and military power structure that consolidated, in the same hands, political and military considerations; and second, the importance of psychological warfare. More specifically, as Paret explained, "proper psychological measures could create and maintain ideological cohesion among fighters and their civilian supporters."[7]

Revolutionary warfare, in Paret's view, boiled down to a simple equation: *Guerrilla warfare + psychological warfare = revolutionary warfare.*[8] And many revolutionary strategies fell under the rubric of psychological warfare, Paret maintained, including at one end of the spectrum terrorist attacks intended to impress the general population, and at the other end, diplomatic interventions at international organizations. In all of these strategies, the focus was on the population, and the medium was psychological. As Paret wrote:

> The populace, according to the formulation by Mao Tse-tung that has become one of the favorite quotations of the French theorists, is for the army what water is for fish. And more concretely, "A Red army . . . without the support of the population and the guerrillas would be a one-armed warrior." The conquest—i.e., securing complicity—of at least sections of the population is accordingly seen as the indispensable curtain-raiser to insurrectional war.[9]

Or more succinctly, drawing on a detailed five-stage process elaborated by another French analyst: "the ground over which the main battle will be fought: the population."[10]

Of course, neither Paret nor other strategists were so naïve as to think that Mao invented guerrilla warfare. Paret spent much of his research tracing the antecedents and earlier experiments with insurgent and counterinsurgency warfare. "Civilians taking up arms and fighting as irregulars are as old as war," Paret emphasized. Caesar had to deal with them in Gaul and Germania, the British in the American colonies or in South Africa with the Boers, Napoleon in Spain, and on and on. In fact, as Paret stressed, the very term "guerrilla" originated in the Spanish peasant resistance to Napoleon after the Spanish monarchy had fallen between 1808 and 1813. Paret developed case studies of the Spanish resistance, as well as detailed analyses of the repression of the Vendée rebellion at the time of the French Revolution between 1789 and 1796.[11] Long before Mao, Clausewitz had dedicated a chapter of his famous work *On War* to irregular warfare, calling it a "phenomenon of the nineteenth century"; and T. E. Lawrence as well wrote and analyzed key features of irregular warfare after he himself had led uprisings in the Arab peninsula during World War I.

But for purposes of describing the "*guerre révolutionnaire*" of the 1960s, the most pertinent and timely objects of study were Mao Zedong and the Chinese revolution. And on the basis of that particular conception of revolutionary war, Paret set forth a model of *counter*revolutionary warfare. Drawing principally on French military practitioners and theorists, Paret delineated a three-pronged strategy focused on a mixture of intelligence gathering, psychological warfare on both the population and the subversives, and severe treatment of the rebels. In *Guerrillas in the 1960's*, Paret reduced the tasks of "counterguerrilla action" to the following:

1. The military defeat of the guerrilla forces.
2. The separation of the guerrilla from the population.
3. The reestablishment of governmental authority and the development of a viable social order.[12]

Paret emphasized, drawing again on Mao, that military defeat is not enough. "Unless the population has been weaned away from the guerrilla and his cause, unless reforms and re-education have attacked the psychological base of guerrilla action, unless the political network backing him up has been destroyed," he wrote, "military defeat is only a pause and fighting can easily erupt again." Rehearing the lessons of the French in Vietnam and Algeria, and the British in Malaysia, Paret underscored that "the tasks of counterguerrilla warfare are as much political as military—or even more so; the two continually interact."[13]

So the central task, according to Paret, was to attack the rebel's popular support so that he would "lose his hold over the people, and be isolated from them." There were different ways to accomplish this, from widely publicized military defeats and sophisticated psychological warfare to the resettlement of populations—in addition to other more coercive measures. But one rose above the others for Paret: to encourage the people to form progovernment militias and fight against the guerrillas. This approach had the most potential, Paret observes: "Once a substantial number of members of a community commit violence on behalf of the government, they have gone far to break permanently the tie between that community and the guerrillas."[14] In sum, the French model of counterrevolutionary warfare, in Paret's view, had to be understood as the inverse of revolutionary warfare.

The main sources for Paret's synthesis were the writings and practices of French commanders on the ground, especially Roger Trinquier and David Galula, though there were others as well.[15] Trinquier, one of the first French commanders to theorize modern warfare based on his first-hand experience, had a unique military background. He had remained loyal to the Vichy government in Indochina during World War II, resulting in deep tensions with General Charles de Gaulle and other Free French officers after the war. But he was retained and respected because of his antiguerrilla expertise. Trinquier became especially well-known for his *guerrilla-style* antiguerrilla tactics during the war in Indochina. He led anti-Communist guerrilla units deep inside enemy territory, and ultimately, by 1951, received command over all of the behind-the-line operations. He was, according to the war correspondent Bernard Fall, the perfect "centurion": he "had survived the Indochina war, had learned his Mao Tse-tung the hard way, and later had sought to apply his lessons in Algeria or even in mainland France."[16]

In his book *Modern Warfare: A French View of Counterinsurgency*, published in France in 1961 and quickly translated into English in 1964, Trinquier announces a new warfare paradigm and at the same time sounds an alarm. "Since the end of World War II, a new form of warfare has been born," Trinquier writes. "Called at times either *subversive warfare* or *revolutionary warfare*, it differs fundamentally from the wars of the past in that victory is not expected from the clash of two armies on a field of battle." The failure to recognize this difference, Trinquier warns, could only lead to defeat. "Our military machine," he cautions, "reminds one of a pile driver attempting to crush a fly, indefatigably persisting in repeating its efforts." Trinquier argues that this new form of modern warfare called for "an interlocking system of actions—political, economic, psychological, military," grounded on "Countrywide Intelligence." As Trinquier emphasizes, "since *modern warfare* asserts its presence on the totality of the population, we have to be *everywhere informed*." Informed, in order to know and target the population and wipe out the insurgency.[17]

The other leading counterinsurgency theorist, also with deep first-hand experience in Algeria, David Galula, also understood the importance of total information and of winning the hearts and minds of the general population.[18] He too had learned his Mao—including the fly analogy, which he quoted in the introduction to his book *Counterinsurgency Warfare: Theory and Practice*, published in 1964: "In the fight between a fly and a lion, the fly cannot deliver a knockout blow and the lion cannot fly." In the late 1940s, Galula had closely studied Mao's writings in their English translation in the *Marine Corps Gazette*, and, according to people close to him, "spoke of Mao and the civil war 'all the time.'"[19]

From Mao, Galula drew the central lesson that societies were divided into three groups and that the key to victory was to isolate and eradicate the active minority in order to gain the allegiance of the masses. Galula emphasizes in *Counterinsurgency Warfare* that the central strategy of counterinsurgency theory "simply expresses the basic tenet of the exercise of political power":

> *In any situation, whatever the cause, there will be an active minority for the cause, a neutral majority, and an active minority against the cause.*
>
> The technique of power consists in relying on the favorable minority in order to rally the neutral majority and to neutralize or eliminate the hostile minority.[20]

The battle was over the general population, Galula emphasized in his *Counterinsurgency Warfare*, and this tenet represented the key political dimension of a new warfare strategy.

US general David Petraeus picked up right where David Galula and Peter Paret left off. Widely recognized as the leading American thinker and practitioner of counterinsurgency theory—eventually responsible for all coalition troops in Iraq and the architect of the troop surge of 2007—General Petraeus would refine Galula's central lesson to a concise paragraph in the very first chapter of his edition of the US Army and Marine Corps Field Manual 3-24 on counterinsurgency, published and widely disseminated in 2006. Under the header "Aspects of Counterinsurgency," Petraeus's field manual reads:

> In almost every case, counterinsurgents face a populace containing an active minority supporting the government and an equally small militant faction opposing it. Success requires the government to be accepted as legitimate by most of that uncommitted middle, which also includes passive supporters of both sides. (See Figure I-2.)[21]

The referenced figure captures the very essence of this way of seeing the world, echoing Galula exactly: "In any situation, whatever

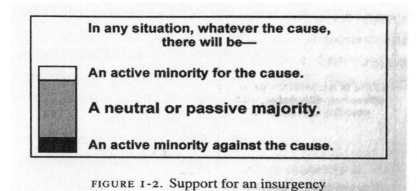

FIGURE 1-2. Support for an insurgency

Figure I-2 from General Petraeus's *Counterinsurgency Field Manual.*

the cause." From Mao and Galula, Petraeus derived not only the core foundations of counterinsurgency, but a central political vision. This is a political theory, not simply a military strategy. It is a worldview, a way of dealing with all situations—whether on the field of battle or off it.[22]

On this political foundation, General Petraeus's manual establishes three key pillars—what might be called counterinsurgency's core principles.

The first is that the most important struggle is over the population. In a short set of guidelines that accompanies his field manual, General Petraeus emphasizes: "The decisive terrain is the human terrain. The people are the center of gravity." David Galula had said the same. "The objective is the population," Galula wrote. "The population is at the same time the real terrain of the war."[23] This first lesson had been learned the hard way in Algeria for the French, and later in Vietnam for the Americans. Galula had made the point in his 1963 memoirs, emphasizing that "support from the population was the key to the whole problem for us as well as for the rebels." But eventually the lesson was learned, and the general population would become central to counterinsurgency theory. In a short "Summary," General Petraeus's field manual stresses that "at its core, COIN [counterinsurgency] is a struggle for the population's support."[24] The main battle, then, is over the populace.

The second principle is that the allegiance of the masses can only be secured by separating the small revolutionary minority from the passive majority, and by isolating, containing, and ultimately eliminating the active minority. In his accompanying guidelines, General Petraeus emphasizes: "Seek out and eliminate those who threaten the population. Don't let them intimidate the innocent. Target the whole network, not just individuals."[25]

The third core principle is that success turns on collecting information on everyone in the population. Total information is essential to properly distinguish friend from foe and then extract the revolutionary minority. It is intelligence—total information awareness—that renders the counterinsurgency possible. It is what makes the difference between, in the words of General Petraeus's field manual, "blind boxers wasting energy flailing at unseen opponents and perhaps causing unintended harm," and, on the other hand, "surgeons cutting out cancerous tissue while keeping other vital organs intact."[26]

Heavily influenced by Galula's writings—as well as by those of the British counterinsurgency theorist Sir Robert Thompson—Petraeus's field manual reads like an ode to early French counterinsurgency theory.

"Counterinsurgency is not just thinking man's warfare—it is the graduate level of war," states the epigraph to the first chapter of General Petraeus's manual. And for Petraeus, the graduate level *was* 1960s French counterinsurgency strategy as reflected in its most theoretical manifestations. Building on his extensive firsthand experience, General Petraeus gravitated toward those early writings and emphasized the political nature of the battle.

The manual's short "Acknowledgements," placed up front right after Petraeus's signature, refers to only two books: David Galula's *Counterinsurgency Warfare: Theory and Practice* and Sir Robert Thompson's *Defeating Communist Insurgency: The Lessons of Malaya and Vietnam*, both from the mid-1960s.

Chapter One of the manual takes a leaf out of Galula's book and, practically paraphrasing the French commander, underscores the primacy of political factors in counterinsurgency. "General Chang Ting-chen of Mao Zedong's central committee once stated that revolutionary war was 80 percent political action and only 20 percent military," the manual reads. Then it warns: "At the beginning of a COIN operation, military actions may appear predominant as security forces conduct operations to secure the populace and kill or capture insurgents; however, *political objectives must guide the military's approach.*"[27]

Chapter Two opens with an epigraph from David Galula's book: "Essential though it is, the military action is secondary to the political one, its primary purpose being to afford the political power enough freedom to work safely with the population." The field manual comes back to Galula several pages later, stating how "David Galula wisely notes" that the soldier must temporarily focus on civilian tasks. "Galula's last sentence is important," Petraeus's manual emphasizes. Redirecting the military from its core military tasks should only be temporary, "one taken to address urgent circumstances."[28]

The influence of Galula is everywhere evident. As Lieutenant Colonel John Nagl, a member of the team that helped write the manual, notes, "Of the many books that were influential in the writing of the Field Manual 3-24, perhaps none was as important as David Galula's *Counterinsurgency Warfare: Theory and Practice.*" The historian Grégor Mathias reports that General Petraeus "encouraged officers serving in Iraq and Afghanistan to read [Galula's book]."[29] General Petraeus himself would later refer to Galula as "the Clausewitz of counterinsurgency" and to his *Counterinsurgency Warfare* as "the greatest book written on unconventional warfare." Petraeus added that Galula was, from this side of the Atlantic, "the most illustrious French strategist of the twentieth century."[30]

And through Galula, Mao Zedong's shadow looms over Petraeus's manual.[31] Mao's central insight—regarding the political nature of counterinsurgency—is front and center. The manual dissects Mao's strategy as it was used during the Chinese Civil War, in Vietnam, and elsewhere—"the Maoist, Che Guevara-type focoist, and urban approaches to insurgency." After reviewing the different types of insurgent approaches, the manual goes into a long exegesis on "**Mao Zedong's Theory of Protracted War**" (bold in original) and describes Mao's three-phase strategy of political and military insurgency. The manual details, in a two-and-a-half-page development, the different phases of Maoist strategy. It then elaborates on the North Vietnamese *dau tranh* ("struggle") tactics that "offers another example of the application of Mao's strategy." Chapter Five contains a history of the defeat of Chiang Kai-shek to the Communist insurgency led by Mao, underscoring Chiang Kai-shek's mistaken strategy of defending only the coastal financial and industrial hubs. The final chapter analyses Mao's logistics theories to establish the importance of nimble logistical practices in a counterinsurgency: "Mao believed the enemy's rear was the guerrillas' front; the guerrillas' advantage was that they had no discernable logistic rear."[32]

The result is that General Petraeus's field manual and its recommendations at times almost sound as if they were written by Mao Zedong. One can hear the words of Mao on the eve of his departure to negotiate with Chiang Kai-shek in 1945: "We must systematically win over the majority, oppose the minority, and defeat [the enemy] one by one."[33] Or Mao's words in 1946: "In order to crush [the opposition] . . . we must co-operate closely with the people, and we must win over all those that can be won over . . . we should try to win over all those who may be opposed to the war and to isolate the war-lovers." Or his words in 1947: "we must resolutely and persistently carry out the policy of winning over the masses by giving them some benefits so that they will come over to our side. Only if we can accomplish these . . . things will victory be ours."[34] Mao is the ghost that haunts Petraeus's field manual.

General David Petraeus learned, but more importantly popularized, Mao Zedong's central lesson: *counterinsurgency warfare is political*. It is a strategy for winning over the people. It is a strategy for governing.

And it is quite telling that a work so indebted to Mao and midcentury French colonial thinkers would become so influential post-9/11. Petraeus's manual contained a roadmap for a new paradigm of governing. As the fog lifts from 9/11, it is becoming increasingly clear what lasting impact Mao had on our government of self and others today.

2

A JANUS-FACED
PARADIGM

THE POLITICAL PARADIGM OF MODERN WARFARE EXISTED IN
two distinct variations: one more explicitly brutal, the other more
legalistic. The tension between the two would arise again and again—
and it plagued counterinsurgency practice as a mode of governing for
decades.

The theorist of the harsh version was Roger Trinquier, author of that
early treatise *Modern Warfare: A French View of Counterinsurgency*.
Trinquier of course shared many core tenets with his counterparts. He
too believed that the most vital objective was to gain the allegiance of
the civilian population: "Military tactics and hardware are all well and
good," Trinquier writes, "but they are really quite useless if one has lost
the confidence of the population among whom one is fighting." But although everyone agreed on the importance of gaining the population's
confidence, they disagreed on *how to* achieve that objective. Trinquier
and some other French commanders in Algeria, like General Paul Aussaresses, resolved the dilemma by heeding Machiavelli's advice to the
letter: "It is much safer to be feared than loved, if you cannot be both."[1]

Trinquier took a harshly realist view of his enemies and, as a result, a take-no-prisoners approach to warfare. He believed that terrorism was the most effective strategy of the insurgents. "We know that the *sine qua non* of victory in *modern warfare* is the unconditional support of the population," he wrote. "If it doesn't exist, it must be secured by every possible means, the most effective of which is *terrorism*." The only way to counter that, he argued, was "the complete destruction" of the insurgent group. This, he emphasized, was "the master concept that must guide us in our study of *modern warfare*."[2] And it entailed using all means necessary—including torture and disappearances.

Terrorism was not a means for the guerrilla opposition only, in Trinquier's view. After having discussed at length the terrorist acts and torture administered by the Front de libération nationale (FLN) in Algeria, Trinquier concluded: "In *modern warfare*, as in the traditional wars of the past, it is absolutely essential to make use of all the weapons the enemy employs. Not to do so would be absurd . . . If, like the knights of old, our army refused to employ all the weapons of *modern warfare*, it could no longer fulfill its mission. We would no longer be defended. Our national independence, the civilization we hold dear, our very freedom would probably perish."[3]

In *Modern Warfare*, Trinquier quietly but resolutely condoned torture. The interrogations and related tasks were considered police work, as opposed to military operations, but they had the exact same mission: the complete destruction of the insurgent group. Discussing the typical interrogation of a detainee, captured and suspected of belonging to a terrorist organization, Trinquier wrote: "No lawyer is present for such an interrogation. If the prisoner gives the information requested, the examination is quickly terminated; if not, specialists must force his secret from him. Then, as a soldier, he must face the suffering, and perhaps the death, he has heretofore managed to avoid." Trinquier described specialists forcing secrets out of suspects using scientific methods that did not injure the "integrity of individuals," but it was clear what those "scientific" methods entailed.[4] As the war correspondent

Bernard Fall suggests, the political situation in Algeria offered Trinquier the opportunity to develop "a Cartesian rationale" to justify the use of torture in modern warfare.[5]

Similarly minded commanders championed the use of torture, indefinite detention, and summary executions. They made no bones about it.

In his autobiographical account published in 2001, *Services Spéciaux. Algérie 1955–1957*, General Paul Aussaresses admits to the brutal methods that were the cornerstone of his military strategy.[6] He makes clear that his approach to counterinsurgency rested on a three-pronged strategy, which included first, intelligence work; second, torture; and third, summary executions. The intelligence function was primordial because the insurgents' strategy in Algeria was to infiltrate and integrate the population, to blend in perfectly, and then gradually to involve the population in the struggle. To combat this insurgent strategy required intelligence—the only way to sort the dangerous revolutionaries from the passive masses—and then, violent repression. "The first step was to dispatch the clean-up teams, of which I was a part," Aussaresses writes. "Rebel leaders had to be identified, neutralized, and eliminated discreetly. By seeking information on FLN leaders I would automatically be able to capture the rebels and make them talk."[7]

The rebels were made to talk by means of torture. Aussaresses firmly believed that torture was the best way to extract information. It also served to terrorize the radical minority and, in the process, to reduce it. The practice of torture was "widely used in Algeria," Aussaresses acknowledges. Not on every prisoner, though; many spoke freely. "It was only when a prisoner refused to talk or denied the obvious that torture was used."[8]

Aussaresses claims he was introduced to torture in Algeria by the policemen there, who used it regularly. But it quickly became routine to him. "Without any hesitation," he writes, "the policemen showed me the technique used for 'extreme' interrogations: first, a beating, which in most cases was enough; then other means, such as electric shocks, known as the famous '*gégène*'; and finally water." Aussaresses explains: "Torture by electric shock was made possible by generators used to power field radio transmitters, which were extremely common in Algeria. Electrodes were attached to the prisoner's ears or testicles, then electric charges of varying intensity were turned on. This was apparently a well-known procedure and I assumed that the policemen at Philippeville [in Algeria] had not invented it."[9] (Similar methods had, in fact, been used earlier in Indochina.)

Aussaresses could not have been more clear:

> The methods I used were always the same: beatings, electric shocks, and, in particular, water torture, which was the most dangerous technique for the prisoner. It never lasted for more than one hour and the suspects would speak in the hope of saving their own lives. They would therefore either talk quickly or never.

The French historian Benjamin Stora confirms the generalized use of torture. He reports that in the Battle of Algiers, under the commanding officer, General Jacques Massu, the paratroopers conducted massive arrests and "practiced torture" using "electrodes [. . .] dunking in bathtubs, beatings." General Massu himself would later acknowledge the use of torture. In a rebuttal he wrote in 1971 to the film *The Battle of Algiers*, Massu described torture as "a cruel necessity."[10] According to Aussaresses, torture was condoned at the highest levels of the French government. "Regarding the use of torture," Aussaresses maintains, "it was tolerated if not actually recommended. François Mitterrand, as minister of justice, had a de facto representative with General Massu in Judge Jean Bérard, who covered our actions and knew exactly what was going on during the night. I had an excellent relationship with him, with nothing to hide."[11]

After torture, in Aussaresses's toolbox, came summary executions. Aussaresses does not minimize the use of these either, nor the fact that they were approved at the highest levels of the French government. "By asking the military to reestablish law and order inside the city of

Algiers, the civilian authorities had implicitly approved of having summary executions," he writes. "Whenever we felt it was necessary to be given more explicit instructions, the practice in question was always clearly approved." In fact, Aussaresses firmly believes from his personal conversations with General Massu that he had been given the express signal that summary executions were approved by the government of Prime Minister Guy Mollet: "When we killed those [twelve] prisoners there was no doubt in our minds that we were following the direct orders of Max Lejeune, who was part of the government of Guy Mollet, and acting in the name of the French Republic."[12]

Suspected insurgents, whether proven guilty or innocent, had to be eliminated. A person who turned out not to have information was just as dangerous as someone who confessed, since the process of interrogation would turn anyone against the French government. Aussaresses explains:

> Only rarely were the prisoners we had questioned during the night still alive the next morning. Whether they had talked or not they generally had been neutralized. It was impossible to send them back to the court system, there were too many of them and the machine of justice would have become clogged with cases and stopped working altogether. Furthermore, many of the prisoners would probably have managed to avoid any kind of punishment.[13]

This too is confirmed by the historian Benjamin Stora, who reports that there were as many as 3,024 disappearances in Algeria.[14]

For his part, Aussaresses legitimized the violence. "I don't think I ever tortured or executed people who were innocent," he writes. He could say this, in part, because he understood guilt as extending so widely. At least twenty people were involved at different stages of a bomb attack, he maintained—from the bomb maker, to the driver, to the lookout, etc. And in contrast to the terrorists, Aussaresses claims, "I had never fought civilians and never harmed children. I was fighting men who had made their own choices."[15]

For Aussaresses, as for Roger Trinquier, torture and disappearances were simply an inevitable byproduct of an insurgency—inevitable on *both* sides of the struggle. Because terrorism was inscribed in revolutionary strategy, it had to be used in its repression as well. In a fascinating televised debate in 1970 with the FLN leader and producer of *The Battle of Algiers,* Saadi Yacef, Trinquier confidently asserted that torture was simply a necessary and inevitable part of modern warfare. Torture will take place. Insurgents know it. In fact, they anticipate it. The passage is striking:

> I have to tell you. Whether you're for or against torture, it makes no difference. Torture is a weapon that will be used in every insurgent war. One has to know that . . . One has to know that in an insurgency, you are going to be tortured.
>
> And you have to mount a subversive organization in light of that and in function of torture. *It is not a question of being for or against torture.* You have to know that all arrested prisoners in an insurgency will speak—unless they commit suicide. Their confession will *always* be obtained. So a subversive organization must be mounted in function of that, so that a prisoner who speaks does not give away the whole organization.[16]

On Trinquier's view, torture was inevitable. It practically defined revolutionary war and counterinsurgency, as opposed to conventional warfare. The FLN engaged in torturous acts, including lethal terror attacks on civilians and torture against ordinary members of the Muslim population who favored the French or were uncommitted, he asserted.[17] And, although the extent of the torture is still in dispute today, it is true that the FLN, like other liberation movements, engaged in acts of terrorism, often aimed at civilian populations, including bombings of restaurants and bars, and targeted assassinations of the police. To *not* torture in response, to *not* torture to gain information about the insurgency, that would have meant to *not* fight the war, Trinquier argued.

The French may as well have decided to simply relinquish their colonial power—which they ultimately would.

"Torture?" asks the lieutenant *aide de camp* in Henri Alleg's 1958 exposé *The Question*. "You don't make war with choirboys."[18] Alleg, a French journalist and director of the *Alger républicain* newspaper, was himself detained and tortured by French paratroopers in Algiers. His book describes the experience in detail, and in his account, torture was the inevitable product of colonization and the anticolonial struggle. As Jean-Paul Sartre writes in his preface to Alleg's book, torture "is the essence of the conflict and expresses its deepest truth."[19] It was inextricably linked to colonialism, racism, and counterinsurgency. For many French officers, like Trinquier, it was an inexorable byproduct of modern warfare.

In an arresting part of *The Battle of Algiers* it becomes clear that many of the French officers who tortured suspected FLN members had themselves, as members of the French Resistance, been victims of torture at the hands of the Gestapo. It is a shocking moment. We know, of course, that abuse often begets abuse; but nevertheless, one would have hoped that a victim of torture would recoil from administering it to others. Instead, as Trinquier suggests, torture became normalized in Algeria. This is, as Sartre describes it, the "terrible truth": "If fifteen years are enough to transform victims into executioners, then this behavior is not more than a matter of opportunity and occasion. Anybody, at any time, may equally find himself victim or executioner."[20]

In contrast, other French commanders abjured torture, at least publicly. David Galula, for instance, knew that torture was used by some French officers in Algeria, but he minimized its occurrence. The complaints of torture were "90 percent nonsense and 10 percent truth," he would say.[21] Galula himself preferred to avoid physical torture and to use instead more psychological means—such as locking a prisoner in an oven and threatening to turn the oven on[22]—or to turn suspects over to units that he knew tortured. Galula bought into a sham legal framework that absolved French paratroopers of responsibility whenever suspects were murdered. He ascribed to a more legalistic version of counterinsurgency and maintained a greater public distance from the practice of torture than other commanders.

Galula acknowledged the need for harsh interrogation. "As the insurgents don't hesitate to employ terrorism, the counterinsurgent must do police work," he wrote, referring to a euphemism for torture. He believed that the paratroopers needed to dirty their hands. "If anyone seriously believes that his purity will allow him to get information, all I can say is that he will learn a lot once he is faced with the problem." But he also believed that torture could backfire, and expressed reservations. "My only interest," he noted, "was to remain within decent limits and do no damage to my more constructive pacification work."[23]

As this reference to "decent limits" suggests, Galula took a more legalistic or procedural approach to the use of brutality. He relied on the legal process to investigate and cover up disappearances. Because no war was declared in Algeria, any death as a result of the conflict would immediately require a homicide investigation. The officer or soldier had to appear before a judge and be charged with manslaughter. There had to be a manslaughter report. But those reports served only to whitewash the deaths. The law would be brought in, would perform a cursory investigation, and declare an accidental killing. On one occasion, when he was involved in the death of a prisoner who was being interrogated and who allegedly tried to run away from captivity, Galula himself underwent the charade. In his own words: "Gendarmes came to Ighouna, interrogated the sentry and me, made the usual manslaughter report, and the case, of course, was dismissed months later."[24]

In effect, Galula used the legal process as a backdoor means of rationalizing practices similar to those that other commanders defended more openly. Rather than embracing brutality outright, Galula relied on legality. He let the legal mechanisms justify any excess.

Galula negotiated a fine line. He was hardheaded about the use of violence, including merciless violence. "It is necessary to punish in exemplary fashion the rebel criminals we have caught," he wrote. "The rebels' flagrant crimes must be punished immediately, mercilessly, and on the very spot where they took place." Elsewhere, Galula emphasized the importance of always brandishing the stick along with the carrot. And in the last section of *Pacification in Algeria*, Galula, like Trinquier, attributed the failure in Algeria to a lack of firmness toward the population.[25] But despite all of this, Galula did not justify torture explicitly, and he did not boast of his brutality—by contrast, say, to General Aussaresses.

It is probably for this reason that American military strategists would later privilege Galula over other French commanders when they would import French modern warfare. Galula always represented the kinder, gentler face of counterinsurgency theory—and still today, in fact, stands for the approach that emphasizes civil society or "population-centric" strategies by opposition to the more military and repressive "global war on terror."[26]

Both versions of French counterinsurgency theory made their way across the Atlantic rapidly. Lieutenant Colonel Trinquier, you will recall, gained a reputation for his guerrilla-style antiguerrilla tactics in Indochina and drew the attention of American officers in Saigon. He was invited to visit US counterinsurgency training facilities in Korea and Japan, and was enlisted to train American commandos in the early 1950s. The United States also began to supply him with equipment for his behind-the-line guerrilla antiguerrilla missions. General Aussaresses traveled to the United States after his command in Algeria to teach counterinsurgency practices to elite American Special Forces. As early as May 1961, Aussaresses served as an instructor at Fort Benning, Georgia, and at Fort Bragg, North Carolina, for soldiers who were being trained for special missions in Vietnam. Some of his students at Fort Bragg would eventually develop the CIA's Phoenix Program, a controversial counterinsurgency program in Vietnam linked to assassinations and torture. Aussaresses then became the military attaché at the French embassy in Washington, DC.[27]

The importation of the harsh version of French counterinsurgency theory continued after 9/11. Shortly after the invasion of Iraq, the formerly banned film, *The Battle of Algiers*, was screened at the Pentagon by the US Department of Defense to serve as the basis of discussions regarding the political situation that the American troops were facing on the ground in Iraq. According to news reports, "The idea came from the Directorate for Special Operations and Low-Intensity Conflict, which a Defense Department official described as a civilian-led group with 'responsibility for thinking aggressively and creatively' on issues of guerrilla war." The idea was to stimulate conversations about the parallels with Algeria. "As the flier for the Pentagon showing suggested, the conditions that the French faced in Algeria are similar to those the United States is finding in Iraq," the report states. An official at the Pentagon said, "Showing the film offers historical insight into the conduct of French operations in Algeria, and was intended to prompt informative discussion of the challenges faced by the French," adding that "the discussion was lively and that more showings would probably be held."[28]

Meanwhile, the more palatable legalistic version was also quickly imported to the United States, especially through the writings of David Galula. Galula was originally identified and invited by the RAND Corporation to attend a gathering of experts in April 1962—a five-day symposium that essentially launched theoretical and comparative research on counterinsurgency practices.[29] The participants at that RAND symposium studied and compared the various counterinsurgency strategies used in Algeria, China, Greece, Kenya, Laos, Malaya, Oman, Vietnam, and the Philippines. At the symposium, Galula seized the conversation right off the bat and laid out his vision of counterinsurgency. The summary of Galula's first intervention goes on for three single-spaced pages. His subsequent interventions were equally impressive. An impartial reading of the symposium minutes clearly shows that Galula dominated the five-day meetings.

Galula so impressed his hosts, especially the RAND analysts, that they would commission him to write his memoirs of Algeria, and then translated and published them in 1963 as a confidential classified report titled *Pacification in Algeria, 1956–1958*. The following year, the RAND Corporation translated and helped publish Galula's more theoretical work, *Counter-insurgency Warfare: Theory and Practice*—in which Galula sets forth his eight steps of counterinsurgency.[30] Galula also lectured at Fort Bragg, spent six months at the Armed Forces Staff College at Norfolk, Virginia, and spent two years at Harvard University's Center for International Affairs as a research associate. Galula's writings had an important influence as well on the development of counterinsurgency strategies in Vietnam.[31]

As both schools of French counterinsurgency gained influence in the United States, the use of torture quickly emerged as a central problem. The historian Peter Paret, who initially popularized *la guerre révolutionnaire*, was one of the first to tackle the problem. His position on torture was carefully nuanced—to the point, possibly, of some ambiguity. Explicitly, Paret opposed torture. "Atrocities made re-education in a nontotalitarian sense impossible," he wrote.[32] But even so, Paret acknowledged, just as David Galula before him had, harsh and sometimes exceptional measures needed to be used—at least at the time Paret was writing, in 1962. "Rarely can guerrillas be isolated from the people without the use of unusually harsh coercive measures," Paret observed. "Unless harsh measures are employed rationally and with the clear understanding by all that they are emergency measures, to be stopped as soon as possible, they may actually break down the sense of security with which the legitimacy of any non-totalitarian government is inextricably linked."[33]

In other words, for Paret, unusually harsh measures were rational so long as they were exceptional. Indeed, Paret noted in passing in *French Revolutionary Warfare from Indochina to Algeria*: "Reprisal and terror could be considered rationally as weapons in an intense struggle between ideologically opposed and necessarily ruthless opponents." On the next page, Paret observed that "the efficacy of terror for immobilizing active opposition among a hostile people can hardly be doubted."[34] Given that eliminating the active minority was at the very core of counterinsurgency, those words were suggestive to some, to say the least.

Decades later, General David Petraeus also carefully distanced himself from the torture that took place in Algeria, while simultaneously extolling French theory in general. His field manual explicitly repudiated torture, portraying it as a counterproductive method. Torture, the manual suggested, is what led to the French defeat. In fact, a central discussion of counterinsurgency practices in Algeria takes place in the context of *avoiding* torture. Torture, the manual noted, "empowered the moral legitimacy of the opposition, undermined the French moral legitimacy, and caused internal fragmentation among serving officers that led to an unsuccessful coup attempt in 1962. In the end, failure to comply with moral and legal restrictions against torture severely undermined French efforts and contributed to their loss despite several significant military victories."[35]

At the same time, General Petraeus's field manual read like a tribute to French modern warfare, which was at best deeply ambiguous about the place of brutality. Petraeus's official biographer notes that he "realized the political sensitivity of the manual" and as a result personally edited the opening chapter "thirty to forty times." His correspondence at the time reflects that he was acutely aware of the tension between the more and less brutal versions, and tried to weave a fine line between the different variants.[36]

It is not surprising, then, that some commentators soon argued it was an odd choice to rely so heavily on the French model. "Why do the manual writers put so much emphasis on that French experience," one reviewer wrote, "given that the French failed strategically, engaged in immoral conduct during the war, provoked a civil-military crisis in France, and tolerated genocide and mass population displacement in northern Africa after the withdrawal of French forces? It seems that the French government could not have achieved a worse set of results, nor could US doctrine have chosen a worse model to admire, if admiration it is."[37]

Preferring to avoid the French connection, the later edition of the US field manual published in 2014 excised all references to Galula and French theory, and expunged the annotated bibliography in which his work had figured prominently.[38] The result was a far less theoretical document, and far more intellectually humble. A certain hubris had surrounded the earlier edition—especially that reference to the "graduate level" of warfare. All that is gone. The manual is now silent about those French commanders. But the tension remains.

The recurring strain between brutality and legality, so evident in Algeria and persistent in the writings of Paret and Petraeus, is inherent to counterinsurgency theory. Modern warfare is grounded on the policing of an entire population and the eradication of a minority; as a result, the specter of torture, disappearances, and terrorizing practices hovers over counterinsurgency, when it does not comprise it. Certainly, those practices alone do not always constitute counterinsurgency warfare. Sometimes its constituent parts are less brutal, even laudable—for instance, the provision of essential goods and services for the general population. But even when they are not laudable, experience shows how easily they can be rendered legal, as we saw in the manslaughter inquests in Algeria. And since 9/11, we have repeatedly witnessed the most brutal practices of counterinsurgency being rendered perfectly legal—as we will see in the lengthy legal memos justifying unconscionable practices in the war on terrorism.

In the end, the counterinsurgency model was—from its inception— Janus-faced. It is only recently that our government learned, or rediscovered, ways to mask this central tension.

PART II

A TRIUMPH IN FOREIGN POLICY

Developed by military commanders and strategists over decades of anticolonial wars, counterinsurgency warfare was refined, deployed, and tested in the years following 9/11. Since then, the modern warfare paradigm has been distilled into a concise three-pronged strategy:

1. Bulk-collect all intelligence about everyone in the population—every piece of data and metadata available. Everything about everyone must be known and rendered accessible for data-mining. All communications must be intercepted. All devices must be known. Every piece of data must be amassed. This is the model of the NSA's Treasure Map program. In the NSA's words, "every single end device that is connected to the Internet somewhere in the world—every smartphone, tablet, and computer" must be known.[1] And not just the data of the active minority, but rather the information of *everyone* and *every citizen* in the population, especially the neutral or passive majority. That is the only way to accurately identify the insurgents. Whether through new digital surveillance technologies or enhanced physical interrogation, all intelligence must be obtained. Under the capitalized header "INTELLIGENCE DRIVES OPERATIONS," General Petraeus's field manual underscores the critical importance of "timely, specific, and reliable intelligence, gathered and analyzed at the lowest possible level and disseminated throughout the force."[2] The key here is *total information awareness.*

2. Identify and eradicate the revolutionary minority. Total information about everyone makes it possible to discriminate between friend and foe. Once suspicion attaches, individuals must

be treated severely to extract all possible information, with enhanced interrogation techniques if necessary; and if they are revealed to belong to the active minority, they must be disposed of through detention, rendition, deportation, or drone strike—in other words, targeted assassination. Unlike conventional soldiers from the past, these insurgents are dangerous because of their ideology, not their physical presence on a battlefield. They need to be sequestered from the general population (when not outright eliminated) so as not to taint it. This corresponds to the "enemy-centric" aspects of counterinsurgency.[3] Under the capitalized header "INSURGENTS MUST BE ISOLATED FROM THEIR CAUSE AND SUPPORT," General Petraeus's manual reads: "Clearly, killing or capturing insurgents will be necessary, especially when an insurgency is based in religious or ideological extremism." It is difficult, though, to kill "every insurgent," and so often more effective "to separate an insurgency from its resources and let it die than to kill every insurgent." But "with respect to the hard-core extremists," the field manual underscores, "the task was more straightforward: their complete and utter destruction."[4] The second objective, then, is to destroy any and all potential insurgents.

3. Pacify the masses. The population must be distracted, entertained, satisfied, occupied, and most importantly, neutralized, or deradicalized if necessary, in order to ensure that the vast preponderance of ordinary individuals remain just that—*ordinary*. This third prong reflects the "population-centric" dimension of counterinsurgency theory. Remember, in this new way of seeing, the population *is* the battlefield. Its hearts and minds must be assured. In the digital age, this can be achieved, first, by targeting enhanced content (such as sermons by moderate imams) to deradicalize susceptible persons—in other words, by deploying new digital techniques of psychological warfare and propaganda.

Second, by providing just the bare minimum in terms of welfare and humanitarian assistance—like rebuilding schools, distributing some cash, and bolstering certain government institutions. As General Petraeus's field manual stresses, "dollars and ballots will have more important effects than bombs and bullets."[5] Third, by demonstrating to the general population who is more powerful and who has control of the territory. One of the most important lessons from prior insurgencies is that it is possible to win the war militarily, but lose it politically and diplomatically.[6] For this reason, it is essential to privilege these *political dimensions* of the counterinsurgency struggle. Under the header "LEGITIMACY IS THE MAIN OBJECTIVE," the field manual emphasizes: "Military action can address the symptoms of a loss of legitimacy. In some cases, it can eliminate substantial numbers of insurgents. However, success in the form of a durable peace requires restoring legitimacy, which, in turn, requires the use of all instruments of national power. A [counterinsurgency] effort cannot achieve lasting success without the [host-nation] government achieving legitimacy."[7]

And this final step, of course, takes us back to the first prong, total information awareness, because in order to achieve state legitimacy it is necessary to know everything about the whole population in order to prevent gains by the active minority. As the former head of the NSA, General Michael Hayden, writes in his book *Playing to the Edge*, the primary task of the signals intelligence agency is essentially preventive counterterrorism.[8] The idea is to identify the revolutionary minority before it materializes. Total awareness is directly tied into the other two prongs of counterinsurgency.

Counterinsurgency theory embraced its political nature and has gradually matured from a localized military strategy to a broader foreign policy. This distilled version of modern warfare was deployed first in Iraq, then more largely in the global war on terror, but now has reached beyond it to countries like Yemen or Somalia with which we are not at war. At first militarily, but now in foreign affairs, the United States governs abroad on the paradigm of modern warfare. In a short summary, General Petraeus's field manual offers a concise table of best practices. It starts with "Emphasize intelligence," "Focus on the population," and "Isolate insurgents."[9] These best practices can now be read as our new paradigm of governing abroad.

3

TOTAL INFORMATION AWARENESS

THE ATTACK ON THE WORLD TRADE CENTER SHOWED THE weakness of American intelligence gathering. Top secret information obtained by one agency was silo'ed from others, making it impossible to aggregate intelligence and obtain a full picture of the security threats. The CIA knew that two of the 9/11 hijackers were on American soil in San Diego, but didn't share the information with the FBI, who were actively trying to track them down.[1] September 11 was a crippling intelligence failure, and in the immediacy of that failure many in President George W. Bush's administration felt the need to do something radical. Greater sharing of intelligence, naturally. But much more as well. Two main solutions were devised, or revived: total surveillance and tortured interrogations. They represent the first prong of the counterinsurgency approach.

In effect, 9/11 set the stage both for total NSA surveillance and torture as forms of total information awareness. The former functioned at the most virtual or ethereal, or "digital" level, by creating the material for data-mining and analysis. The latter operated at the most bodily or physical, or "analog" level, obtaining information directly from suspects and detainees in Iraq, Pakistan, Afghanistan, and elsewhere. But both satisfied the same goal: total information awareness, the first tactic of counterinsurgency warfare.

The first, total NSA surveillance. In the aftermath of 9/11, the US government put in place a web of illicit and licit signal intelligence programs with the ambition to capture and collect all communications around the world. This effort gave birth to bulk data collection programs ranging from the Section 215 program of the USA PATRIOT Act to those myriad NSA programs made public through the Edward Snowden revelations. With names like PRISM, UPSTREAM, and BOUNDLESS INFORMANT, these surveillance programs would give the US government access to all communications flowing through the underwater cables and satellites orbiting around earth, as well as through the servers of Internet companies and social media. These post–9/11 intelligence programs provide the US government direct access to any foreigner's e-mails, attachments, videos, VoIP calls—in sum, practically all foreign digital communications and Internet traffic. The different programs are targeted at different systems and use different techniques—from simple cable-splicing in order to make integral copies of all the digital data flowing through fiber-optic cables, to the more complex introduction of malware into intercepted and surreptitiously opened hardware being sold to foreigners. What they aim for is *totality*.

You may recall the Total Information Awareness (TIA) program that Admiral John Poindexter tried to pioneer in the late 1990s and to resuscitate in the wake of 9/11. The program had that ominous image of an eye at the top of a pyramid seeing the entire world, with the Baconian logo *scientia est potentia* ("knowledge is power"). The objective was a massive surveillance system that would capture absolutely all communications. The TIA program was originally shelved in 1999 in part because of the controversy surrounding Admiral Poindexter, who had been the highest-ranking official in the Reagan administration found guilty during the Iran-Contra affair. The TIA program was revived and funded for a while after 9/11, before eventually being scrapped again because of the renewed storms surrounding Poindexter.[2] But the architecture, vision, and ambition of "total information awareness" captured perfectly the first prong of counterinsurgency strategy.

The ambition here was *total information*, and our new digital technologies have now made this possible. American Civil Liberties Union (ACLU) legal director David Cole reminds us of a PowerPoint slide leaked by Edward Snowden that gives a sense of the capabilities and the ambition. The NSA document reveals, Cole writes, that "the NSA's 'new collection posture' is to 'collect it all,' 'process it all,' 'exploit it all,' 'partner it all,' 'sniff it all,' and, ultimately, 'know it all.'"[3] Yes, "know it all": that is the goal. US government today tries to gain access, to monitor and surveil practically all foreign communications, including e-mails, Facebook posts, Skype messaging, Yahoo video-chat platforms, Twitter tweets, Tumblr photos, Google searches, etc.—in sum, all telecom data including social media and Internet traffic. And of course, it is not only the US government that tries to achieve these capabilities, but also its Five Eyes partners—the intelligence agencies of Australia, Canada, New Zealand, and the United Kingdom—and other allies like France and Germany, as well as the intelligence agencies of most developed countries large and small, from China or Russia to Israel. And in our new digital age, such surveillance is becoming easier, cheaper, and more efficient daily.

The goal of total information awareness has been carried out through licit and illicit activities—the latter most dramatically illustrated by the infamous hospital episode the night of March 10, 2004. The NSA had been carrying out, for two years, a warrantless eavesdropping program known as Stellar Wind that monitored telecom and e-mail communications between US citizens and foreign citizens if either party was linked to a terrorist group. The warrantless program was ultimately deemed illegal by the Department of Justice. Despite that, and shortly thereafter, then White House counsel Alberto Gonzales and President

Bush's chief of staff rushed to the hospital late at night to get the ail-
ing attorney general, John Ashcroft, semiconscious and in his sickbed
in the intensive-care unit, to reauthorize the warrantless eavesdropping program. Ashcroft was so sick, in fact, that his powers had been
transferred to his deputy, James Comey. Significant legal controversy
also surrounded the Section 215 program, which was deemed illegal
by several federal judges—before it was eventually modified, ever so
slightly, in June 2015 to require that the telecoms hold the metadata
rather than the NSA, at taxpayer's expense.[4] The full scope and reach of
the NSA programs, and their constitutionality, have not, to date, been
sufficiently recognized or properly adjudicated.

What is clear, though—as I document in *Exposed*—is that the myriad NSA, FBI, CIA, and allied intelligence agencies produce total information, the first and most important prong of the counterinsurgency
paradigm. Most important, because both of the other prongs depend
on it. As the RAND Corporation notes in its lengthy 519-page report
on the current state of counterinsurgency theory and practice, "Effective governance depends on knowing the population, demographically
and individually." The RAND report reminds us that this insight is not
novel or new. The report then returns, pointedly for us, to Algeria and
the French commander, David Galula: "Galula, in *Counterinsurgency
Warfare*, argued that 'control of the population begins with a thorough
census. Every inhabitant must be registered and given a foolproof identity card.'"[5] Today, that identity card is an IP address, a mobile phone, a
digital device, facial recognition, and all our digital stamps. These new
digital technologies have made everyone virtually transparent. And
with our new ethos of selfies, tweets, Facebook, and Internet surfing,
everyone is now exposed.

Second, tortured interrogation. The dual personality of counterinsurgency warfare is nowhere more evident than in the intensive use of
torture for information gathering by the United States immediately
after 9/11. Fulfilling the first task of counterinsurgency theory—total

surveillance—this practice married the most extreme form of brutality associated with modern warfare to the formality of legal process and the rule of law. The combination of inhumanity and legality was spectacular.

In the days following 9/11, many in the Bush administration felt there was only one immediate way to address the information shortfall, namely, to engage in "enhanced interrogation" of captured suspected terrorists—another euphemism for torture. Of course, torture of captured suspects would not fix the problem of silo'ed information, but they thought it would at least provide immediate information of any pending attacks. One could say that the United States turned to torture because many in the administration believed the country did not have adequate intelligence capabilities, lacking the spy network or even the language abilities to infiltrate and conduct regular espionage on organizations like Al Qaeda.[6]

The tortured interrogations combined the extremes of brutality with the formality of the rule of law. We are familiar with the first, but the details nevertheless remain stunning—and numbing. Waterboarding a suspect over 183 times. Forcing a detainee to remain in a standing stress position for 7.5 days, or almost 180 hours. Locking a prisoner in a coffin-sized confinement box for nearly 2 weeks. These unconscionable practices were administered by CIA agents and contractors, including psychologists, beginning in 2002, in black-site prisons far and wide—from Afghanistan to Thailand—many times after extensive and lengthy FBI interrogations.

Even the more ordinary instances of "enhanced interrogation" were harrowing—and so often administered, according to the Senate report, after the interrogators believed there was no more information to be had, sometimes even before the detainee had the opportunity to speak. One prisoner, named Ridhar al-Najjar, is described as "having been left hanging—which involved handcuffing one or both wrists to an overhead bar which would not allow him to lower his arms—for 22 hours each day for two consecutive days." Another prisoner, Gul Rahman, was subjected to "48 hours of sleep deprivation, auditory overload, total darkness, isolation, a cold shower, and rough treatment," before then being "shackled to the wall of his cell in a position that required [him] to rest on the bare concrete floor [. . .] wearing only a sweatshirt." (He was found dead the next day. The cause of death was hypothermia.) Another prisoner, Abd al-Rahim al-Nashiri, was placed "in a 'standing stress position' with 'his hands affixed over his head' for approximately two and a half days," and then later, a CIA officer "placed a pistol near al-Nashiri's head and operated a cordless drill near al-Nashiri's body."[7]

Ramzi bin al-Shibh was subjected to this type of treatment immediately upon arrival in detention, even before being interrogated or given an opportunity to cooperate—in what would become a "template" for other detainees. Bin al-Shibh was subjected first to "sensory dislocation" including "shaving bin al-Shibh's head and face, exposing him to loud noise in a white room with white lights, keeping him 'unclothed and subjected to uncomfortably cool temperatures,' and shackling him 'hand and foot with arms outstretched over his head (with his feet firmly on the floor and not allowed to support his weight with his arms).'" Following that, the interrogation would include "attention grasp, walling, the facial hold, the facial slap . . . the abdominal slap, cramped confinement, wall standing, stress positions, sleep deprivation beyond 72 hours, and the waterboard, as appropriate to [bin al-Shibh's] level of resistance."[8] This template would be used on others—and served as a warning to all.

The more extreme forms of torture were also accompanied by the promise of life-long solitary confinement or, in the case of death, cremation. Counterinsurgency torture in the past had often been linked to summary disappearances and executions. Under the Bush administration, it was tied to what one might call virtual disappearances.

During the Algerian war, as noted already, the widespread use of brutal interrogation techniques meant that those who had been victimized—both the guilty and innocent—became dangerous in the eyes of the French military leadership. FLN members needed to be silenced, forever; but so did others who might be radicalized by the waterboarding or *gégène*. In Algeria, a simple solution was devised: the tortured would be thrown out from helicopters into the Mediterranean. They became *les crevettes de Bigeard*, after the notorious French general in Algeria, Marcel Bigeard: "Bigeard's shrimp," dumped into the sea, their feet in poured concrete—a technique the French military had apparently experimented with earlier in Indochina.[9]

The CIA would devise a different solution in 2002: either torture the suspect accidentally to death and then cremate his body to avoid detection, or torture the suspect to the extreme and then ensure that he would never again talk to another human being. Abu Zubaydah received the latter treatment. Zubaydah had first been seized and interrogated at length by the FBI, had provided useful information, and was placed in isolation for forty-seven days, the FBI believing that he had no more valuable information. Then the CIA took over, believing he might still be a source.[10] The CIA turned to its more extreme forms of torture—utilizing all ten of its most brutal techniques—but, as a CIA cable from the interrogation team, dated July 15, 2002, records, they realized beforehand that it would either have to cover up the torture if death ensued or ensure that Zubaydah would never talk to another human being again in his lifetime. According to the Senate report, "the cable stated that if Abu Zubaydah were to die during the interrogation, he would be cremated. The interrogation team closed the cable by stating: 'regardless which [disposition] option we follow however, and especially in light of the planned psychological pressure techniques to be implemented, we need to get reasonable assurances that [Abu Zubaydah] will remain in isolation and incommunicado for the remainder of his life.'"[11] In response to this request for assurance, a cable from the CIA station gave the interrogation team those assurances, noting that "it was correct in its 'understanding that the interrogation process takes precedence over preventative medical procedures,'" and then adding in the cable:

> There is a fairly unanimous sentiment within HQS that [Abu Zubaydah] will never be placed in a situation where he has any significant contact with others and/or has the opportunity to be released. While it is difficult to discuss specifics at this point, all major players are in concurrence that [Abu Zubaydah] should remain incommunicado for the remainder of his life.[12]

"Incommunicado for the remainder of his life": this statement may explain why the Guantánamo prison camp remained operative for so long. Abu Zubaydah made his first public appearance at a Periodic Review Board hearing at Guantánamo fourteen years later, on August 23, 2016—after fourteen years incommunicado. As of this writing, he remains detained at Guantánamo. The agency was given a governmental promise, at the highest levels.

Such measures and assurances, of course, were not the product of a demented interrogator, a deranged superior, or commanders gone native or mad. These routines were approved at the uppermost level of the US government, by the president of the United States and his closest advisers. These practices were put in place, designed carefully and legally—very legalistically, in fact—to be used on suspected enemies. They were not an aberration. There are, to be sure, long histories written of rogue intelligence services using unauthorized techniques; there is a lengthy record, as well, of CIA ingenuity and creativity in this domain, including, among other examples, the 1963 KUBARK Counterintelligence Interrogation manual.[13] But after 9/11, the blueprint was drawn at the White House and the Pentagon, and it became official US policy—deliberate, debated, well-thought-out, and adopted as legal measures.

President George W. Bush himself specifically approved the transfer of the first detainee who would be interrogated by the CIA, Abu Zubaydah, to a black site in a foreign country because (among other reasons which are blacked out in the report) there would be a "lack of US court jurisdiction" there. "That morning, the president approved moving forward with the plan to transfer Abu Zubaydah to Country [redacted]," the Senate report states. Thereafter, and deliberately, the president kept willfully ignorant of the location of detainees "to avoid inadvertent disclosures," but he tacitly approved it all.[14]

In this context, the explicit decisions regarding the transfer and treatment of detainees, and the interrogation methods used, fell to the secretaries of defense and of state, the attorney general, and, whenever possible, the vice president. John Ashcroft, the attorney general of the United States and the highest-ranking lawyer in the country, on July 24, 2002, "verbally approved the use of 10 interrogation techniques, which included: the attention grasp, walling, the facial hold, the facial slap (insult slap), cramped confinement, wall standing, stress positions, sleep deprivation, use of diapers, and use of insects." Two days later, the Senate report states, *the attorney general verbally approved the use of the waterboard.*" And in early August, according to the Senate report, "the National Security Council legal advisor informed the DCI's chief of staff that '[National Security Adviser] Dr. Rice had been informed that there would be no briefing of the President on this matter,' but that the DCI had policy approval to employ the CIA's enhanced interrogation techniques."[15]

A year later, in July 2003, after being briefed by the DCI and CIA General Counsel on the enhanced interrogation techniques—including a description of the waterboard techniques that substantially understated the number of times it had been used on detainees Khalid Sheikh Mohammed and Abu Zubaydah—Vice President Cheney and Rice spoke on behalf of the White House and reauthorized the use of torture.[16]

Practically every enhanced interrogation measure used—except perhaps the use of a drill and a broom handle—was also vetted at CIA headquarters and approved as an interrogation plan at the top level of the CIA. Prior to using "enhanced interrogation techniques," multiple cables and authorizations went back and forth between the detention facilities and CIA headquarters.[17] These uses of torturous methods were planned, authorized, supervised, analyzed, and reconfirmed and reinforced by the highest government authorities.

In 2003, the CIA General Counsel communicated with the National Security Council principals, White House staff, and Department of Justice personnel, and expressed concern that CIA interrogation methods "might be inconsistent with public statements from the Administration that the US Government's treatment of detainees was 'humane.'" The result was not what one might have expected. As the Senate torture report indicates, instead of putting a halt to these practices, following the communiqué, "the White House press secretary was advised to avoid using the term 'humane treatment' when discussing the detention of al-Qa'ida and Taliban personnel."[18] Clearly, these were not accidental practices. They were fully discussed, deliberated, and made legal. The government's decision to avoid talk of "humane treatment" perfectly embodies the combination of brutality and official government sanction characteristic of a counterinsurgency regime.

The Janus face of torture was its formal legality amidst its shocking brutality. Many of the country's best lawyers and legal scholars, professors at top-ranked law schools, top government attorneys, and later federal judges would pore over statutes and case law to find legal maneuvers to permit torture. The felt need to legitimate and legalize the brutality—and of course, to protect the officials and operatives from later litigation—was remarkable.

The documents known collectively as the "torture memos" fell into two categories: first, those legal memos regarding whether the Guantánamo detainees were entitled to POW status under the Geneva Conventions (GPW), written between September 25, 2001, and August 1, 2002; and second, starting in August 2002, the legal memos regarding whether the "enhanced interrogation techniques" envisaged by the CIA amounted to torture prohibited under international law.

The first set of memos, dealing with the Geneva Conventions, ultimately led President Bush to declare, on February 7, 2002, that the

GPW did not apply in the conflict against Al Qaeda. Secretary of State Colin Powell had previously asked President Bush to reconsider that conclusion, arguing that the GPW should apply.[19] In the ensuing exchange, it became clear that one of the principal concerns within the administration was whether the president or other US officials were opening themselves up to criminal liability for violating the GPW.

Alberto Gonzales, then White House counsel, made this concern clear. In his recapitulation of the pros and cons of changing views on the GPW, Gonzales focused on the risk of prosecution. Sticking with the view that the GPW did not apply, he argued,

> substantially reduces the threat of domestic criminal prosecution under the War Crimes Act (18 U.S.C. 2441). [. . .] It is difficult to predict the motives of prosecutors and independent counsels who may in the future decide to pursue unwarranted charges based on Section 2441. Your determination would create a reasonable basis in law that Section 2441 does not apply, which would provide a solid defense to any future prosecution.[20]

Secretary Colin Powell also emphasized that his proposal to apply the GPW would not entail "any significant risk of domestic prosecution against US officials." President Bush ultimately denied GPW status to the detainees, but ordered that they would nevertheless be treated humanely. The problem of the "rogue prosecutor" loomed large in the torture memos.[21] The president, his cabinet, and closest advisers were trying to ensure that they would never be prosecuted or that they would have a defense in case they were prosecuted for violating the ban on torture. The extensive legal back and forth would have been offered to prove that these officials were trying to comply with the law. And after the publication of the Senate torture report revealed the use of certain extreme forms of torture (such as "rectal rehydration"), John Yoo, who had been at the Office of Legal Counsel and authored several of the torture memos, stated he was not aware of that type of torture being used and that it would probably violate the prohibition on torture. This defensive maneuver was precisely the kind of protection sought and provided by the legal documentation.

The next set of memos concerned the use of torture. These memos began immediately after the first wave, on February 26, 2002, and reached a climax during August 2002. The timing is important. The Senate torture report reveals that Zubaydah was being waterboarded in August 2002, and other reports suggest he was being tortured earlier in the summer. These torture memos were being written to justify practices that were *already taking place.* They justified torture by setting the threshold of torture so high that protections would only trigger in the case of extreme physical abuse with specific intent to cause death or organ failure. As Jay Bybee, then at the Office of Legal Counsel and now a federal judge, wrote in his August 1, 2002, memo:

> We conclude that torture as defined in and proscribed by [18 US Code] Sections 2340-2340A, covers only extreme acts. Severe pain is generally of the kind difficult for the victim to endure. Where the pain is physical, it must be of an intensity akin to that which accompanies serious physical injury *such as death or organ failure.* Severe mental pain requires suffering not just at the moment of infliction but also requires lasting psychological harm, such as seen in mental disorders like post-traumatic stress disorder. [. . .] Because the acts inflicting torture are extreme, there is significant range of acts that though they might constitute cruel, inhuman, or degrading treatment or punishment fail to rise to the level of torture.[22]

This definition of torture was so demanding that it excluded the brutal practices that the United States was using. It set the federal legal standard, essentially, at death or organ failure.

By October 2002, the interrogation teams were asking for permission to use methods including waterboarding—"Use of a wet towel and dripping water to induce the misperception of suffocation"—and other forms of generally recognized torture. Secretary of Defense Donald Rumsfeld approved a number of techniques on December 2, 2002, adding, in a handwritten note, that he himself stands eight hours a day. By the time Rumsfeld finally approved a longer list of techniques on April 16, 2003, they were twenty-four in number and were written in such a way as to seem innocuous. Gone also is waterboarding.[23] They resembled more the type of forensic interrogation techniques discussed in *Miranda v. Arizona*, or in the infamous police interrogation manuals of the time. The Senate torture report, however, documents the unusually brutal ways in which they were actually implemented.

The turn to legality and legal process—the turn to the most legalistic treatment at the highest levels of United States law making, including the attorney general and the Office of Legal Counsel—is telling. The authors of the torture memos were not military officers improvising on the field of battle under hostile gunfire. Nor were they under the pressure of a ticking time bomb.[24] Instead, they participated in a slow, bureaucratic, deliberate legal negotiation, fully reasoned, regarding the government regulation of prohibited conduct at a time when a deep international consensus—including international treaties and customary law—held that actions like waterboarding would violate sovereign responsibilities.

None of it is unprecedented, of course. In fact, for centuries torture was fully legal and deeply regulated—both inquisitorial torture to gain information and punitive torture for corporal or capital punishment. The history of the oversight and minute regulation of torture—state sanctioned at the highest level—goes far back. The Justinian *Digest* codified the strict regulation of the use of torture on slaves and served as a model to later codifications during the early Middle Ages and to the practices of the Inquisition. A good illustration of the latter, for instance, is the methodical and meticulous recitation of waterboarding—the *toca*, the classic, definitional form of torture during the Spanish Inquisition—at the formal inquisition of Marina González in Toledo in 1494, as reported by the notary at trial. This interrogation would typically have occurred in a separate, secret chamber, where only Ma-rina González, the inquisitor, and the notary would be present. Here is a literal translation from the fifteenth-century archive:

> She was stripped of her old skirts and put on the rack, and her arms and legs were tied tightly with cords. She also had a cord tied tightly around her head. They put a hood in front of her face, and with a jar that held three pints, more or less, they started to pour water down her nose and throat.
>
> [. . .]His reverence ordered her to be given water until the three-pint jar ran out; she never said a word. [. . .] They tied her up again and began to give her more water from the jar, which they had refilled [. . .]
>
> They gave her more water, and she said that she would tell everything, for Holy Mary's sake.[25]

These practices were highly regulated and limited, but fully codified in law and supervised by magistrates during the Inquisition. They were also tame compared to the practices in the new millennium.

The torture memos effectively tried to replicate this legal framework, but it did so in a unique manner. Instead of officially codifying the practices—which would have been impossible given the treaties and laws on the books and customary international law—the executive branch assumed a quasi-judicial function. The Bush administration formed itself as a minijudiciary, with legal briefs going back and forth, legal arguments, and pretend judicial opinions. It "legalized" the practices by constituting itself as its own judicial system.

Through the process of legalization, the president's men appropriated the judicial function. The lawyers at the White House and departments of justice, state, and defense filed briefs with each other, trying to persuade each other, contesting but ultimately deciding the questions at issue: they rendered judgment. The memos became "legal briefs"—in fact, it says so on many of them[26]—and then, effectively, judicial opinions. The executive branch became a minijudiciary, with no effective oversight or judicial review. And in the end, it worked. The men who wrote these memos have never been prosecuted nor seriously taken to task, as a legal matter, for their actions. The American people allowed a quasi-judiciary to function autonomously, during and after. These self-appointed judges wrote the legal briefs, rendered judgment, and wrote the judicial opinions that legitimized these brutal counterinsurgency practices. In the process, they rendered the counterinsurgency fully legal. They inscribed torture within the fabric of law.

One could go further. The torture memos accomplished a new resolution of the tension between brutality and legality, one that we had not witnessed previously in history. It was an audacious quasi-judicial legality that had rarely been seen before. And by legalizing torture in that way, the Bush administration provided a legal infrastructure for counterinsurgency-as-governance more broadly.

In this sense, it is illusory to draw distinctions, as contemporary counterinsurgency theorists do, between good and bad forms of modern warfare—between what are referred to as the "kill-capture" or "win-the-population" approaches, between the "enemy-centric" and "population-centric" strategies, or even between President Bush's "war on terror" and the newer "global war on terror" (GWOT).[27] These variations are all simply different *versions* of the counterinsurgency paradigm, revolving around the same three central strategies.[28] Some parts of that paradigm are more enemy-centric, such as extracting information through brutal means and eradicating the active minority. Other pieces of the paradigm are more population-centric, such as total information awareness and winning the hearts and minds. But they do not represent distinct models of warfare, just variations on the theme of the counterinsurgency model. And the Bush administration's turn to legality created a legal prototype for the counterinsurgency paradigm to become a form of governing—to unleash its *political* nature.

Ultimately, turning torture into this legal practice—outside the formal legal system but regulated by this new quasi-judiciary—loosened all the constraints: torture began to pervade the liminal spaces and to exceed the bounds of mere extraction of information. Abu Ghraib, black sites, Guantánamo—these spaces became places of torture, not only in the interrogation rooms, but through the solitary confinement, the horrid conditions, even the ordinary custodial measures.[29] The entire spaces filled up with torture as torture became the new legal norm.

And through this process of legalization, these broader torturous practices spilled over into the second prong of counterinsurgency: the eradication of an active minority. Torture began to function as a way to isolate, punish, and eliminate those suspected of being insurgents.

4

INDEFINITE DETENTION AND DRONE KILLINGS

"**M**P, Sir, I cannot breathe! . . . MP, *sir*, please," Mohamedou Slahi begged, as he was transported from Bagram Air Base in Afghanistan. With a bag over his head, a mask over his mouth and nose, strapped tightly around the stomach by a belt fastened to his straight-back seat, shackled by the hands and feet to his waist, Slahi could barely breathe. He thought he was going to die, smothered by the security measures imposed for transportation. "Now I couldn't endure the pain," Slahi recounted in the 466-page manuscript he handwrote in his Guantánamo prison cell in 2005.[1] Written to serve as a legal chronicle for purposes of a habeas corpus challenge, the manuscript was subsequently published for a general readership under the title *Guantánamo Diary*.

This particular ordeal was not another CIA interrogation scene, though it surely was torturous. "I felt I was going to die. I couldn't help asking for help louder. 'Mister, I cannot breathe . . . ,'" Slahi writes. "'I cannot breathe!' I said, gesturing to my nose."[2] Slahi was being transported to the prison camp at Guantánamo for an indeterminate period of detention. He would remain at Guantánamo from 2002 to October 2016 without ever being tried, convicted, or sentenced. Treated as an "enemy combatant" in an undeclared war on terrorism, Slahi was now incommunicado. While at Guantánamo, he would be tortured, placed in solitary confinement, beaten and humiliated, and taken out to sea on a helicopter for a mock execution.

Indefinite detention at Guantánamo served as one of two principal strategies to eradicate the active minority. The use of drone strikes was the other—both entirely consistent with the dictates of counterinsurgency theory. With the transition from the Bush to the Obama administration, we observed a distinct shift in emphasis from the first to the second. But that did not suggest a weakening of counterinsurgency's influence. If anything, drone strikes represented counterinsurgency's deepening hold over American foreign policy.

The second prong of counterinsurgency theory—to eliminate the active minority—was first accomplished right after 9/11 by the capture and indefinite detention of suspects in black sites, American prisons abroad, and Guantánamo Bay camp. Indefinite detention in isolation for months is in itself a form of torture, of course; but it is also an effective way to eliminate people. A particularly torturous way to do so, from start to finish.

Mohamedou Slahi's account is chilling. Eight months in complete isolation, the beatings, the sleep deprivation, the colored blinkers, the ear-piercing music—and then over a dozen years of indefinite detention. One of the more striking features of Slahi's account is precisely how torturous even the ordinary moments and day-to-day treatment were. We already encountered in the last chapter the extreme brutality—the waterboarding, the coffin-sized boxes, the isolation. But the other, more banal custodial experiences were also deeply brutalizing.

In the everyday moments, the routinized security measures turned violent. The devices of restraint—the handcuffs and ankle-cuffs that dug into the skin, the chains on the waist, the straight chair, for hours and hours, the fellow inmate who accidentally or carelessly yanked the chain, driving the metal cuffs into one's bones. The inability to change position, the numbing, the tingling, the limbs that fell asleep, for hours. These too became torturous. "A guard appeared and took the mask off my nose," Slahi tells us. "I took a deep breath and felt really relieved. But to my dismay, the guard put the mask back on my nose and mouth. 'Sir, I cannot breathe . . . MP . . . MP.' The same guy showed up once more, but instead of taking the mask off my nose, he took the plug out of my ear and said, 'Forget about it!' and immediately put the ear plug back. It was harsh [. . .] I was panicking, I had just enough air, but the only way to survive was to convince the brain to be satisfied with the tiny bit of air it got."[3]

There is a numbing quality to Slahi's account—perhaps the indefiniteness of time and torture themselves becomes numbing. Perhaps becoming numb is the only way to bear it. A chronology, a log—a chronicle of abuse, an obscene list of gratuitous violence:

> By now the chains on my ankles were cutting off the blood to my feet. My feet became numb. I heard only the moaning and crying of other detainees. Beating was the order of the trip. I was not spared: the guard kept hitting me on my head and squeezing my neck against the rear end of the other detainee.[4]

The indefinite detention and brutal ordinary measures served as a way to eliminate these men—captured in the field or traded for reward monies, almost like slaves from yonder. The incommunicado confinement itself satisfied the second prong of counterinsurgency theory.[5] But somehow it also reached further than mere detention, approximating a form of disappearance or virtual death. The conditions these men found themselves in were so extreme, it is almost as if they were as good as dead.

Reading Slahi's numbing descriptions, one cannot help but agree with the philosopher Giorgio Agamben that these men at Guantánamo were, in his words, no more than "bare life."[6] Agamben's concept of bare existence captures well the dimensions of dehumanization and degradation that characterized their lives: the camp inmates were reduced to nothing more than bare animal existence. They were no longer human, but things that lived. The indefinite detention and torture at Guantánamo achieved an utter denial of their humanity.

Every aspect of their treatment at black sites and detention facilities reinforced this notion of bare life: not just the torturous physical and psychological methods that reduced them to their bodies only, not just the coffin-sized boxes and waterboards, but the fact that their bodies would have been anonymously cremated; that the president did not even need to be briefed about them; that the black sites were geographically located to avoid US court jurisdiction; that the tortured detainees would remain incommunicado for the remainder of their lives, never again to have significant contact with others. All these practices evacuated their humanity, excluded them as humans, wiped them off the face of the earth. Indefinite detention was a method to eliminate them.

Since then, a large number of Guantánamo prisoners have been deported to foreign countries under strict security agreements with foreign governments that are intended to ensure their continued surveillance and monitoring. Some have been prosecuted in their countries upon return. Some are now held in prisons abroad. For the most part, their lives have been shattered and destroyed—even those who are now free have effectively been eliminated.[7]

Decades later, the United States continued to be embroiled in debate over those prisoners who remained at Guantánamo—most of whom had never appeared before a court or been tried or judged. The Republican members of Congress refused to allow Guantánamo to be closed, despite President Obama's pledge to do so during his 2008 presidential campaign.[8] President Donald Trump came into office explicitly vowing to keep Guantánamo open, even to fill it with new terrorist suspects from the war against ISIS, including US citizens.

In these contentious public debates, the voices and experiences of those who had been virtually disappeared rarely received much attention, far less certainly than the more positive filmic representations of the war on terror. Despite the fact that Slahi's book cracked Amazon's top one hundred bestselling books in January 2015, and was chosen for the *New York Times* notable books of 2015, his readership paled in comparison to the viewership of *Zero Dark Thirty*, a thriller movie depicting the capture and assassination of Osama bin Laden—which had over sixteen million viewers and grossed more than $132 million worldwide.[9]

The depiction of indefinite detention in a movie like *Zero Dark Thirty* shaped the American public's imagination, not Slahi's account. *Zero Dark Thirty*, and movies like it, manufacture a different truth about the counterinsurgency: namely that, however begrudgingly, brutal violence and indefinite detention pay off. The filmic representation in *Zero Dark Thirty* subtly convinces the viewer, slowly, patiently, of the benefits of these counterinsurgency strategies. It ultimately valorizes the techniques of modern warfare, in a number of ways. First, by convincing viewers that these methods of indefinite detention and torture are effective. Second, by making it seem that the detainees recover fully from their detention and torture. And third, by dehumanizing the detainees and valorizing the counterinsurgency operatives. Films like *Zero Dark Thirty* serve as the popular brief for the efficacy of detention and torture. Just treating indefinite detention or torture as an ordinary event, as a routine, daily occurrence, serve to normalize and naturalize it, as the philosopher Slavoj Žižek suggests.[10] And this normalization, of course, ties neatly to the third prong of the counterinsurgency—winning the hearts and minds of the people, which we will come to in a moment.

The Predator drone armed with a Hellfire AGM-114C missile is the other principal method used to eliminate the active minority. As noted earlier, the US government began drone operations shortly after 9/11 in Afghanistan, then accelerated their use in Pakistan during the Obama administration. Drones have been deployed in waves in Yemen and Somalia as well. Under the Obama administration, a "kill list" would be drawn up every Tuesday at a weekly gathering of over one hundred national security experts to recommend to President Obama who should be targeted next—a weekly meeting that was dubbed "Terror Tuesday."[11]

The mobile application, Dronestream, listed the following drone strikes for May 2016:

> May 27, 2016: On Friday, in south-central Somalia, the United States fired a missile at Mr. Da'ud (Somalia) washingtonpost.com/news
>
> May 21, 2016: Maybe it was Mr. Mansour. Several US drones lit up a car near Ahmad Wal, killing 2 people (Pakistan) nytimes.com /2016/05/22
>
> May 19, 2016: On Thursday, in the middle of the desert, two drone missiles destroyed a car. 2 people killed (Yemen) pic.twitter.com /7vIoJV7rBI
>
> May 12, 2016: Two people wounded. Five people killed (Somalia) nbcnews.com/news/us-news

As of April 2017, the Bureau of Investigative Journalism had documented 2,250 confirmed drone strikes, resulting in the deaths of between 6,248 and 9,019 persons, of which 736 to 1,391 were innocent civilians, including 242 to 307 children killed.[12] Despite these significant civilian casualties, drone strikes continued at a constant rhythm. In fact, under President Trump, the strikes accelerated. NBC News reported twenty strikes on a single day, March 2, 2017, launched in the Yemeni governorates of Abyan, Al Bayda, and Shabwah.[13] In the first four months of the Trump administration, the average monthly rate of lethal strikes in Pakistan, Somalia, and Yemen increased almost fourfold over the prior administration's average.[14]

There is an ongoing debate among military strategists about whether drone warfare fits within the counterinsurgency paradigm. The debate, however interesting, misses the key point: counterinsurgency practice comes in different variations and any apparent contradiction regarding drone strikes reflects perfectly the internal tensions at the heart of counterinsurgency: precisely the same tensions we saw in the context of torture. Examining whether drone warfare fits into counterinsurgency theory, however, does help us better understand the deeper logic of modern warfare.

As Grégoire Chamayou points out in his book *A Theory of the Drone*, in a chapter titled "Counterinsurgency from the Air," the traditionalists of counterinsurgency always argued that modern warfare was supposed to be about "boots on the ground." From the early days of counterinsurgency theory, airpower was conventionally understood to be counterproductive to the stated goal of winning over the passive masses.[15] In line with this traditional view, many commentators have argued that drone strikes do not fit within the counterinsurgency paradigm because the collateral damage inflicted by drone attacks, especially on innocent civilians, alienates the general population—an argument that, as you will recall, mirrors similar debates over the use of torture in counterinsurgency operations.

In their *New York Times* editorial "Death from Above, Outrage Down Below," David Kilcullen and Andrew McDonald Exum, two counterinsurgency experts, take this view. They argue that drone strikes defy the logic of modern warfare—just as earlier airborne attacks, during the colonial wars, were counterproductive and served to alienate the local populations. "The drone strategy is similar to French aerial bombardment in rural Algeria in the 1950s," they suggest, "and to the 'air control' methods employed by the British in what are now the Pakistani tribal areas in the 1920s. The historical resonance of the British effort encourages people in the tribal areas to see the drone attacks as a continuation of colonial-era policies."[16]

Others, on the other hand, argue that drones fit perfectly within the counterinsurgency paradigm because the precision and the targeted nature of the drone strikes are a safer way to eradicate an active minority: they cause as few side effects or as little collateral damage as possible. Some add that the drone itself, because it is unmanned and invisible, effectively deprives the insurgents of a tangible target—in the words of Chamayou, they "deprive the enemy of an enemy."[17] As a result, the drone in this view undermines a central recruitment strategy of the insurgency.

This debate between more population-centric proponents and more enemy-centric advocates of counterinsurgency should sound familiar. It replays the controversy over the use of torture or other contested methods within the counterinsurgency paradigm. It replicates the strategic debates between the ruthless and the more decent. It rehearses the tensions between Roger Trinquier and David Galula.

Yet just as torture is central to certain versions of modern warfare, the drone strike too is just as important to certain variations of the counterinsurgency approach. Drone strikes, in effect, can serve practically all the functions of the second prong of counterinsurgency warfare. Drone strikes eliminate the identified active minority. They instill terror among everyone living near the active minority, dissuading them and anyone else who might contemplate joining the revolutionaries. They project power and infinite capability. They show who has technological superiority. As one Air Force officer says, "The real advantage of unmanned aerial systems is that they allow you to project power without projecting vulnerability."[18] By terrifying and projecting power, drones dissuade the population from joining the insurgents.

And drones surely are terrorizing—but that, again, is a double-edged sword. As Kilcullen and Exum write, "the drone war has created a siege mentality among Pakistani civilians." They add: "The strikes are now exciting visceral opposition across a broad spectrum of Pakistani opinion in Punjab and Sindh, the nation's two most populous provinces. Covered extensively by the news media, drone attacks are popularly believed to have caused even more civilian casualties than is actually the case. The persistence of these attacks on Pakistani territory offends people's deepest sensibilities, alienates them from their government, and contributes to Pakistan's instability."[19]

In July 2016, the Obama administration released a report estimating the number of civilian casualties resulting from its drone operations *outside* conventional war zones, such as Afghanistan, Iraq, and Syria. The report included drone strikes in Libya, Pakistan, Somalia, and Yemen during the period from 2009 to 2015—countries that were not theatres of war for the United States—and therefore for which strikes would have to have been justified as targeted assassinations in furtherance of self-defense. The Obama administration reported between 64 to 116 civilian bystander fatalities and between 2,372 and 2,581 deaths of purportedly terrorist militants during the course of 473 strikes outside of active war areas over the period from January 20, 2009, to December 31, 2015.[20]

In other words, during the period, there were 64 to 116 officially recognized innocent civilian deaths that were bystander deaths for our—Americans'—self-defense outside a theater of war. The Obama administration made a clear distinction between drones used in conventional war zones in situations of armed conflict and drones used outside these areas in "the exercise of a state's inherent right of self-defense." The administration identified these situations as presenting a "continuing, imminent threat to US persons" and where there is a "near certainty" of avoiding civilian casualties.[21]

Western NGOs that document civilian casualties claimed these numbers underestimated the true number of civilian deaths. Independent agencies estimated the number at between 200 to 800 civilian casualties, outside of war zones, since 2009. Human Rights Watch, for instance, investigated seven deadly drones strikes, a small portion of the 473 acknowledged by the Obama administration, and documented civilian deaths reaching 57 or 59 killed—nearly as many as the lower end of the administration's estimate regarding all of the acknowledged strikes. The Bureau of Investigative Journalism investigated closely 12 strikes in 2012 and documented 57 civilian deaths.[22] The Human Rights Clinic at Columbia Law School and the Sana'a Center for Strategic Studies estimate that the US government has only acknowledged one-fifth, or 20 percent, of its lethal strikes.[23]

These numbers also do not include those civilians killed *in* war zones, such as in Afghanistan or Iraq. In Afghanistan alone, the

Bureau of Investigative Journalism documented between 1,544 confirmed drone strikes that have killed a total of between 2,580 and 3,376 persons, of which 142 to 200 were bystander civilians and between 24 and 49 were children, occurring over a period of just 27 months from January 2015 to April 2017.[24]

Those in the affected countries typically receive far higher casualty reports. The Pakistan press, for instance, reported that there are about 50 civilians killed for every militant assassinated, resulting in a hit rate of about 2 percent. As Kilcullen and Exum argue, regardless of the exact number, "every one of these dead noncombatants represents an alienated family, a new desire for revenge, and more recruits for a militant movement that has grown exponentially even as drone strikes have increased."[25]

To those living in Afghanistan, Iraq, Pakistan, Somalia, Yemen, and neighboring countries, the Predator drones are terrifying. But again— and this is precisely the central tension at the heart of counterinsurgency theory—the terror may be a productive tool for modern warfare. It may dissuade people from joining the active minority. It may convince some insurgents to abandon their efforts. Terror, as we have seen, is by no means antithetical to the counterinsurgency paradigm. Some would argue it is a necessary means.

Drones are by no means a flawless weapons system even for their proponents. There has been some backlash within the US military. A few drone operators came out and criticized drone warfare, publicizing the psychological trauma they experienced. In their documentary titled *National Bird*, filmmakers Wim Wenders and Errol Morris explore the psychological damage that drones may inflict even on those who administer them in utter safety. The director, Sonia Kennebeck, emphasizes, with reference to the drone operators, "They talk about how difficult it is to be in the US and be deployed and fighting, while still being at home in safety." She goes on to explain: "I think the human mind has an issue dealing with that, because you go into this secret environment and you're in a real warzone: you're killing people. Then you go home and sit at the dinner table with your family. It's schizophrenic in a way, to work like that. Your family doesn't have a clue and you're not allowed to talk to them about your experiences."[26]

Similarly, in the context of torture, some men have come out and exposed the psychological effects of torturing others. Eric Fair, who worked for a private security contractor, CACI, was a civilian interrogator during the early months of the war in Iraq tasked with administering the mechanical aspects of the enhanced interrogation program: waking detainees up to ensure sleep deprivation, disrobing the detainees, making them stand and experience stress positions, slapping them—those menial tasks of enhanced interrogation that had to be done by someone. Fair, who did them for three months in early 2004, soon realized that he was not the right man for the job, and left. He had been raised Presbyterian in Bethlehem, Pennsylvania, and felt that he identified more with the men who were being tortured than with the torturers. He felt that he should be tending to their needs rather than exploiting their weaknesses.

The experience nevertheless left Fair damaged. "A man with no face stares at me from the corner of a room," Fair writes in a 2007 essay. "He pleads for help, but I'm afraid to move. He begins to cry. It is a pitiful sound, and it sickens me. He screams, but as I awaken, I realize the screams are mine. That dream, along with a host of other nightmares, has plagued me since my return from Iraq in the summer of 2004." Fair is still haunted, he explains in his book *Consequence*, by "the voice of the general from the comfortable interrogation booth, the cries from the hard site, the sobs from the Palestinian chair and the sound of the old man's head hitting the wall."[27] And the fact that the methods were rendered fully legal made little difference to him. Fair notes:

> Our interrogations used approved techniques. We filed paperwork, followed guidelines, and obeyed the rules. But with every prisoner forced up against a wall, or made to stand naked in a

cold cell, or prevented from falling asleep for significant periods
of time, we felt less and less like decent men. And we felt less and
less like Americans.[28]

These men—drone operators and former torturers—have offered
chilling accounts.[29] Their interviews and stories are haunting. Sadly,
though, they are few. Of the legions of soldiers, agents, and contractors
who have participated in drone strikes, torture, and terror, only a handful have spoken out about the psychological repercussions.

In the end, drones may not be flawless from a counterinsurgency
perspective, but no weapon system is perfect. Drones ensure the elimination of the active minority, while serving other terrorizing goals
of modern warfare. In this sense, drones must be understood as an
alternative tactic to indefinite detention, disappearances, or summary
executions within the framework of the counterinsurgency paradigm.
In the view of many in the US government, drones are far more sani-
tized, virtual, and safe than the alternatives. From the perspective of
the target, of course, there is hardly any distinction: there is psychological harm as well as the raw lethality of the drone with its fifteen
meters of death. But to the drone operator, the harm, if any, is psychological, not directly physical. From the attacker's perspective, the
drone is a safer means—and merely a variation on the second prong of
counterinsurgency.

Grégoire Chamayou asks how particular weapon systems affect both
the relationship of the attacker to its enemy and, in his words, "the
state's relation to its own subjects."[30] The two aspects are linked, of
course, and what Chamayou suggests is that, in the case of the Predator
drone, the utter safety to the drone operators, the fact that they return
home to their families at the end of their shift, the global reach, and
the surgical nature of the drone strike have dramatically altered our
social and political reality and the democratic decision to kill. It has
been years since critical theory has addressed the question of drones.

Perhaps the last time was when Theodor Adorno wrote about Hitler's robot-bombs, the infamous V-1 and V-2 rockets the Nazis launched toward London.[31] But new circumstances call for renewed attention.

Regarding the first question, a drone should be understood as a blended weapons system, one that ultimately functions at several levels. It shares characteristics of the German V-2 missile, to be sure, but also the French guillotine and American lethal injection. It combines safety for the attacker, with relatively precise but rapid death, and a certain anesthetizing effect—as well as, of course, utter terror. For the country administering the drone attack, it is perfectly secure. There is no risk of domestic casualties. In its rapid and apparently surgical death, it can be portrayed, like the guillotine, as almost humane. And drones have had a numbing effect on popular opinion precisely because of their purported precision and hygiene—like lethal injection has done, for the most part, in the death-penalty context. Plus, drones are practically invisible and out of sight—again, for the country using them—though, again, terrifying for the targeted communities.

Chamayou's second question is, perhaps, the most important. This new weapons system has changed the US government's relationship to its own citizens. There is no better evidence of this than the deliberate, targeted drone killing of US and allied nation citizens abroad—as we will see.[32] It is here that we can identify a real drone effect. A conventional targeted assassination by a CIA agent, especially of a US citizen abroad, would surely shock the American conscience. It would raise political and legal issues that are simply elided by the use of a Predator drone, remote-controlled thousands of miles away. Even though there is no difference in objective and result, the novelty of the drone means it does not carry the symbolic baggage of CIA targeted assassinations and the long history of debate regarding their legality. It is not loaded with the weight of past excess.

An analogy from the death penalty may be helpful. There too, the means employed affect the ethical dimensions of the practice itself. The gas chamber and the electric chair—both used in the United States even after the Holocaust—became fraught with meaning. Their symbolism soured public opinion on the death penalty. By contrast, the clinical or medical nature of lethal injection at first reduced the political controversy surrounding executions. Only over time, with botched lethal injections and questions surrounding the drug cocktails and their true effects, have there been more questions raised. But it has taken time for the negative publicity to catch up with lethal injection. Drones, at this point, remain far less fraught than conventional targeted assassinations.

The newness of the drone, its surgical nature, and the fact that there are no domestic casualties, no body counts on nightly television, not even the possibility of a domestic death—these all ease their use. But the point is not just that drones are easier to use. More importantly, they make the counterinsurgency paradigm an easier framework to embrace. They make killing even US citizens abroad far more tolerable. And this tolerance is precisely what ends up eroding the boundaries between foreign policy and domestic governance, something we will come to shortly in Part III.

Like every new military technology that seems at first invincible—the submarine, the V-2, the machine gun—drone technology will one day be less omnipotent. One day, in all likelihood, even newer technology will allow the targets to hack into the remote-control system and send the Hellfire missiles back to the Predator drone, or even worse, into civilian populations. And then a new, perfectly safe killing device will be invented. But for the time being, these drones epitomize the logic of counterinsurgency theory: a deadly machine that eliminates the revolutionary minority, terrorizes their neighbors, and projects the power of the US government—in such a way as to convince the general population of their greater strength and dependability. It is a lethal new addition to modern warfare.

The drone has provided real momentum in the historic transformation we have witnessed over the past few decades. Part of what has contributed to the triumph of counterinsurgency strategy as a foreign policy—and to its domestication—is precisely the technological advances that have made the dream of total information awareness a possibility and the aspiration to surgically eliminate the active minority attainable. Technological innovation—the ability to capture all digital traffic or safely direct a drone strike oceans away—these technologies make it possible to imagine that we have come closer to the ideal that counterinsurgency theory envisioned. These new technologies help realize modern warfare. And they ultimately set the stage for the domestication of the counterinsurgency-warfare paradigm.

5

WINNING HEARTS
AND MINDS

T HE THIRD PRONG OF COUNTERINSURGENCY THEORY CON-
sists in winning the hearts and minds of the general population
to stem the flow of new recruits to the active minority and to seize
the upper hand in the struggle. This goal can be achieved by actively
winning the allegiance of the population, or by pacifying an already
passive population, or even simply by distracting the masses. The bar,
ultimately, is low since, on the counterinsurgency view, the people are
mostly passive. As Roger Trinquier noted in 1961, "Experience has
demonstrated that it is by no means necessary to enjoy the sympathy
of the majority of the people to obtain their backing; most are amorphous, indifferent." Or, as General Petraeus's manual states, the vast
majority is "neutral" and "passive"; it represents an "uncommitted middle" with "passive supporters of both sides."[1] The third prong, then, is
aimed mostly at assuaging, pacifying perhaps, or merely distracting the
indifferent masses.

In the case of the wars in Iraq and Afghanistan, and broader foreign
policy, the third prong has translated, principally, into three tactics:

investments in infrastructure, new forms of digital propaganda, and generalized terror. Together, they juxtapose the beneficent and humanitarian with the terrifying and terrorizing. They include some innovations, especially new digital technologies that update more traditional approaches to wooing a population. And over time—from the occupation of Iraq to the war on ISIS—the emphasis has shifted from infrastructure investment to digital propaganda. Undergirding them both, though, is the third tactic, the threat of generalized terror, that serves as a foundational method and looming constant.

In *How Everything Became War and the Military Became Everything*, Rosa Brooks writes that since 9/11 we have witnessed the expansion of the military and its encroachment on civilian affairs. "We've seen," in her words, "the steady militarization of US foreign policy as our military has been assigned many of the tasks once given to civilian institutions." Brooks warns us of a new world where "the boundaries between war and nonwar, military and nonmilitary have eroded." It is a world in which, Brooks notes, the military is no longer confined to guns and battles, but does all kinds of civilian tasks—like "train Afghan judges and parliamentarians, develop television soap operas for Iraqi audiences, and conduct antipiracy patrols off the Somali coast . . . They monitor global email and telephone communications, pilot weaponized drones from simulated airplane cockpits thousands of miles away, and help develop and plan for high-tech new modes of warfare, from autonomous weapons systems operated by computers using artificial intelligence to DNA-linked bioweapons."[2]

We are indeed facing, as Brooks powerfully demonstrates, a new world of an ever-encroaching military. But what this reveals, more than anything, is the rise of the counterinsurgency paradigm of government. It is the model of counterinsurgency warfare—of Galula's early turn to building schools and health facilities, to focusing on the hearts and minds of the general population—that has pushed the military into these traditionally civilian domains, including total surveillance, rule-of-law projects, artificial intelligence, entertainment, etc. In effect, *it is the counterinsurgency paradigm of government* that has become every-thing, and *everything that has become counterinsurgency.* The blurring of boundaries between war and peaceful governance is not merely the contingent result of 9/11, it is instead the culmination of a long and deliberate process of modernizing warfare.

Brooks's diagnosis—of a military encroaching on civilian realms since 9/11—can best be understood in the broader framework of the as-cent of counterinsurgency as foreign policy. The blurred lines between war and foreign policy, embodied for instance in the development of soap operas and social projects in Iraq, was not some sort of fluke. It represented instead the growing influence of counterinsurgency thinking.

The first tactic, then, is the investment in infrastructure and civil soci-ety—a strategy that has, at least at the outset, a humanitarian character. This was one of David Galula's key strategies of modern warfare, and Galula himself invested an enormous amount of time in Algeria in set-ting up schools, constructing roads and forts, and enhancing medical care.[3] General Petraeus followed suit, and his field manual stressed the importance of engaging in social projects. Many on the ground recog-nized the reluctance of some in the military to engage in social work—as well as the military's lack of competence in the area. Nevertheless, General Petraeus's manual underscored that "durable policy success requires balancing the measured use of force with an emphasis on non-military programs. Political, social, and economic programs are most commonly and appropriately associated with civilian organizations and expertise; however, effective implementation of these programs is more important than who performs the tasks."[4]

Providing basic necessities, labeled "essential services" in the field manual, is a key counterinsurgency practice. It consists primarily of ensuring that there is "food, water, clothing, shelter, and medical treat-ment" for the general population. General Petraeus's manual explains the rationale in very simple terms: "People pursue essential needs until they are met, at any cost and from any source. People support the source that meets their needs. If it is an insurgent source, the population is likely to support the insurgency. If the [host nation] government provides reliable essential services, the population is more likely to support it. Commanders therefore identify who provides essential services to each group within the population."[5]

General Petraeus's field manual gave the example, for instance, of the development efforts in the city of Tal Afar in northern Iraq, which was the target of heated insurgency in early 2005. The 3rd Armored Cavalry Regiment—under the leadership of Lieutenant General H. R. McMaster, who would later become national security adviser under President Donald Trump[6]—reclaimed the area in the summer of 2005, and after expelling the insurgents, began a project of reconstruction. The manual describes the efforts in these terms:

> With the assistance of the Department of State and the US Agency for International Development's Office of Transition Initiatives, efforts to reestablish municipal and economic systems began in earnest. These initiatives included providing essential services (water, electricity, sewage, and trash collection), education projects, police stations, parks, and reconstruction efforts. A legal claims process and compensation program to address local grievances for damages was also established.
>
> As security and living conditions in Tal Afar improved, citizens began providing information that helped eliminate the insurgency's infrastructure. In addition to information received on the streets, multinational forces established joint coordination centers in Tal Afar and nearby communities that became multinational command posts and intelligence-sharing facilities with the Iraqi Army and the Iraqi police.
>
> Unity of effort by local Iraqi leaders, Iraqi security forces, and US forces was critical to success. Success became evident when many families who had fled the area returned to the secured city.[7]

General Petraeus also emphasized the correlative need to relate positively to the local population. You will recall Mao's "Eight Points of Attention" to his fighters mentioned earlier, that reminded them to "talk to people politely," "observe fair dealing in all business transactions," and "return everything borrowed from the people." Galula had similar prescriptions, such as to deploy counterinsurgency forces "where the population actually lives and not on positions deemed to possess a military value."[8] General Petraeus learned Mao's and Galula's lessons well. Here are some of Petraeus's twenty-four commandments that accompanied, by memo, his field manual:

LIVE WITH THE PEOPLE. We can't commute to the fight. Position joint bases and combat outposts as close to those we're seeking to secure as feasible . . .

WALK. Stop by, don't drive. Patrol on foot whenever possible and engage the population. Take off your sunglasses. Situational awareness can only be gained by interacting face-to-face, not separated by ballistic glass or Oakleys.

BE A GOOD GUEST. Treat the Afghan people and their property with respect. Think about how we drive, how we patrol, how we relate to people, and how we help the community. View our actions through the eyes of the Afghans and, together with our partners, consult with elders before pursuing new initiatives and operations.[9]

Note that, in his original version of this last point, General Petraeus had written: "View your actions through the eyes of the Afghans. Alienating Afghan civilians sows the seeds of our defeat."[10]

In order to make good on all these promises and invest in civil society, the American government flooded the occupied territories with money. The United States spent $113 billion in Afghanistan between 2001 and early 2016 for reconstruction, which represented far more than the Marshall Plan in postwar Europe. It spent about $14 billion a year on contracted work. General Petraeus aggressively promoted "the practice of pumping money into the economy of Afghanistan," arguing that dollars would buy peace. "Employ money as a weapons system," Petraeus wrote in 2008. "Money can be 'ammunition.'"[11] Most of these dollars went to American private companies and to local establishments, serving another objective of minimizing American casualties.

The result was a dizzying distribution of cash, marked by extreme corruption. With very little oversight of procurement bidding and with the strategic need to rely on apparent friends and allies, contracts were dished out in ways that created instant fortunes for the lucky and the connected. From 2007 to 2014 alone, the United States gave out $89 billion in contracted moneys in Afghanistan.[12] As Matthieu Aikins reported in the *New Yorker*:

> "There were so many contracts out there that you could win anything you wanted," Simon Hilliard, a former British soldier who worked on KAF [the main US base, known as Kandahar Airfield] as the managing director of Watan Risk Management, an Afghan-owned security company, told me. "The margins were insane." He said that, in eighteen months, Watan's revenues increased from five hundred thousand dollars to fifty-eight million.[13]

The corruption was documented in cases like *United States of America v. Sum of $70,990,605, et al.*, in which the US Justice Department accused one Afghan entrepreneur of bribery; and criminal cases surrounding these, like the ones in which eight US soldiers pleaded guilty on related charges. The Center for Public Integrity published a study in May 2015 that found that "at least a hundred and fifteen US service members who deployed to Iraq and Afghanistan have been convicted of bribery, theft, and contract-rigging charges since 2005."[14] Naturally, much of the money found its way back with the Taliban and the forces that the American military were fighting. A forensic audit conducted in 2010 by the military, Task Force 2010, discovered for instance that, of about $31 billion in contracts inspected, about $360 million ended up in the hands of the Taliban, corrupt officials, or criminals; and that was only what could be directly accounted for. Recognizing some of these problems, General Petraeus put in place, in September 2010, guidelines to reduce corruption and stem the flow of moneys going to the Taliban. "The scale of our contracting in Afghanistan represents both an opportunity and a danger," Petraeus said. "With proper oversight contracting can spur economic growth and development."[15]

Ultimately, counterinsurgency theory calls for providing social goods and building infrastructure, but in Iraq and Afghanistan the government followed this dictate somewhat partially and lazily, leading to much corruption. This result reflects, of course, the difficulty of hewing to counterinsurgency theory, as well as the imperfect embrace of it. But as we will see, it also reveals a more solid undercurrent of modern warfare, namely, the use of terror.

A second approach to securing the neutrality of the majority is more psychological. In the early days of modern warfare, examples of this approach included measures such as the resettlement of populations, in the words of counterinsurgency experts, "to control them better and to block the insurgents' support." This is what the British did in Malaya, and the French in Algeria. Other examples included basic propaganda campaigns.[16]

As time has gone by, new digital technologies have enabled new forms of psychological counterinsurgency warfare. One of the newest involves digital propaganda, reflected most recently in the Center for Global Engagement set up under the Obama administration in early 2016. Created with the objective to prevent the radicalization of vulnerable youth, the center adopted strategies pioneered by the giants of Silicon Valley—Google, Amazon, Netflix—and was originally funded at the level of about $20 million. It targeted susceptible persons suspected of easier radicalization and sent them enhanced and improved third-party content in order to try to dissuade them, subliminally, from radicalizing or joining ISIS. In the words of an investigative journalist, "The Obama administration is launching a stealth anti-Islamic State messaging campaign, delivered by proxies and targeted to individual would-be extremists, the same way Amazon or Google sends you shopping suggestions based on your online browsing history."[17]

There were several steps to this approach, and they were all modeled on the latest algorithmic recommendation techniques of digital giants like Google and the most sophisticated digital advertising methods of Facebook and social media.

The first step was to collect and data mine the digital traces that all Internet users leave on social media, retail sites, web browsing, video games, and other digital venues to identify persons at risk of radicalization by ISIS or other extremists. Just as the retail giant Target could identify pregnant women through their digital traces before other family members could, the Global Engagement Center would data mine all our digital traces in order to identify those susceptible to radical influences even before they began to fall prey to those influences themselves.[18]

The second step was to identify third-party content that has a moderating, rather than radicalizing, effect, and then to enhance and improve that content so that it was even more effective. Providing consultation and financial support to third parties, the center ensured that they were using the best practices of the digital advertising industry— for instance, more images and better rhetorical strategies. The idea here, according to reports, was to "give local nonprofits, regional leaders, or activists invisible financial support and technical expertise to make their videos or websites or radio programs look and sound professional—and let them own and distribute the message." In these efforts, the center took its cue from the private sector, relying especially on the best practices of the digital advertising industry. Apparently, the center worked directly with Facebook, and its spokesman, Jodi Seth, indicated that Facebook shared their research with the center in order to show administration officials "factors that help make counter-speech more successful," such as better formatting of content (for example, it is now believed that including photos and videos will increase the likelihood that posts are read) and improving the tone of the content (here, for instance, it is believed that it is better to be constructive and to use satire or humor rather than just attack ads).[19]

The third step, then, was to measure the success of the targeted information, to determine whether the information was received, opened, viewed, and clicked on. Here again, the center used the most cutting-edge methods of the digital advertising business, which had made it its mission to measure impressions and reception. After directing the enhanced third-party content to the targets that had been identified, the center measured in real time the reception of the information. This was a critical step where big data really mattered: it was not enough to simply identify targets, it was even more important to determine whether the targeted content was being opened and viewed. For this, the center contracted with private companies that did the data mining to parse the digital traces that the targeted users left behind.[20]

The idea was to mimic what the enemy did itself, which, apparently, was to copy the Google and Amazon approach. According to the head of the center, Michael Lumpkin, the strategy was to "emulate how ISIS goes after its followers": "Usually it starts on Twitter, then it goes to Facebook, then it goes to Instagram, and ultimately, it goes to Telegram or some other encrypted, point-to-point discussion," Lumpkin explains. "They are doing what Amazon does. They are targeting selected information to an individual based on their receptivity. We need to do the same thing."[21]

In all this, the Center effaced, naturally, all the "Made in USA" labels. "The new center 'is not going to be focused on US messages with a government stamp on them, but rather amplifying moderate credible voices in the region and throughout civil society,' said Lisa Monaco, speaking at the Council on Foreign Relations. [. . .] 'Recognizing who is going to have the most legitimate voice and doing everything we can to lift that up and not have it be a US message.'" The head of the Center, Michael Lumpkin added: "In the face of a nimble, adaptive opponent unconstrained by truth or ethics, our people are left swimming in bureaucracy, using outdated technology."[22] The idea behind the center was to update our technology and become more nimble.

And of course, it relied on all of us sharing all our information via social media and invasive digital technologies that feed what I call our expository society. As David Galula emphasizes in his 1963 memoirs, *Pacification in Algeria*, intelligence is "the key to success."[23] We must now understand our expository society as the essential underpinning of a new counterinsurgency paradigm of government. The approach of the Global Engagement Center captures perfectly these new digital techniques and algorithms—and how they blend, exploit, and deploy the latest and best practices of digital advertising and entertainment, subliminal messaging, and soft propaganda.[24] And here, of course, the boundaries between counterinsurgency as foreign policy and counterinsurgency as domestic governance begin to crumble as more and more data is necessary for more effective data mining. As the battle against terror goes global, so do the populations to target—including our own.

The third set of measures was even more basic: terror. The most formidable way to win hearts and minds is to terrorize the local population to make sure they do not sympathize with or aid the active minority. When Paul Aussaresses described his brutal treatment of suspected FLN members and the torturous methods he used in Algeria—the *gégène*, the waterboard, the summary executions—the French general subsumed these practices under the rubric and chapter heading: *La Terreur*.[25] "The Terror." He knew what he was talking about. Since 9/11, the same idea has come to guide US foreign policy. Strategies like social spending and digital propaganda, in truth, are merely ornaments to a more basic and enduring structure of terror.

The brutality of counterinsurgency serves, of course, to gather information and eradicate the revolutionary minority. But it also aims higher and reaches further: its ambition, as General Aussaresses recognized well, is to terrorize the insurgents, to scare them to death, *and* to frighten the local population in order to prevent them from joining the insurgent faction. Today, the use of unusually brutal torture, the targeted drone assassination of high-value suspects, and the indefinite detention under solitary conditions aim not only to eviscerate the enemy, but also to warn others, strike fear, and win their submission and obedience. Drones and indefinite detention crush those they touch, and strike with terror anyone else who might even imagine sympathizing with the revolutionary minority. They display a mastery that appeals and seduces the masses. They legitimize the counterrevolutionary minority. Terror, it turns out, is what truly conquers and colonizes the hearts and minds of the masses. And in US foreign policy since 9/11, terror has served as a way of securing the submission of the passive majority, not just the active minority. Terror, in the end, is a key component of the third core strategy of counterinsurgency.

Since antiquity, terror has served to demarcate the civilized from the barbarian, to distinguish the free citizen from the enslaved. The free male in ancient Greece had the privilege of swearing an oath to the gods, of testifying on his word. The slave, by contrast, could only give testimony under torture. Torture, in this sense, defined freedom and citizenship by demeaning and marking—by imposing stigmata—on those who *could* be tortured. It served to demarcate the weak. It marked the vulnerable. And it also, paradoxically, served to delineate the "more civilized." This is perhaps the greatest paradox of the brutality of counterinsurgency: *to be civilized is to torture judiciously.* This paradox was born in antiquity, but it journeys on. There is a striking passage in an interview with the French general Jacques Massu, notorious for having brutally commanded the Battle of Algiers, in which he compares the French torturers to "choir boys." "I am not afraid of the word torture," Massu explains, "but I think in the majority of cases, the French military men obliged to use it to vanquish terrorism were, fortunately, choir boys compared to the use to which it was put by the rebels. The latter's extreme savagery led us to some ferocity, it is certain, but we remained within the law of eye for eye, tooth for tooth."[26] Torture was, in Massu's words, "a cruel necessity," but it apparently revealed, more than anything, how civilized the French were.

The judicious administration of terror is the hallmark of civilization. To be civilized is to terrorize properly, judiciously, with restraint, according to the rules. Only the barbarians tortured savagely, viciously, unrestrainedly. The civilized, by contrast, knew how and when to tame torture, how to rein it terror, to apply it with judgment and discretion. Compared to the barbarians—the beheadings of ISIS is a modern case on point—*we* are tame and judicious, even when we torture, not like those barbarians. And since 9/11, the judicious use of terror has been a key US strategy. In the end, terror functions in myriad ways to win the hearts and minds of the masses under the counterinsurgency paradigm of governing.

6

GOVERNING THROUGH TERROR

WATERBOARDING, INDEFINITE DETENTION, ISOLATION AND solitary confinement, drone strikes, the live entombing in coffin-size boxes and barbed-wire pens—these practices are, to be sure, strategic components of counterinsurgency warfare: they work well to extract information, to eliminate the radical minority, and to control the masses. In this sense, they serve well the three prongs of counterinsurgency theory. But there is more to it than that.

Terror is not only the thread that ties together the three core strategies of counterinsurgency, it also functions in myriad ways to advance counterinsurgency as a paradigm of governing—by producing the truth of the efficacy of terror, by legitimizing the regime of terror, by creating fear and discipline within the counterrevolutionary minority, and more. Terror does much more than expected. It produces a whole much greater than the sum of its parts.

Terror, for instance, is what renders counterinsurgency theory so resilient, despite the fact that modern warfare rarely, if ever, has succeeded at the military level. Practically all counterinsurgencies ended in national independence for the insurgents and resounding failure for its architects. But counterinsurgency was perfectly resilient at the broader political level because its proponents could and always would argue that their defeat was attributable to a lack of resolve. It was never the logic of counterinsurgency that failed, but rather the failure to follow through on that logic—the failure to be tough enough. Every time the counterinsurgency miscarried—in Indochina, in Algeria, in Vietnam—it was always because the military had not shown sufficient harshness to the insurgent minority. "We lost the war in Indochina largely because we hesitated to take the necessary measures or took them too late," Roger Trinquier emphasized. "For the same reason," he predicted, "we are going to lose the war in Algeria."[1] It was always a lack of sufficient resolve—a lack of sufficient terror—that proved to be the culprit. This resilience fueled the counterinsurgency paradigm.

Terror, it turns out, has always been a linchpin of counterinsurgency. Some advocates explicitly embraced it. Others tiptoed around it, conceding the power of terror but trying to ignore or avoid it. Yet it was always present, even as a shadow. It haunted the sham judicial inquest. It cast a shade over the torture memos. It was right there in the recognition that terrorism is the insurgents' most effective tool. Or in the suggestion that no methods should be taken off the table. It was always there because, in the end, *modern warfare is a paradigm of governing through terror.*[2]

Now, terror is not an unprecedented component of governing, even if its role in the counterinsurgency model may be uniquely constitutive. It has been with us since slavery in antiquity, through the many inquisitions, to the internment and concentration camps of modern history. And there too, in each of its manifestations, it functioned at multiple levels to bolster different modes of governing. Looking back through history, terror has done a lot of work. Today as well. And to see all that terror achieves today—above and beyond the three prongs of counterinsurgency theory—it is useful to look back through history and recall its different functions and the work it has done. The reflections today are stunning.

This chapter—somewhat more historical and theoretical—will return, then, in some detail, to five episodes that reveal the work that terror has done historically, and how that work is refracted today in the counterinsurgency paradigm of governing. The ambition of this chapter is to show how important brutal excess, torture, and terror are to counterrevolutionary strategies. Much of this, but not all, will circle back to torture—where our discussion of post–9/11 US policy began, with torture-as-intelligence gathering, now torture-as-terror. But terror has other manifestations, which is why the broader category is ultimately the more fitting one today.

The first episode reaches back to antiquity, but represents a recurring theme throughout history: terror has often served to manufacture its own truth—especially in terms of its efficacy. "They all talk." That is a constant refrain in so many texts on tortured interrogation. It is the opening scene of *The Battle of Algiers.* "He finally spit it out!" says the young interrogator. They all say it to Mohamedou Slahi. They say it to Henri Alleg. Not just once, but throughout: "You'll answer, I promise you." "Everybody talks. You'll have to tell us everything—and not only a little bit of the truth, but everything!" "You're going to talk! Everybody talks here!"[3]

Trying to convince a suspect that he will talk, telling him that he will—this is, of course, a psychological technique, but it is more than that. It is also a firm belief of counterinsurgency theorists outside the interrogation room. Roger Trinquier, for instance, insists on this in his televised debate with Saadi Yacef in 1970—and he is not, there, trying to soften up another suspect. Even the FLN apparently believed it, which is why it ordered its members to resist for just twenty-four hours, the amount of time necessary for other FLN members to go in hiding. Everyone says it, and everyone begins to believe it. It becomes, eventually, the truth of terror.

Manufacturing truth: that is, perhaps, the first major function of terror. It is the power of terror, especially in the face of ordinary men and women, of humans, all too human. It has been that way since the inquisitions of the Middle Ages, and before, since antiquity. On this score, little has changed.

In her book on slavery in Greek antiquity, *Torture and Truth*, Page duBois argues that the idea of truth dominant today in Western thought is indissolubly tied to the practice of torture, while torture itself is deeply connected to the will to discover something that is always beyond our grasp. As a result, society after society returns to torture, in almost an eternal recurrence, to seek out the truth that is always beyond our reach. In ancient times, duBois shows, torture functioned as the metaphorical touchstone of truth and as a means to establish a social hierarchy. In duBois's words, "the desire to create an other and the desire to extract truth are inseparable, in that the other, because she or he is an other, is constituted as a source of truth." Truth, in sum, is always "inextricably linked with the practice of torture."[4]

DuBois opens her book with an etymological discussion of the Greek term for torture, *basanos*—which referred to the touchstone that was used in ancient practice to test the mettle of gold, a practice of the money changers. DuBois shows how, in antiquity, the Greeks believed that the torture of a slave was the preeminent source of attaining truth and served as the best and most reliable proof. "The evidence derived from the slave's body and reported to the court," duBois writes, "is considered superior to that given freely in the court, before the jury, in the presence of the litigants." Slave torture produced truth of such a high quality, in fact, that torture achieved the triple functions of demarcating freedom, of instantiating social order, and of fulfilling the search for truth. Truth, duBois argues, "resides in the slave body."[5]

In this sense, slave torture in antiquity became the touchstone of truth: the ultimate test of the veracity, of the metal, of the genuineness or authenticity of what was said. As duBois suggests, "The Greeks first use the literal meaning for *basanos* of 'touchstone,' then metaphorize it to connote a test, then reconcretize, rematerialize it to mean once again a physical testing in torture."[6] There is, oddly, an uncanny similitude between the actual operation of the *basanos*—the tool itself—and the operation of torture: with the tool, the Lydian stone, one rubs gold against the slate, physically ripping pieces of the gold off to see the color of the mark made and left on the slate. Physical torture, it seems, mimics that physical act: it is a rubbing of the physical body against all kinds of tools—in ancient times, the rack or water, still today the wall slam, the slap, the waterboard, the electrical charge—in order to *see* the truth. The metaphor of scraping the body, like one scrapes gold, to see the residue of truth, is haunting.

Even more, terror produced social difference and hierarchy. The limits on torture in ancient societies served to define what it meant to be among those who could be tortured—what it meant to be a slave or to be free. In ancient times, the testimony of a slave could only be elicited, and only became admissible in litigation, under torture. Only free male citizens could take an oath or resolve a controversy by sermon. The rules about who could be tortured in ancient times did not just regulate the victims of torture, the rules themselves were constitutive of what it meant to be a slave. The laws demarcated and defined freedom itself—what it looked like, what it entailed.

Sophocles's tragedy *Oedipus Rex* has captured our imagination for centuries on questions of fate and power. But it is perhaps on the question of terror and truth that the play turns. At the climax of Sophocles's tragedy—at the pivotal moment when truth finally emerges for all to see and to recognize—there is a scene of terror. The shepherd slave who held the knowledge of Oedipus's ancestry is threatened with torture. And that threat of torture alone—at the culmination of a whole series of unsuccessful inquiries—produces the truth: torture provokes the shepherd's confession and that allows Oedipus to recognize his fate. But more than that, torture reaffirms the social order in Thebes—a social order where gods rule, oracles tell truth, prophets divine, fateful kings govern, and slaves serve. It is, ultimately, the right to terrorize that reveals Oedipus's power and the shepherd's place in society. Torture constituted servitude: only those who could not swear an oath had to be terrorized. But it also returns the gods and prophets to their rightful place.

In a similar way, terror today produces its own truth—about the effectiveness of torture in eliciting truth, about its effectiveness in subjugating the insurgents, about the justness of counterinsurgency.

Second, terror—or more specifically the regulatory framework that surrounds terror—legitimizes the practices of terror itself. This may sound paradoxical or circular—but it has often been true in history. The structures that frame and regulate the administration of terrorizing practices have the effect, unexpectedly, of legitimizing the use of brutal methods and the regimes of terror.

The strict Justinian codification of the use of torture on slaves in Book 48 of the *Digest* served to inscribe the practices of terror within law, in a process that would simultaneously contain the barbarity of these extreme practices and empower the authorities that oversaw them. The extreme nature of torture, once brought within the fabric of the law, concentrated power in the hands of those who had the knowledge and skill, the *techne*, to master the brutality. The Justinian codification served as a model to later codifications during the early Middle Ages and to the practices of the Inquisition.

Extreme practices call for expert oversight and enable a concentration of power in the hands of those who know best. In this sense, torture not only provides information and eliminates the active minority, but also concentrates power into the hands of the administrators. It centralizes power, produces a new judiciary, and immunizes the torturers—precisely because they are the ones who have asserted and assume the greatest power of all, the power over life and death. Others yield to their audacity. The concentration of power through terror has a long history.

Centuries after the Justinian code, in the twelfth and thirteenth centuries, Roman law resurfaced and began to compete with Visigothic and other Germanic legal regimes. Torture was reinscribed in legal codes in the Middle Ages, once again forming part of fully coherent codified legal systems. Alfonso X of Castile's codification of laws, *Las Siete*

Partidas, drafted by a collective body of jurists in the mid-thirteenth century and completed around 1265—which the legal historian Jesús R. Velasco has brilliantly elucidated for us—integrated torture into the fabric of the law, just as the *Digest* had before it.[7] Specifically, the *Partidas* incorporated torture into Part Seven, Title 30, "Concerning Torture," simultaneously valorizing torture and at the same time taming it—protecting against it, rarifying its practice, ensuring against excess. Torture was only permitted under an order of a judge and could only be administered if there was one credible witness and the suspect was "a man of bad reputation or of inferior rank." Certain classes of individuals could be tortured, others not. A certain restraint in questioning had to be respected. Even more importantly, and by contrast to much of the Spanish Inquisition, the risk of harm fell on the inquisitor, not on the tortured victim.[8] There would be consequences for abuse.

Torture was being regulated and regularized in those early centuries. These same routines were replicated in the Spanish Inquisition, which extended from 1478 to 1834, as is reflected in the various inquisitorial instruction manuals, like that of Gaspar Isidro de Argüello in 1627, *Instructions of the Holy Office of the Inquisition* (1484–1561), which refer to half proofs and penance, to confiscations, to perpetual prisons, and to other regulated practices of punishment.[9] Torture was brought into the fabric of the law and rarified at the same time. The rarefication in the Medieval Period served a political end: to make torture even more foreboding. Had torture become too generalized or too frequent, it might have lost its exceptionality and terrorizing effect.

Torture was rarely applied, and, as one historian notes, inflicted with "the utmost care and moderation."[10] Look, for instance, at the archive of the Inquisition court at Pamiers headed by Bishop Jacques Fournier from 1318 to 1325 in southern France, described masterfully by Emmanuel Le Roy Ladurie in *Montaillou: The Promised Land of Error* (1978). The archive is striking in part for the lack of confessional torture and the low number of death sentences. During the period in which it operated, between 1318 and 1325, the Inquisition court at Pamiers conducted 578 interrogations, consisting of 418 interrogations of accused persons and 160 of witnesses, in a total of 98 cases that involved 114 persons accused of being heretics, mostly of Albigensian persuasion. Of those 98 cases, only one was accompanied by torture. According to Le Roy Ladurie, "In only one instance did Jacques Fournier have his victims tortured: this was in the trumped-up case in which French agents made him bring against the lepers, who brought forth wild and absurd confessions about poisoning wells with powdered toads, etc."[11]

The rarity achieved by the limited use and legal regulation of torture in the Medieval Period served to ensure its persistence and role as a social epistemological device—as a producer of truths, especially truth about itself. Centuries later, the Bush administration and its top lawyers re-created a legal architecture surrounding the use of torture. It included a list of approved torture techniques. It also included a requirement that Secretary of Defense Donald Rumsfeld himself approve a small subset of the more torturous techniques. This creation of an internal legal framework to carry out torture, through legal memoranda and cable authorizations, had the very same effect: to centralize power, to appropriate judicial decision-making, to authorize the administrators, to empower them, and to immunize them. The legal framework served to legitimate the practices themselves.

Third, the legal regulation of terror also legitimizes the larger political regime. Here too there is a long history, as evidenced by the surprising but highly regulated practices of torture on slaves during the antebellum period in the American South. Once again, these effects live on.

In the antebellum period, the southern judiciary proactively policed the admissibility at trial of slave confessions given under torture—at a time when even more brutal treatment of slaves by their masters was commonplace. Those remarkable judicial decisions rendered the system of chattel slavery more palatable, and stable. The judicial oversight subtly negotiated an equilibrium that served to maintain the political economy of slavery. Still today, the use and legal regulation of torture or drone strikes by American presidents work in a similar way: they stabilize and balance American interests in such a way as to secure and steady the political regime. The intricate legal negotiation over the use of torture during the Bush administration, for instance, as well as President Obama's decision not to prosecute anyone for the excesses, were carefully negotiated efforts at stabilizing the United States during a time of global political turmoil.[12]

Chattel slavery in this country was, without doubt, a form of terror. One need only glance at antebellum judicial decisions, which regularly and nonchalantly recount inhuman forms of terror routinely administered on slaves. "Bob [a slave] was taken out by Joshua Morse, a son-in-law of his master, and some of the other neighbors, and severely whipped, and afterwards salted, by pouring the salt upon the wounds made by the blows inflicted," a typical decision reads.[13] The system of slavery was inhuman, perpetrating a permanent state of terror among a whole class of society.

But remarkably, within that tortured system, the state judiciaries tinkered with the admission of coerced confessions. In Alabama, for instance, in a series of judicial decisions regarding tortured slave confessions beginning at least in 1847, the Alabama Supreme Court developed a strict evidentiary rule policing the admissibility of slave confessions at trial. As the Alabama justices declared in 1860 in *Mose (a slave) v. The State*—a case in which the slave, Mose, alias "Moses," was charged with the murder of his overseer, a white man named Martin Oaks—"It is a rule of great strictness, that if a confession has once been obtained by undue means, no subsequent confessions of like character are evidence, unless it be shown that the influence has been removed."[14] On the basis of those decisions, the Alabama justices would reverse slave convictions and sentences of death, even in the most extreme cases of injury or death to the slave owner.

The State of Alabama v. Clarissa, a slave is a good illustration. The slave Clarissa, whose attorney won a retrial from her sentence of death, was convicted for attempting to poison her master, Hezekiah Bussey, and her overseer, Nelson Parsons—two white men. There was evidence of poisoning, Clarissa had confessed at least twice, and her mother had admitted to seeing Clarissa spike their coffee. Clarissa's first confession, the clear product of a severe whipping, was not admitted at trial, but her second tacit admission was presented to her jury. Defense counsel moved to suppress it, on the grounds that it was not reliable, but the trial court allowed it in. On appeal, the Supreme Court of Alabama declared that it should not have been admitted at trial, and indicated that, at any retrial, the second confession would not be admissible. The Alabama Supreme Court recognized that, ordinarily, a slave's confession obtained without brutality should be admissible, even though it alone should not be used to prove a slave's guilt. As Justice James Ormond explained, "The confessions of slaves, freely and voluntarily made, uninfluenced by threats or promises, must, as in the case of white persons, be received in evidence"; but the justice immediately added that "it must be admitted, their condition in the scale of society, throws a certain degree of discredit over any confession of guilt they may make, and renders it unsafe if not improper, to act upon such evidence alone, without other corroborating proof."[15]

Without deciding whether a second confession *always* had to be excluded after a first coerced confession, the Alabama Supreme Court intimated that it would be better practice never to admit a second confession after a beating: "When a confession has been extorted by threats or punishment, or obtained by promises of favor, it would seem that no subsequent confession of the same facts, ought in the case of slaves, under any circumstances to be admitted, as even a recantation of what was once admitted, would be to expose the accused again to punishment."[16] In the end, however, the Alabama Supreme Court refrained from articulating such a strict rule, declaring instead that in this case, on the limited facts of the case, there was a clear and independent reason to exclude the second confession and reverse the conviction.

It may seem surprising or paradoxical that the antebellum courts would protect a slave accused of poisoning her master. But there is an explanation: the intricate legal framework surrounding the criminalization and punishment of errant slaves during the antebellum period served to maintain and stabilize chattel slavery in the South—it served to equilibrate the political economy of slavery. It served to balance interests in such a way that neither the slave owners nor the slaves would push the whole system of slavery into disarray. And the courts and politicians carefully handled this delicate balance.

So, for instance, to avoid the excess of slave owners taking justice into their own hands and murdering their slaves—or on the other hand, simply selling an accused slave without disclosing their alleged crime, or covering up for a slave because of the possible loss—the state of Alabama would compensate an owner for half the value of his slave if the slave was sentenced to death at a criminal trial and executed.[17] This was a delicately negotiated arrangement that was understood by all parties—including the slaves. In the 1858 case of *Bob v. State*, for instance, it is reported that the jailor who held the slave, Bob, in custody, told him that he might as well confess to avoid being lynched and so that his master could at least get compensated for his value.[18]

In fact, the financial loss associated with the execution of a slave was viewed as the only way to guarantee that owners made sure their slaves received a fair trial. During the 1842–1843 legislative session, the general assembly passed a bill providing for full compensation for executed slaves—increasing the restitution from 50 percent to 100 percent. The governor, Benjamin Fitzpatrick, vetoed the provision because it eliminated any incentive to ensure slaves received a fair trial. In a veto message to the general assembly, the governor wrote that "humanity alone, as the statute now stands, is the only inducement to the master to take that interest which is essential to insure his slave a fair and impartial trial when implicated."[19]

Other complex rules surrounding slave trials served to optimize the risk of abuse and to stabilize the system. Throughout the nineteenth-century antebellum period, for instance, slaves charged with a capital offense in Alabama were afforded legal counsel at trial at their owner's expense. Slaveholders also managed the slave criminal process by means of the slave's right to a jury trial and the fact that slaveholders had to sit on slave juries. Slaveholders were also guaranteed a certain number of votes at a slave's trial—again, a delicate balance. There were other accommodations in the law of slave trials. For instance, rules allowed slaveholders to be competent witnesses at the trial of their slaves—even though they were interested parties. The courts also placed discretion in the hands of slaveholders, who not only determined guilt, but punishment, value, and reimbursement as well.[20]

These complex negotiations over the criminal rules accompanied the practices of slavery in Alabama—a form of terror—and served to legitimize the larger political economy of chattel slavery. They offered stability to the slave economy by making the different participants in the criminal process and in slavery—the slave owners, the foremen, the magistrates, and the public at large—more confident in the whole enterprise. The extensive legal regulation of the torture of slaves was not about justifying torture, nor about resolving philosophical or ethical questions. Instead, it served to strike a balance and stabilize the institution of slavery.

Throughout the history of the regulation of terror—from the antebellum period to the regulation of drone strikes—we have seen formal legal frameworks serve the larger ends of legitimizing the institutions of power, and, more generally, the prevailing political economy. In the end, the legal memos on the applicability of the Geneva Conventions, on the use of torture, and on the propriety of using drones against US citizens all served to legitimize the war on terrorism—and, more generally, the counterinsurgency paradigm of warfare.

Fourth, the ability to terrorize—and to get away with it—has a powerful effect on others. The audacity and the mastery impress the general masses. Something about winning or beating others seduces the population. People like winners, and winning is inscribed in terrorizing others.

The desire to dominate, the will to win, the ambition to beat others—it is impossible to extricate these deep impulses from the reality of terror. Dostoyevsky said it best, perhaps, through the voice of his Grand Inquisitor in the *Brothers Karamazov*: "We will force them into obedience, and it is they who will admire us the most. They will regard us as gods, and feel grateful to those who have consented to lead the masses and bear their burden of freedom by ruling over them—so terrible will that freedom at last appear to men!"[21] Succeeding, winning—these are inscribed at the heart of terror, and they resonate deeply with men and women. The fact of winning is somehow tied to domination, mastery, victory—to beating the other. Perhaps we should not be surprised at the double meaning of that expression: "beating the other." It seamlessly combines torture and victory. Victory persuades and comforts. It assuages others, and gives them the confidence to follow. Victory, in the end, is the essence of terror, because winning will ultimately win over the hearts and minds of the population.

President Donald Trump's embrace of torture was woven into this winning, this beating. "My life is winning," Trump told the *New York Times* before his election. "I win. I know how to win. Most people don't know how to win. In golf, in sports, in life—I win, always." Elsewhere, Trump declared, "I've been in competitions all my life and there's nothing as exciting as winning this stuff," after taking the Louisiana primary and the Kentucky Republican caucus. "Winning deals, or winning club championships, or whatever you want to say, there's nothing like this," Trump announced; in fact, Trump added during the campaign, "We will have so much winning if I get elected that you may get bored with winning."[22]

"Winning" against the terrorists, for President Trump, meant pushing the limits of terror. As Trump announced in his campaign, he favored torture techniques even worse than waterboarding. Trump said that he was prepared to torture the families of suspected terrorists—completely innocent family members. This zeal, this excess of terror, and especially his getting away with it, was tied to winning over the masses.

Similarly, the ruthlessness of the president of the Philippines, Rodrigo Duterte, is what led to his popularity. A vocal law-and-order proponent, who declared a war against drug addicts, Duterte oversaw the killing by police and others of around 3,600 addicts and dealers in the nine months after he took office in June 2016 (some reliable sources put that number at 7,000). Duterte's worldview was simple: he killed, literally, by his own hand, suspected criminals. He admitted this openly. He called for their murder. Referring to drug addicts, he said, "I would be happy to slaughter them." "I have my own political philosophy," Duterte explained. "Do not destroy my country because I will kill you."[23] Despite all this, or perhaps precisely because of it, Duterte was elected president by a strong majority and only gained in popularity since then. There can be no doubt that his popularity was linked to his audacity, to his willingness to terrorize. "I might go down in the history as the butcher," Duterte admitted in January 2017.[24]

In the end, there is something to what Roger Trinquier said: terror is integral to colonial insurgency and to counterinsurgency. But not just because both sides expect it. Not just because revolutions and counterinsurgencies must anticipate it. Terror is integral to the colonial struggle because it is tied to showing one's dominance, one's willingness to do whatever it takes to win. And when it comes time to convince others to follow, or when it comes time to reassure, such dominance is often the most important characteristic. Because we all respect winners—at least, practically all of us. Most of us side with the victor.

Fifth, and relatedly, terror is gendered, which also tends to reinforce the power and appeal of the more brutal counterinsurgency practices. Brutality is most often associated with the dominant half of the couple, the one who controls, and however much we might protest, this tends to strengthen the attraction.

Notions of dominance lace most accounts of torture. A striking passage, for instance, at the end of Henri Alleg's memoire, *The Question*, reflects well the masculinity of torture. After all his torture is over, Alleg writes:

I could sense from the different attitude of the [paratroopers] toward me, that they regarded my refusal to speak as "sporting."
Even the big para in Lo___'s group had changed his attitude. He
came into my cell one morning and said to me:

"Were you tortured in the Resistance?"

"No; it's the first time," I replied.

"You've done well," he said with the air of a connoisseur.
"You're very tough."[25]

There was, in effect, a male sportsman-like aspect to his ordeal, as
though it were a sporting game among athletes or even gladiators. Alleg's torture was a test of his virility. Another soldier would admire him
for not giving in to torture. Alleg continues:

During the evening another para, whom I did not know, came in
on his round. [. . .] He said to me with a big smile: "You know, I
was present all the time! My father talked to me about the Com-
munists in the Resistance. They died, but they never talked. That's
very fine!" I looked at this youth with his sympathetic face, who
could talk of the sessions of torture I had undergone as if they
were a football match that he remembered and could congratulate
me without spite as he would a champion athlete.[26]

The man—note, we are talking mostly about men here, though
many women too were the victims of torture in Algeria, as Marnia
Lazreg documents[27]—but here, the *man* who can resist torture becomes
a champion athlete. This theme runs throughout Alleg's account, and it
gives credence to the notion that we are dealing with a form of competition. Again, when Alleg was still being tortured, a young paratrooper
praised him. "Why are you so determined not to talk?" he asked. "You
have to have courage to hold out like that." Similarly, when Alleg encountered, later in his captivity, General Massu's *aide de camp*, the latter confided in him: "I admire your resistance."[28]

His resistance—at least as Alleg recounts it—is admirable. And, quite understandably, Alleg's courage becomes a part of his own identity. Alleg prides himself on not having divulged the location of his protectors or the identity of other collaborators. Understandably so—I do not intend in any way to minimize or trivialize his courage, and I form no opinion on its veracity. "I was exalted by the fight which I had survived without weakening," Alleg writes at the end of the book, "and by the thought that I would die as I had always hoped to die, true to my beliefs and to my companions in battle."[29] Alleg went on: "I suddenly felt proud and happy. I hadn't given in. I was now sure I could stand up to it if they started again, that I could hold out to the end, and that I wouldn't make their job easier by killing myself."[30]

The reader too gets caught up in this pride. The reader respects Alleg because he does not talk. Jean-Paul Sartre captures these feelings well: "Alleg has saved us from despair and shame because he is the victim himself and because *he has conquered torture.* [. . .] Because of him we regain a little of our pride: we are proud that he is French." Or, as Sartre writes at the end of his preface, buying into the heroic storyline, "Alleg is the only really tough one, the only one who is really strong."[31] Notice, again, the masculinity.

The execution of the men, at the end of Alleg's book, was male martyrdom, martyrdom that called forth the voices of women from "the women's section of the prison."[32] The voices of the women singing—the women singing about men:

> Out of our struggle
> Rise the voices of free men:
> They claim independence
> For our country.
> I give you everything I love,
> I give you my life,
> O my country . . . O my country.[33]

Sartre betrays this, perhaps unintentionally. Alleg, he writes, "paid the highest price for the simple right to remain a man among men."[34]

Masculinity permeates these exchanges—and it permeates terror. The torture of men, as we see here. But even more, the rape and sexual humiliation of women. Marnia Lazreg meticulously documents that "rape by troops was systematic in rural villages and scattered hamlets [in Algeria] where the population was defenseless." Rape not only pervaded the military occupation, it also saturated the very language of military discourse, with constant references to "psychological rape," "inviolate regions," and "penetrating" areas.[35]

There is a distinct machismo to being a torturer—it goes with all the winning, dominating, mastering of the other. And there is a masculinity to withstanding it. More generally, most terror contains a gendered or sexual dimension. When the tormentor is a woman, as in the case of Lynndie England at Abu Ghraib, the degradation and humiliation has a distinct sexualizing element. As Lazreg writes, "Torture *is* sexual in nature . . . Toying with a person's sexual identity, violating her most private domain by compelling her to act out the pornographic desires of the torturer *is* physical and mental torture."[36] Torture is often explicitly sexualized, especially but not only in the cases of the legion of women who have been victims of torture across the globe—in Argentina during the dictatorship, in Rwanda during the genocide, in Algeria and Vietnam. Rape and sexual abuse of women and men form integral components of torture—again, predominantly in a masculinist fashion.

This dimension resonates when one reads about the young men of ISIS who envisage what awaits them in their martyrdom, or the new bands of anti-ISIS mercenaries in Syria—or when one recalls President George W. Bush, in his flight jacket, pretending to be a war hero on the deck of the USS *Abraham Lincoln*, declaring "mission accomplished." Ideals of masculinity permeate those moments. "The American idea of masculinity," James Baldwin writes in his essay "Here Be Dragons:"

"There are few things under heaven more difficult to understand or, when I was younger, to forgive."[37] This idea of masculinity somehow seduces the masses and ultimately empowers brutality.

James Baldwin located the root of much harm, including racism and homophobia, in our ideals of masculinity themselves. In Baldwin's words, "The American ideal of masculinity [. . .] has created cowboys and Indians, good guys and bad guys, punks and studs, tough guys and softies, butch and faggot, black and white."[38] The ideal of masculinity, Baldwin asserted, served simultaneously to reify the distinctions between black and white, man and woman, gay and straight, and at the same time fuel the fear, or even "terror" in his words—as well as the desire—for the other.

Baldwin put his finger on the uncanny relationship between racism and masculinity, helping us see well how the masculinity of terror nourished other forms of domination. For example, the torture at Abu Ghraib and Guantánamo simultaneously racialized the Muslim minority. There and elsewhere in the war on terrorism, the victims of torture have practically all been Muslims, and in part, this has transformed the suspected active minority into *all* Muslims—in addition, that is, to Mexican Americans and African American and Hispanic communities especially in neighborhoods like Baltimore or Ferguson or Oakland. As the philosopher Jean-Paul Sartre notes in the case of Algeria, terror there was "demanded by racial hatred."[39]

In the aftermath of 9/11, the use of torture served to dehumanize men and women along distinct racial and ethnic lines—lines that blurred color, ethnicity, religion into the dark-skin of Middle Eastern Muslims.[40] This has long been one of torture's functions: to racialize its victims. It was certainly the case during the Holocaust, as it was during American slavery. The Nazi concentration camp functioned—in part only, of course, it did so much other evil work—to degrade the Jew, the gypsy, the homosexual, the disabled. It served to debase, to exclude from humanity, those whom it confined and ultimately murdered. In a similar way, the use of torture at Abu Ghraib and elsewhere against Muslims suspected of being enemies served to racialize and dehumanize them.

The philosopher Giorgio Agamben refers to the Nazi treatment of Jews as "bare life." This notion, discussed earlier, captures well this dimension of dehumanization and degradation: the concentration camp inmates were reduced to nothing more than mere existence. All of their humanity was stamped out, annihilated. This is precisely what terror does: it denies humanity. One need only read Agamben's wrenching account of one of the first Nazi human experiments, on a young Jewish woman, thirty-seven years of age, who unwillingly became a "VP," a *Versuchsperson*, a human guinea pig, tested for the effect of high-altitude pressure.[41] That is, surely, bare life. We witness there the sovereign right to kill in its most pristine form.

In a frightening twist that could hardly have been anticipated, the iconic figure of bare life, for Agamben, was "the Muslim," *der Muselmann*. Not the Muslim believer, not the person of Muslim faith. Agamben was referring to the Jew in the concentration camp "for whom humiliation, horror, and fear had so taken away all consciousness and all personality as to make him absolutely apathetic." "Hence," Agamben adds, "the ironical name given to him." The Muslim was the figure that Primo Levi famously described for us. The Muslim no longer even belonged to his own community, to the community of Jews. He had become withdrawn from everything. "Mute and absolutely alone, he has passed into another world without memory and without grief."[42]

Tragically, Agamben's paradigm of bare life—the figure of *homo sacer*, the one who "may be killed and yet not sacrificed"[43]—is not exceptional, but rather captures our present reality too well. Looking back today at the images of Guantánamo or Abu Ghraib or other detention facilities in Iraq, those prisoners too are no more than bare life. Without question, terror served to racialize and dehumanize these men and women. Part of the use of terror, of its deployment, is precisely to turn the active minority into mere animals in the eyes of the general population.[44]

Terror works in other ways as well, and many other historical episodes could shed light on the complex functioning of terror today—of what Adriana Cavarero refers to as "horrorism."[45] Terror, for instance, operates to control and manage one's comrades. It can serve to keep the counterrevolutionary minority in check. The willingness to engage in extreme forms of brutality, in senseless violence, in irrational excess signals one's own ruthlessness to one's peers or inferiors. It can frighten and discipline both inferiors and superiors. It demonstrates one's willingness to be cruel—which can be productive, in fact necessary, to a counterinsurgency. The excesses of the guillotine, for instance, served to discipline the ranks of the revolutionary committees during The Terror. The use of terror by Cardinal Richelieu and Chancelier Séguier to suppress the 1639 uprisings of the *Nu-pieds* peasants in Normandy served to rein in the Normand bourgeoisie and parliamentarians.[46] The brutal repression of the prison riots at Attica in 1971 served to reassert Governor Nelson Rockefeller's control—as well as to tar the prisoners and racialize them, as Heather Ann Thompson shows in her brilliant account of the repression of the uprising, *Blood in the Water*.[47] Violence and terror can also produce fraternity, as Jean-Paul Sartre would remind us— what he called "a bond of immanence through positive reciprocities."[48]

In the end, terroristic methods do not just extract information, nor do they simply eliminate insurgents or win hearts and minds—they do much more work. They make counterinsurgency a powerful governing paradigm. And, as we will see in the next part, they help break down the boundaries between the foreign and the domestic.

―――――――――

"The Grand Inquisitor" is Dostoyevsky's sketch of a poem presented by Ivan Karamazov to his brother, Alyosha. It recounts the fictitious return of Christ at a difficult time in history—during the Spanish Inquisition.

In Ivan's poem, Christ comes face to face with the Grand Inquisitor, who had replaced Christ's word with terror—the terror of the Inquisition. The challenge, the Grand Inquisitor tells Christ, was to govern ordinary, weak men. And to succeed, he explains, the Grand Inquisitor had to rework and improve Christ's message. He had to harness its power in order to win over the passive masses.

Ivan's story captures a moral and political evolution. In the words of the Grand Inquisitor, speaking to Christ at the height of the Inquisition:

> We corrected and improved Thy teaching and based it upon 'Miracle, Mystery, and Authority.' And men rejoiced at finding themselves led once more like a herd of cattle, and at finding their hearts at last delivered of the terrible burden laid upon them by Thee, which caused them so much suffering. Tell me, were we right in doing as we did? Did not we show our great love for humanity, by realizing in such a humble spirit its helplessness, by so mercifully lightening its great burden, and by permitting and remitting for its weak nature every sin, provided it be committed with our authorization?[49]

And the Grand Inquisitor asks Christ, "For what, then, hast Thou come again to trouble us in our work?"

In the Grand Inquisitor's account, Christ's teaching proved inadequate to the Church's task. What the Church needed was authority and mastery. And in order to achieve mastery over the people, the Inquisitor had to reverse Christ's message: "We took Rome from him and the glaive of Caesar, and declared ourselves alone the kings of this earth, its sole kings," the Grand Inquisitor declared. The Inquisitor achieved mastery by placing evil above good, authority above compassion, Caesar above Christ.

That reversal ultimately produced a new truth: Christ's method—courageous freedom for the chosen few—could never succeed as a style of governing. No, not for the "weak, vicious, miserable nonentities born wicked and rebellious," as the Grand Inquisitor would say.

Even Christ understood this well, and ultimately forgives the Grand Inquisitor: "Suddenly He rises; slowly and silently approaching the Inquisitor. He bends towards him and softly kisses the bloodless, four-score and-ten-year-old lips. That is all the answer. The Grand Inquisitor shudders. There is a convulsive twitch at the corner of his mouth."

It is all understood. Everyone knows that mastery is the most important thing to achieve. And at the end of the parable, the Grand Inquisitor "goes to the door, opens it, and addressing Him, 'Go,' he says, 'go, and return no more . . . do not come again . . . never, never!' and—lets Him out into the dark night."

"The prisoner vanishes." Christ departs once again.

Post 9/11, in our new era of counterinsurgency warfare, I fear, we would not have opened the door. No, today, many, too many, would have tortured Christ more and better. Today, it seems, we would have terrorized Christ to death, once again.

PART III

THE DOMESTICATION OF COUNTERINSURGENCY

Once counterinsurgency warfare has taken hold in foreign affairs, it is but a small step to extend its logic to one's own citizens. Barely noticeable, the strategies are first applied in the same field of battle, but this time to different targets. The line between foreign combatant and suspect citizen begins to fade. Boundaries and borders become porous. Gradually we start to target our own in those foreign lands.

The year 2013 marked the first use of a targeted drone strike to assassinate a US citizen abroad. The target was born in Las Cruces, New Mexico, and raised in Nebraska, Minnesota, and Yemen. He obtained his undergraduate degree from Colorado State University, and did his graduate studies at San Diego State and George Washington Universities, before returning to Yemen in 2004. He became an imam there, and started posting videos of himself preaching radical sermons on the Internet. At that point, Anwar al-Awlaki, an American citizen residing in Yemen, was marked for death.[1]

His assassination was planned for several years by the Obama administration. As early as July 2010, David Barron, at the time an attorney at the Office of Legal Counsel and now a federal judge, wrote a forty-one-page legal memorandum detailing the legal justifications for killing a US citizen abroad. Barron concluded that the use of legal force was acceptable where, in his words, "the target's activities pose a 'continued and imminent threat of violence or death' to US persons" and high-level intelligence officers have determined that "a capture operation would be infeasible."[2] Academics and civil-liberties advocates criticized the rationale for being too vague and for failing to set standards for what is imminent or infeasible, threatening to create a dangerously broad justification for extrajudicial killing of American citizens. National security leaders, on the other hand, defended drone strikes on our citizens abroad in situations limited to those described in Barron's memorandum, under a wartime emergency justification.[3]

In March 2012, President Obama's attorney general officially declared that US citizens abroad "may be killed by US forces, but are still protected under the Fifth Amendment's due process clause" and that "it would be lawful to target a US citizen if the individual poses an imminent threat, capture is not feasible, and the operation were executed in observance of the applicable laws of war."[4] By 2013, Anwar al-Awlaki was dead, the victim of a targeted assassination against an American citizen abroad—without ever having been charged, tried, convicted, or sentenced to death.

In addition to al-Awlaki, nine other American citizens were killed by United States drone strikes between 2001 and 2015—although, according to official sources, they were not explicitly designated as assassination targets.[5] In 2002, American citizen Kemal Darwish was killed in the first American drone strike in Yemen. In 2013, the US Justice Department confirmed, along with the targeted killing of al-Awlaki, the purportedly inadvertent killing of three other American citizens. The same strike that killed al-Awlaki killed another US citizen named Samir Khan, who was suspected of being an Al Qaeda militant. Al-Awlaki's sixteen-year-old son, Abdulrahman al-Awlaki, was coincidentally killed in another drone strike the month after his father was assassinated. Jude Kenan Mohammad, another American suspected of recruiting for Al Qaeda, was killed in Pakistan in 2011. A CIA drone strike on the Pakistani border of Afghanistan in January 2015 killed an American hostage, Warren Weinstein, and a suspected American Al Qaeda militant named Ahmed Farouq. Within a week of that strike, another strike in the same region killed Adam Gadahn, an American citizen who was suspected of running Al Qaeda's propaganda department. Although Farouq and Gadahn were allegedly high-ranking members of Al Qaeda, according to the *New York Times*, "there had never been a Justice Department determination that they could be marked for death."[6] Administration officials claim that all of these victims were simply in "the wrong place at the wrong time" despite the fact that they were terrorist suspects.

The United States has also targeted nationals of allied countries. On November 12, 2015, the US military sent an MQ-9 Reaper drone and killed Mohammed Emwazi, a British citizen. Emwazi grew up in London and was a naturalized British citizen. He was detained by British authorities in 2010 and barred from leaving the United Kingdom, but eventually got to Syria and purportedly joined the Islamic state. Prime Minister David Cameron described the strike as a "combined effort" between US and British forces, and defended it as "an act of self-defense" and "the right thing to do."[7] On October 16, 2015, a US airstrike targeted German hip-hop artist Denis Cuspert in Syria. Early claims that he had been killed later proved false, but US officials acknowledged that Cuspert, who left Germany to join ISIS in 2012, was the target of the attack. Cuspert converted to Islam around 2007 and began going by the name Abu Malik in 2011, using his social media platforms to disseminate Islamic devotional music (*nasheeds*) and rap videos purportedly to recruit young Western Muslims. Cuspert was labeled a "Specially Designated Global Terrorist" by the Department of State on February 9, 2015. In confirming the targeted airstrike, Department of Defense spokeswoman Elissa Smith said that Cuspert's death would "contribute to our efforts to stop foreign fighter recruitment."[8]

All in all, as of April 23, 2015, the Bureau of Investigative Journalism reported that there have been thirty-eight intentional and unintentional Western drone deaths, which "include ten Americans, eight Britons, seven Germans, three Australians, two Spaniards, two Canadians, one Belgian or Swiss national, and now one Italian. There have also been four 'Westerners' of unidentified nationality."[9] And from there, it's a mere baby step to bring the counterinsurgency back home onto American soil.

7

COUNTERINSURGENCY COMES HOME

IN THE EARLY MORNING HOURS OF FRIDAY JULY 8, 2016, THE Dallas Police Department cornered a suspect believed to have shot and killed five police officers and wounded another seven officers and two civilians at a peaceful protest against police violence. The suspect, an army veteran named Micah Johnson, was negotiating with the police, exchanging gunfire, and claimed to have explosives on him. As the standoff wore on, Dallas police chief David O. Brown shifted gears. At his command, Dallas police officers carefully attached an explosive device to the arm of a robot and sent the robot in the direction of the suspect. Usually used to disable explosives, the tactical robot was turned into a robot-bomb. When it got sufficiently close to Micah Johnson, the Dallas police detonated the bomb, killing the suspect.[1]

The use of essentially a lethal drone in a civilian context on American soil was unprecedented. It raised a number of questions about police use of new drone technologies, about the increased militarization of the police, and about the proper boundary between policing and warfare. These questions were particularly salient because there was no indication that Johnson was tied, in any way whatsoever, to an international terrorist organization or to global terrorism. There was no suggestion he had any connection, other than being an army veteran, to the "war on terror." Instead, Johnson was an "ordinary" criminal suspect believed to have committed multiple common-law felony homicides.

On one level, these were legal questions surrounding the reasonableness of using such military-style weaponry—specifically, a weapon that is designed to kill an enemy, rather than to demobilize or neutralize a common-law suspect—in the civilian policing context. There is no license to kill in the civilian context, as there might be under ordinary combat situations during wartime. The use of deadly force is permitted in very limited contexts in police encounters, and is tightly constrained by necessity. The reason, of course, is that there had been no trial or finding of guilt, and therefore the suspect was entitled to a presumption of innocence. Johnson may have been mentally ill and not legally responsible for his actions. There are any number of scenarios that could have exculpated him—which is why there are, for good reason, far greater restrictions on the use of deadly force in the civilian context. As a legal matter, the constitutional-law scholar Noah Feldman notes, "It would have been better to use a police shooter, who might have been able to wound or incapacitate the [suspect] without killing him, and might have been in the best position to determine whether killing him was legally necessary."[2]

But the more pressing questions, for our purposes, are not narrowly legal, but instead larger political and strategic questions. The use of the robot-bomb in Dallas reflected a broader military turn in domestic civilian affairs, evident in the militarization of both policing equipment and strategy. Specifically, it illustrated a shift in domestic policing in the United States toward a counterinsurgency war paradigm. As Feldman remarks, "The step from the robot bomb to a drone strike is barely even incremental: morally and technologically, they're basically the same."[3]

The Dallas incident was a vivid illustration of the increasing domestication of the counterinsurgency warfare paradigm. Since 9/11, we have witnessed, in area after area, the government turn these methods back on its own citizens.[4] Total surveillance was extended to the American population. Law-enforcement agencies monitored mosques and Muslims on American soil. Police forces were outfitted with counterinsurgency equipment and began to deploy counterinsurgency tactics. Policing, it turns out, has been a particularly conducive vector through which the counterinsurgency paradigm has moved from military and foreign policy to the domestic context. But the domestication has been far broader than just in the criminal-justice area—as we will see.

Counterinsurgency strategies seeped into the streets and homes of America. As a result of Department of Defense programs that distribute excess military equipment, millions of dollars' worth of armored vehicles, military weapons, and tactical equipment reached local police forces across the country. According to the *Washington Post*, transfers through one such program, the Excess Property Program, increased exponentially since the war in Iraq. In 2006, the program was transferring $33 million worth of excess property to law-enforcement agencies; by 2013, that number rose to $420 million. In the first four months of 2014 alone, the agency made $206 million in transfers. Overall, the Excess Property Program transferred military equipment worth more than $5 billion since it began operating in the mid-1990s.[5]

Police forces across the country have stockpiled over 500 military-grade aircrafts, 44,000 night-vision devices, 93,000 assault weapons, 200 grenade launchers, and 12,000 bayonets. The Excess Property Program funneled to local law enforcement, over the period from 2006 to 2014, over 600 mine-resistant ambush-protected vehicles (MRAP), 475 bomb-detonator robots, 50 airplanes, 400 helicopters, as well as thousands of combat knives, night-vision sniper scopes, and camouflage gear.[6] The total dollar value of this military equipment is staggering. According to the *Congressional Digest*, between 2009 and 2014, the federal government "provided nearly $18 billion in funds and resources to support programs that provide equipment and tactical resources to state and local LEAs [law-enforcement agencies]."[7]

Radley Balko traced the history of the gradual militarization of local police forces in his stunning book *Rise of the Warrior Cop: The Militarization of America's Police Forces*. His conclusion there perfectly summarized our condition today: "Police today are armed, dressed, trained, and conditioned like soldiers."[8] This has been nowhere more evident than in the policing of protests.

In Ferguson, Missouri, during the protests following the shooting death of Michael Brown in August 2014, the local police responded in a heavily militarized way. The police "employed armored vehicles, noise-based crowd-control devices, shotguns, M4 rifles like those used by forces in Iraq and Afghanistan, rubber-coated metal pellets and tear gas," the *Washington Post* reported.[9] The images of unarmed, unprotected protesters facing militarized tactical SWAT teams visualized the new dynamics of the militarized police.

Ordinary police forces and military units can hardly be distinguished any longer. And the military buildup of civilian police forces also resulted in an increased use of militarized tactics.

Alongside the tanks, military-assault rifles, and camouflage apparel, local police forces are increasingly deploying counterinsurgency practices learned in the villages and moats of Iraq and Afghanistan. Civilian law enforcement now regularly responds to 911 calls about suspicious persons with the exact same techniques that would be used in a raid in Iraq or Afghanistan. In part, this is due to the porous nature of police, military, and reserve personnel and training. Many police officers are in the reserves, and vice versa. In part, it is due to the dominance of the counterinsurgency paradigm in the law-enforcement imagination.

Police watch protesters in Ferguson, Missouri, on August 13, 2014. (AP Photo/Jeff Roberson, reproduced by permission.)

Police face unarmed protesters in Ferguson, Missouri, on August 13, 2014. (AP Photo/Jeff Roberson, reproduced by permission.)

A former infantryman with the US Army's 3rd Stryker Brigade, 2nd Infantry Division in Iraq, Alex Horton conducted countless counterinsurgency raids against suspected guerrilla fighters in Iraq. When he returned stateside, Horton accidentally found himself at the other end of the barrel. He had been temporarily placed in a model unit in his apartment complex while his rental unit was being repaired, and one evening he was suspected of being a squatter. Three police officers barged into his temporary unit, guns drawn, sweeping the place, backing into corners, pointing their weapons at him. "In the shouting and commotion, I felt an instant familiarity," Horton wrote. "I had done this a few dozen times myself, 6,000 miles away from my Alexandria, Va., apartment . . . I had conducted the same kind of raid on suspected bombmakers and high-value insurgents."[10]

The same techniques, the same movements, practically the same equipment. "Their tactics were similar to the ones I used to clear rooms during the height of guerrilla warfare in Iraq," Horton observed. "I could almost admire it—their fluid sweep from the bedroom doorway to the distant corner. They stayed clear of one another's lines of fire in case they needed to empty their Sig Sauer .40-caliber pistols into me."

The counterinsurgency model has seeped into ordinary domestic policing. The result are scenes like this in homes and on the streets of heartland America, where the target is not a suspected bombmaker, but a suspected vagrant. In fact, the experience has become so commonplace in the United States that people began abusing the 911 system—out of vengeance or for a prank—by calling a SWAT team out on unsuspecting victims. The phenomenon has now entered the public imagination and has its own top definition in the urban dictionary: *swatting* is defined as tricking the police into sending a fully equipped SWAT team "to an unsuspecting victim's home under false pretenses."[11] The phenomenon began around the same time as the war in Iraq, as more and more American towns began to have SWAT teams. By the mid-2000s, 80 percent of police forces in small towns with populations between twenty-five and fifty thousand had a military-style SWAT unit.

And with those units came increased swatting. The *New York Times* reports that "the phenomenon is touching more and more lives in more serious ways."[12]

Meanwhile, in 2015, North Dakota became the first state to authorize the use of armed drones by law-enforcement agencies. The weapons permitted must be "less than lethal," according to the new law; but they can include Tasers, rubber bullets, tear gas, and pepper spray. And, following the July 2016 robot-bomb incident in Dallas, a leading police research institute, the Police Foundation, released a 311-page report with guidelines to assist police departments in using drones in such a way, as its title suggests, "to Enhance Community Trust."[13]

As suggested earlier, counterinsurgency logics have also seeped into the way that police officers think and imagine the world. By way of illustration, an editorial by a former St. Louis police officer and police reformer, Redditt Hudson, under the caption "I'm a Black Ex-cop, and This Is the Real Truth About Race and Policing," declares: "On any given day, in any police department in the nation, 15 percent of officers will do the right thing no matter what is happening. Fifteen percent of officers will abuse their authority at every opportunity. The remaining 70 percent could go either way depending on whom they are working with."

These are precisely the foundational principles of counterinsurgency theory. And they are not just this officer's intuitions. They represent the wisdom of experts who, as the editorial notes, have "trained thousands of officers around the country in use of force." The obvious danger, from this perspective, is that the rogue minority will taint the 70 percent who could go either way—especially because, as Hudson notes, "that remaining 70 percent of officers are highly susceptible to the culture in a given department." Everything turns, then, on those passive masses and protecting them against the corrupting influence of the rogue minority and its "outsize influence."[14]

The logic of an active minority being responsible for the vast majority of the problems recurs in a wide range of law-enforcement areas. A small minority of police officers conduct the vast majority of arrests. A small minority of cops are responsible for the majority of complaints of police misconduct. A small minority of homeless individuals account for the vast majority of hospitalizations and homeless incidents. In the words of a leading police administrator, there is only a small minority of dedicated and hardworking police officers and "those 10 percent do 90 percent of the work."[15] And the same holds true "among the bad guys" as well, he tells us. There is a small minority of young men responsible for the vast majority of violent crime. The list goes on and on. And in all of them, the foundational elements of the counterinsurgency rationale are there, often in a subliminal way, infusing the way that we imagine the world.

The domestication of counterinsurgency strategies started early, in the 1950s and 1960s, and predominantly in the context of policing and law enforcement. Although it accelerated and became widespread after 9/11, it first made its appearance at exactly the time when these tactics were being developed and refined in Vietnam.

The operations of COINTELPRO—the Counter Intelligence Program developed by the FBI in the 1950s to disrupt the American Communist Party, and extended into the 1960s to eradicate the Black Panthers—took precisely the form of counterinsurgency warfare. The notorious August 1967 directive of FBI director J. Edgar Hoover to "expose, disrupt, misdirect, discredit, or otherwise neutralize the activities of black nationalist, hate-type organizations and groupings, their leadership, spokesmen, membership, and supporters";[16] the police raids on Black Panther headquarters in 1968 and 1969; the summary execution of the charismatic chairman of the Chicago Black Panther Party, Fred Hampton; the first SWAT operations carried out against the Panthers in Los Angeles—these all had the trappings of modern warfare.

Hoover's FBI targeted the Panthers in a manner that drew on the foundational principles of counterinsurgency: first, to collect as much intelligence on the Black Panther Party as possible through the use of FBI informants and total surveillance; second, to isolate the Panthers from their communities by making their lives individually so burdened with surveillance and so difficult that they were forced to separate themselves from their friends and family members; third, to turn the Panther movement into one that was perceived, by the general population, as a radicalized extremist organization, as a way to delegitimize the Panthers and reduce their appeal and influence; and ultimately, to eliminate and eradicate them, initially through police arrests, then through criminal prosecutions (for instance, of the New York 21) and justified homicides (for instance, of Bobby Hutton in 1968 and others in Los Angeles), and ultimately by fomenting conflict and divisiveness within the party, especially between Huey Newton and Eldridge Cleaver in 1971.[17] The logics of counterinsurgency could be heard clearly in Hoover's notorious memo from March 1968 setting out the very objectives of COINTELPRO: to "prevent militant black nationalist groups and leaders from gaining respectability, by discrediting them to [. . .] both the responsible community and to liberals who have vestiges of sympathy," and to "prevent the long-range growth of militant black organizations, especially among youth."[18]

Similarly, the armed takeover of the Attica Prison by the New York State Police troopers during the Attica uprising had all the trappings of a counterinsurgency operation, as Heather Thompson documents in her book, *Blood in the Water*. There too, the political leaders, especially Governor Nelson Rockefeller, portrayed the inmate population as a radical fringe minority. Rather than pursue further negotiations and allow them to gain momentum, Rockefeller opted to annihilate them through a military-style operation that ultimately killed thirty-three inmates as well as ten correctional officers. The assault on Attica and the repression of other prison revolts in the early 1970s had precisely the effect that counterinsurgency operations aim at: to separate and isolate the radical minority from the general population—literally, here, the general prison population—and then eliminate them.

The domestic use of counterinsurgency strategies continued sporadically over the 1980s and 1990s. In 1985, for instance, the Philadelphia

Police Department used a Pennsylvania State Police helicopter to drop two bombs on the compound of a black-liberation organization called MOVE, resulting in the death of eleven members, including five children and the leader of the movement, John Africa. The resulting fire destroyed around sixty-five row houses in the neighborhood. As *Time* magazine reported, "It looks just like a war zone."[19] In 1993, the ATF, FBI, and Texas National Guard mounted a raid on the Branch Davidian compound that resembled another counterinsurgency attack—resulting in the deaths of eighty-seven men, women, and children. Throughout the 1980s, the United States experimented with the domestication of counterrevolutionary practices in Central America, especially with its covert support of the Contras in Nicaragua. And there were similar domestic uses of counterinsurgency in other countries as well, notably by the British government during the struggle against the Irish Republican Army. There too, counterinsurgency strategies developed and refined in the colonies—in Palestine and Malaya—were brought back home to repress insurgents and minorities favoring Irish independence.

But since 9/11, the domestication of counterinsurgency accelerated exponentially with the hypermilitarization of local police forces and the coming of total information awareness. What is happening today is that foreign warfare, domestic antiterrorism policing, and ordinary domestic policing have all converged on the counterinsurgency model. Modern warfare has now colonized our ordinary forms of domestic policing and governance.

Police departments are increasingly adopting the logic of the counterinsurgency model. Professors Charles Sabel and William Simon at Columbia University document this trend and the emerging contrast between an earlier strategy of policing modeled on large-scale warfare and a newer policing approach modeled on counterinsurgency.[20]

The earlier model can be illustrated by the NYPD order-maintenance approach. Mayor Rudolph Giuliani and his first police commissioner, William Bratton, inaugurated the strategy in 1994 under the rubric "broken-windows policing" or the "quality-of-life initiative."[21] Giuliani's successor, Michael Bloomberg, and his police commissioner, Ray Kelly, modified the strategy to prioritize "stop-and-frisk" practices in the early 2000s. With the return of Bill Bratton as police chief under mayor Bill de Blasio from 2014 to 2016, the NYPD strategy reverted to an aggressive misdemeanor arrest policy under the broken-windows theory. At all times, though, the NYPD emphasized a massive campaign of either aggressive misdemeanor arrests or stop-and-frisk practices—modeled on large-scale warfare.[22]

One of the main architects of broken-windows policing, Jack Maple, referred to the strategy as all-out "war." Bratton, Maple asserted, had "clearly communicated a revolutionary goal—to 'win the war on crime.'"[23] "Maple and others called Chief of Patrol Louis Anemone 'our Patton,'" Sabel and Simon add, "invoking the World War II general associated with mobile tank warfare."[24] The metaphor could hardly be more on point: the approach was modeled on the kind of large-scale warfare characteristic of World War II and the policy interventions that were designed in its mold, like the War on Poverty and later the War on Crime.

In his own descriptions of broken-windows policing, Maple referred repeatedly to war strategists from Sun Tzu, the ancient Chinese general and strategist from the fifth century BCE (544–496 BCE), to Hannibal in the Alps, to Admiral Lord Nelson at Trafalgar, to General Patton. Napoleon appears over and over. Marine Corps strategy and maneuver warfare became the model. The World War II motif was everywhere. General Patton surfaced again and again. So did Eisenhower. The police officers were referred to as "troops in the field." The police captains were referred to as "skilled, audacious commanders." And they were each—or practically each—given a field marshal equivalent right out of World War II.[25] As Maple wrote:

> Bratton was our George C. Marshall, the man of vision who shook the US armed forces out of their sleep in 1941 and demonstrated an infallible instinct for identifying talent. Chief of Department

John Timoney was our Eisenhower, as respected by the soldiers in the field as he was knowledgeable about the intricacies of managing a mammoth fighting organization. Chief of Patrol Louie Anemone was our Patton, a tireless motivator and brilliant field strategist who could move ground forces at warp speed. First Deputy Commissioner Dave Scott didn't have a World War II counterpart: He was Burt Lancaster in *Trapeze*. He wanted to help the young acrobats learn to fly, but he was also there to catch us if we fell.[26]

Today, by contrast to this earlier battlefield logic, a number of cities are turning to a very different approach. In Cincinnati, for instance, new strategies are being developed under the express rubric of SARA (Scanning, Analysis, Response, Assessment), imposed on the city by a consent decree settling civil-rights lawsuits against the city for excessive use-of-force practices. The SARA approach is reminiscent of systems analysis—the type of recursive systems planning perfected by RAND in the 1960s. As Sabel and Simon describe it, the approach "begins with a precise definition of a problem, proceeds to look for well-configured interventions, implements them, assesses the results, and then if the problem persists, begins the cycle anew with a revised account of the problem in the light of experience." The approach is based on the idea of "problem-solving policing," and it targets whatever needs are identified, whether it is shoplifting, street prostitution, "Assaults in and Around Bars," or "Disorder at Day Laborer Sites."[27]

Many of these new policing interventions engage with the communities and involve local stakeholders. They may implicate social-service agencies as well, or job-related services, or community volunteers depending on the needs—notice the resonance with winning hearts and minds in the traditional counterinsurgency context. Some of the officers involved in these efforts draw a comparison to the strategies used in the war in Afghanistan. "In discussing his work with a community development organization in Cincinnati's Walnut Hills neighborhood,"

Sabel and Simon report, "Captain Daniel Gerard noted that he saw similarity between this work and that of a friend serving as an army officer in Helmand Province, Afghanistan." In Afghanistan, the army officer had been involved in "economic and institutional development efforts." Sabel and Simon comment:

> The implication is that Problem-Oriented Policing more resembles the counterinsurgency model of warfare associated with General David Petraeus than General Patton's mobile tank tactics invoked by Bratton to explain Compstat. Like POP, the counterinsurgency approach prescribes that patrol, response to incidents, and use-of-force be coordinated with diverse proactive initiatives that engage civilians with a stake in achieving security. The goal is to secure terrain by building a viable community, not by attempting to annihilate all potentially hostile forces. As POP-influenced police offers often say "we couldn't arrest our way out of this problem," David Petraeus reports that he often said in Iraq that "we would not be able to kill or capture our way out of" problems there.[28]

Today, a counterinsurgency mindset has begun to dominate ordinary policing. Increasingly, it seems, there is an active minority that needs to be identified and eliminated—predominantly susceptible Muslims, Mexican "bad *hombres*," inner-city black youths, and unruly police protesters. We are told about the dangers of ISIS followers who are now "home grown" in the heartland of the United States—not to mention in the *banlieus* of Paris, in the outskirts of London, in the center of Brussels. A counterinsurgency mentality is beginning to pervade the streets. Everything is perceived through an "us versus them" lens, the law-abiding citizens versus the criminals. There is constant talk about the "criminal element" and "criminal invasion"—terms that appear in the early writings of James Q. Wilson, Edward Banfield, and George Kelling, and have now become routine. So, for instance, the former police chief of St. Louis, Sam Dotson, was quoted saying that, in the wake of the Black Lives Matter protests, the "criminal element is feeling empowered."[29] Meanwhile, the *Washington Post* and *Guardian* have begun documenting the high rate of lethal police shootings in the United States, fueling a siege mentality in certain neighborhoods in inner cities: 1,091 police shootings in 2016 according to the *Guardian*, 963 according to the *Post*.[30]

Policing at the national level as well has seen a noticeable shift. The War on Crime, during the second half of the twentieth century, involved large-scale military-style operations—especially the federal War on Drugs in Latin America, which included widespread eradication and blanketing of poppy fields, and military campaigns in the countryside. These campaigns had dramatically disparate effects on African Americans and Hispanics at home. In both their foreign and domestic manifestations—the eradication of cocaine abroad, the elimination of crime domestically—the political interventions had Patton-like ambitions. Presidents from Richard Nixon through Ronald Reagan promoted massive prison construction and juvenile detention facilities, mostly for minority youths, and increasingly militarized the policing of housing projects.

But as the historian Elizabeth Hinton shows in her compelling book *From the War on Poverty to the War on Crime*, the model of large-scale warfare has increasingly tilted toward counterinsurgency strategies.[31] Federal officials began to view black militant activists as a revolutionary minority that needed to be repressed, violently. President Ronald Reagan signed a Comprehensive Crime Control Act in 1984 under which most of the $900 million that Congress allotted for drug rehab programs was spent on intelligence facilities, warplanes, and helicopters. In the early 1990s, the federal government began experimenting with a "Weed and Seed" approach that mirrored the counterinsurgency paradigm: to weed out drug users, dealers, and traffickers, and seed the neighborhoods with social and economic revitalization programs. The weed-and-seed approach sought to "mobilize community residents in the target areas to assist enforcement in identifying and removing violent offenders and drug traffickers from the community."[32] Through federal grants, the approach was implemented in more than 150 communities across the United States. And through programs like the Excess Property Program and others, the federal government began funding the increasingly counterinsurgency-modeled militarization of local police forces.

Today, all three central strategies of counterinsurgency have been turned back on the American people. Americans are now caught in total information awareness. American Muslims and other minorities have become the active minority that is targeted for elimination. And it is, more broadly, the American people whose hearts and minds are being sought. The counterinsurgency paradigm has come home.

8

SURVEILLING AMERICANS

IGHT AFTER 9/11, HIGH-RANKING OFFICIALS IN THE BUSH administration devised an illicit eavesdropping program and cast as wide a net possible, covering both foreign and domestic communications. The NSA began eavesdropping inside the United States— without court order. Congress soon passed Section 215 of the USA PATRIOT Act that provided for the bulk collection by the NSA of all telephony metadata held by American telecommunications companies like AT&T, Verizon, and Sprint. The FBI began a massive campaign of information gathering targeting over five thousand Muslims. Local police departments, such as the NYPD, implemented surveillance programs directed at mosques and Muslim communities, and began infiltrating domestic Muslim organizations. Through both digital and analog methods, the government turned total information awareness on the American people.

The linchpin of a domesticated counterinsurgency is to bring total information awareness home. Just as it was developed abroad, it is total surveillance alone that makes it possible to distinguish the active minority on domestic soil from the passive masses of Americans. A fully transparent population is the first requisite of the counterinsurgency method. In General Petraeus's field manual, it received a full chapter early on, "Intelligence in Counterinsurgency," with a pithy and poignant epigraph: "Everything *good* that happens seems to come from good intelligence." And as the manual began, so it ended, with the following simple mantra: "The ultimate success or failure of the [counterinsurgency] mission depends on the effectiveness of the intelligence effort."[1]

The government is supposed to treat domestic surveillance differently than foreign intelligence—which explains, among other things, the separation and different legal standards that apply to the FBI and the CIA. Under federal law, domestic communications receive greater protections and require a warrant from a judicial officer to intercept. Foreign communications related to terrorism investigations pass through a more expedited process at the Foreign Intelligence Surveillance Court (FISC), but nevertheless also require approval from that court. Stringent but graduated rules on domestic and foreign intelligence gathering had been put in place in the 1970s as a result of illicit domestic wiretapping programs like COINTELPRO and the subsequent investigation and recommendations of the Church Committee. Limits had been placed especially on domestic surveillance as a result of the excesses of Hoover's FBI investigations into the personal lives of Martin Luther King and others.

Despite all of these restrictions, after 9/11 the government swept aside many of the intelligence reforms from the 1970s and put in place a massive surveillance network at the local, national, and global level to achieve total information awareness of the American people. Programs created after 9/11 for foreign intelligence gathering were turned on Americans. Plus, new technological capabilities made it possible to sweep Americans up with foreign surveillance—both incidentally and intentionally. The digital revolution made the intelligence community's wildest dreams come true. The perceived crisis of global terrorism, of course, naturalized and justified the gradual encroachments. But the domestication of total surveillance had deeper roots in the very logic of counterinsurgency warfare. The fact is, in this new governing paradigm, *every* American is a potential insurgent.

Constant vigilance of the American population is necessary—hand in hand with the appearance of trust. Appearances are vital. A domesticated counterinsurgency must suspect everyone in the population, but not let it be known. This posture, developed in counterinsurgency theory decades ago, was at the core of the paradigm. David Galula had refined it to a witty statement he would tell his soldiers in Algeria: "One cannot catch a fly with vinegar. My rules are: outwardly you must treat every civilian as a friend; inwardly you must consider him as a rebel ally until you have positive proof to the contrary."[2] This mantra has become the rule today—at home.

In the wake of the Twin Tower attacks, the NYPD started surveilling hundreds of mosques, Muslim businesses, associations, and student groups—infiltrating dozens of them—without any evidence they were tied to terrorism or had engaged in wrongdoing. The NYPD recruited "mosque crawlers" to infiltrate and monitor Islamic places of worship, and "rakers" to infiltrate Muslim bookstores, cafés, and bars. (They were called *rakers* because the head of intelligence, who came from the CIA, would say he wanted his unit to "rake the coals, looking for hot spots.") The NYPD infiltrated student groups at Brooklyn College and City College of New York, and accessed student records under false pretenses.[3]

"Place Mosque under observation before and during Jumma (Friday Prayers), record license plates and capture video and photographic record of those in attendance. Pay special attention to all NY State License plates." Those were the directions given to NYPD undercover agents in the "Target of Surveillance" directive regarding the Majid Omar Mosque in Patterson, New Jersey.[4] An "NYPD Secret Weekly MSA Report" dated November 22, 2006, recounted the activities of the Muslim Student Associations at Buffalo, at NYU, and at Rutgers–Newark.[5] The

NYPD intelligence officer reported visiting, in his words, "as a daily routine," the websites, blogs, and forums of the Islamic student organizations there and at Albany University, Baruch College, Brooklyn College, Columbia University, LaGuardia Community College, University of Pennsylvania, Rutgers–New Brunswick, Stony Brook, SUNY Potsdam, Syracuse University, Yale University, and others. He detailed an upcoming scholarly conference at the Toronto Convention Center, discussing the background and visa status of the invited speakers.

In a secret intelligence briefing for the head of intelligence, dated April 25, 2008, the NYPD reported being worried about the verdict in the Sean Bell case—the acquittal of three NYPD detectives charged in the multiple-shooting death of an unarmed man in Jamaica, Queens. The briefing reported that the agency was "especially concerned with and keying on our convert mosques i.e. Ikhwa, Taqwa, Iqquamatideen and MIB (Mosque of Islamic Brotherhood)" and asked a confidential informant to get "involved with the New Black Panther Party."[6]

The same briefing detailed another covert NYPD operation to infiltrate a whitewater rafting-trip by students at City College of New York. The briefing recounted that an undercover NYPD operative, named "OP# 237," left for the "Whitewater Rafting trip Monday, April 21, 2008 and returned Wednesday night April 23, 2008." It explained, "The trip was hosted by the EXTREMEGOERS CCNY SPORTS GROUP; which is essentially run by the MSO [Muslim Student Organization]." It detailed the names and status of many of the nineteen CCNY students, noting that "Ali Ahmed was in charge and did orchestrate the events." It emphasized, "In addition to the regularly scheduled events (Rafting), the group prayed at least four times a day, and much of the conversation was spent discussing Islam and was religious in nature."[7] Although the report spoke in conspiratorial terms, there was no prior reason—and none developed—to suspect the college students of anything.

The NYPD prepared analytic reports with maps and intelligence covering every mosque within one hundred miles of the city, including in Newark, New Jersey, and Suffolk and Nassau Counties, detailing their addresses, telephone numbers, pictures, ethnic affiliation, and "information of note," with entries such as "During visit 3 African Muslim males and an Egyptian male customer were observed dining within" and "Observed a lot of products made in Egypt were sold inside the location."[8] These secret "Demographics Unit" reports mapped mosques, madrassahs, and Muslim population density by ethnicity. They included surveillance photos and intelligence notes on every mosque and Muslim businesses (see surveillance reports on next page).

The Associated Press described the program, in a Pulitzer Prize–winning series, as a "human mapping program" of American Muslims that amounted to "an unusual partnership with the CIA that has blurred the line between foreign and domestic spying." This kind of monitoring of Muslims without any suspicion would have run afoul if it had been done by the federal government, which may explain, as AP suggested, why the CIA worked surreptitiously with the NYPD to ramp up this domestic spying program and also why the federal government gave the NYPD more than $1.6 billion over the decade following 9/11.[9]

Several years later, in August 2016, the Office of the Inspector General for the NYPD issued a report detailing the extent of the targeting of Muslims. It reviewed a random sample of NYPD intelligence investigations from 2010 to 2015 and found that 95 percent of the investigations of political activities targeted Muslims or activity associated with Islam.[10] It also found that over 50 percent of those investigations continued after outliving their authorization.

Following the revelations by the AP, the ACLU filed suit in June 2013 on behalf of plaintiffs challenging the surveillance of mosques. The litigation captured well the historical trajectory of the domestication of counterinsurgency practices. The 2013 case, *Raza v. City of New York*, was folded back into an earlier federal case known as the *Handschu* litigation. The *Handschu* case had been filed in 1971 and challenged NYPD surveillance of the Black Panthers, antiwar protesters, the ACLU, NAACP, and others.[11] *Handschu* addressed precisely the first domestic uses of counterinsurgency strategies—the early antecedents

Name:	Masjid ▮▮▮
Address:	▮▮▮Ave. Newark, New Jersey 071▮▮
Phone Number:	973-▮▮▮▮▮
Building Type:	Private House
Sect:	Sunni
Ethnic Composition:	Nigerian, West African
Imam:	
Capacity:	
Precinct:	4th Precinct
Note(s):	Mosque in private house without any signs. Observed 25 to 30 worshipers exiting after Jumma prayer.

Location Name:	▮▮▮'s Cafe & Snack Shop
Location Type:	Cafe
Ethnicity:	African American
Address:	▮▮▮Avenue
City:	NEWARK
State:	New Jersey
Telephone:	973▮▮▮
Zip code:	07▮▮
Precinct:	3rd

Information of Note:

Owned and operated by African American Muslim.
Small cafe that advertises all halal products.
Same owner owned the body shop next door.
Location is in good condition and has seating capacity for 10-12 customers.
Location is in close proximity of Islamic Cultural Center of New Jersey located at 20 Branford Place.

Location Name:	▮▮▮'s Body Shop
Location Type:	Body shop
Ethnicity:	African American
Address:	▮▮▮Avenue
City:	NEWARK
State:	New Jersey
Telephone:	973▮▮▮
Zip code:	07▮▮
Precinct:	3rd

Information of Note:

Owned and operated by African American Muslim.
Small store that advertises Islamic products, health & beauty supplies, incense, health food and Islamic clothing.
Location is in close proximity of Islamic Cultural Center of New Jersey located at ▮▮▮Place.

NYPD surveillance report on mosque and Islamic businesses in Newark, New Jersey (redacted here to protect privacy). (NYPD Intelligence Division, Demographics Unit, "Newark, New Jersey, Demographics Report," September 25, 2007, pp. 31, 46.)

to today's more coordinated and systemic counterinsurgency. It would serve as the framework to assess the new more systematic surveillance programs targeting mosques, Muslims, and Islamic-related businesses and student groups.

Federal judge Charles S. Haight Jr. of the Southern District of New York oversaw the *Handschu* litigation from its inception, including a settlement agreement in 1985 that led to the famous *Handschu* guidelines for oversight of the NYPD's investigations of political activity. For years, the police department was under an agreement that prevented its intelligence unit from instigating investigations of political activity, and required that any such investigations be based on evidence of a crime. That original agreement was modified shortly after 9/11 to allow the NYPD more flexibility in its investigations of political activity. But even under those more relaxed standards, the NYPD surveillance of mosques and student groups pushed the boundaries of legality, resulting in new modifications of the *Handschu* guidelines.

In various interviews during the 2016 presidential campaign, President Donald Trump endorsed the continued surveillance of mosques and Muslim groups. President Trump indicated that he favored increased surveillance of American Muslims, possible registration of American Muslims in a government database, and even issuing special identifications for Muslims noting their religious faith.[12] "You're going to have to watch and study the mosques, because a lot of talk is going on in the mosques," Trump told MSNBC's *Morning Joe* in November 2015. Referring specifically to the NYPD intelligence programs that monitored New York's Muslims, Trump said that "from what I heard, in the old days—meaning a while ago—we had a great surveillance going on in and around the mosques of New York City."[13]

While the NYPD was ramping up a dragnet surveillance program of Muslims with the aid of the CIA, the FBI and federal prosecutors launched a massive nationwide information gathering campaign targeting Middle Eastern men from predominantly Muslim countries living in the United States on nonimmigrant visas. About two months after 9/11, US attorney general John Ashcroft announced a national campaign to interview as many as five thousand of these men. Federal authorities in Michigan rapidly responded and started the initiative, sending out over 560 letters to the targeted minority, identified as men being between the ages of eighteen and thirty-three from Middle Eastern Muslim countries. Here too, the authorities had no evidence or any reason to believe that any one of them was connected to terrorism or wrongdoing; in fact, the federal officials emphasized as much in those letters, saying, "We have no reason to believe that you are, in any way, associated with terrorist activities."[14] But despite the complete absence of suspicion, the federal authorities pressured the men to meet and talk to federal agents and local police. In order to conduct all these interviews, Ashcroft had asked local police enforcement to pitch in, further domesticating the strategies.

"Please contact my office to set up an interview at a location, date, and time that is convenient for you," the letter stated. "While this interview is voluntary, it is crucial that the investigation be broad-based and thorough, and the interview is important to achieve that goal. We need to hear from you as soon as possible—by December 4. Please call my office between 9 a.m. to 5 p.m. any day, including Saturday and Sunday. We will work with you to accommodate your schedule." Signed by the US attorney for the eastern district of Michigan, these letters couched voluntariness in terms of "needing" to hear back within a week. And given that the targeted men were on nonimmigrant visas, these invitations in truth read as commands.

In addition to these local and domestic national surveillance programs, foreign-style intelligence collection was turned on the American masses. The Bush administration put in place an infamous NSA eavesdropping program inside the United States without prior court approval or any court orders. Congress passed the Section 215 program that collected data from American telecommunications companies.

The NSA put in place a number of signal intelligence programs that captured and monitored all telecommunications data including that of American citizens. Through private sector cooperation with Microsoft, AT&T, and social media, the FBI and NSA increasingly get backdoor access to e-mail services and cloud storage facilities, and direct access to the servers of Yahoo, Google, Facebook, etc.

The NSA's core programs worked in tandem and piggy-backed off the collection and mining of all our personal data by social media and retailers. Since the advent of free e-mail, storage, and social-media services, such as Gmail by Google, Outlook and SkyDrive by Microsoft, or Facebook, these digital giants began collecting all our personal data that crossed their servers. Their business models depended on it, insofar as the only source of income related to these free services was digital advertising. Other digital merchants, such as Amazon, Netflix, and other online retailers, also began capturing all their customers' personal information as well, for purposes of advertising and pushing targeted products on consumers. All of these private giants of the digital age began collecting everyone's data for their own commercial interests. The NSA, who figured this out quickly, soon received access to this data through licit and illicit means. Through programs like PRISM and UPSTREAM, the NSA gained total access to their servers and to the cables through which all of this data streamed.

The PRISM program, discussed earlier in the context of foreign intelligence collection, allowed the NSA to directly access the servers of most of the American digital giants, meaning that agents at the NSA and delegated consultants could directly access the servers of these companies to field inquiries and searches on foreigners as well as Americans. The agency gained direct access to the content of e-mails, attachments, VoIP calls, and all digital communications, allowing access to the personal data of foreigners as well as the information of American citizens. The UPSTREAM program provided the NSA with a copy of all the digital traffic going through undersea cables. And other NSA programs for the collection and mining of our personal digital data proliferated, resulting in a stunning level of access to the private information of Americans.

The invasiveness of today's digital surveillance is truly breathtaking. The creation of these programs coincided with the explosive growth of digital technologies, all of which are rooted in and enable invasive surveillance of those who use them. Our network service providers, search engines, and social-media companies monitor our every digital trace to recommend products, sell advertisements, and fuel consumption. Google collects and mines our Gmail e-mails, attachments, contacts, and calendars. Netflix and Amazon use our data to recommend films, and Twitter tracks our Internet activity on all the websites that carry its little icon. Facebook's smartphone app collects information from our other phone apps and pushes advertisements onto them. Instagram verifies ad impressions, measures their success, and provides feedback to the advertisers as to which are most effective. Neighbors use packet sniffers or free Mac software, like Eavesdrop, to tap into our unsecured networks. Google's street-view cars captured and recorded our usernames, passwords, and personal e-mails on unencrypted Wi-Fi traffic.

And as Edward Snowden's revelations demonstrated, the NSA has practically free access to all of this information through multiple means. A quick look at the top-secret PRISM slides reminds us of the reach into our personal lives: Microsoft, Yahoo, Google, Facebook, Paltalk, YouTube, Skype, AOL, Apple, etc. All of these companies gave the NSA access to communications conducted through them under the PRISM program, and they did so for a trifling sum. According to the Snowden revelations, the entire PRISM program cost the NSA a mere $20 million per year. For that tiny amount, the NSA had direct access to their servers—over and above the cutting and splicing into telecom cables that gave the NSA direct access to all digital communications.

As a result, in the United States today, ordinary citizens face a multifaceted web of surveillance. Social media, retailers, smartphone applications, Internet providers, and web browsers are all collecting our private data, and making them available to the intelligence agencies.

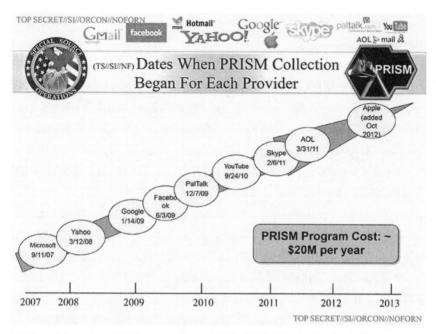

NSA PowerPoint slide on PRISM program history (2013). ("NSA Slides Explain the PRISM Data-Collection Program," *Washington Post*, June 6, 2013.)

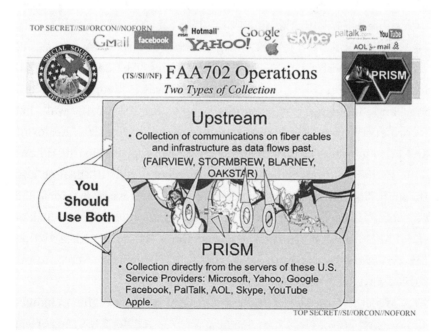

NSA PowerPoint slide on PRISM and UPSTREAM programs (2013). ("NSA Slides Explain the PRISM Data-Collection Program," *Washington Post*, June 6, 2013.)

Most new technology and apps—even games, like Pokémon GO—thrive on accessing our contacts, our GPS location, our calendar, our webcam, and all our private information. We are surrounded by a Lernaean Hydra of telecoms, social media, Google platforms, Facebook apps, Microsoft products, retailers, data brokers, multinational corporations, hackers—including foreign government hackers—*and* our own intelligence agencies, each of which is trying to outdo the other to collect and mine our personal information, each of them pursuing total information awareness with unparalleled vigor.

In *Exposed*, I proposed a new way to understand how power circulates in the digital age and, especially, a new way to comprehend our willingness to expose ourselves to private corporations and the government alike. The metaphors commonly used to describe our digital condition, such as the "surveillance state," Michel Foucault's panopticon prison, or even George Orwell's Big Brother, are inadequate, I argued there. In the new digital age we are not forcibly imprisoned in panoptic cells. There is no "telescreen" anchored to the wall of our apartments by the state. No one is trying to crush our passions, or wear us down into submission with the smell of boiled cabbage and old rag mats, coarse soap, and blunt razors. The goal is not to displace our pleasures with hatred—with "hate" sessions, "hate songs," "hate weeks." Today, instead, we interact by means of "likes," "shares," "favorites," "friending," and "following." We gleefully hang smart TVs on the wall that record everything we say and all our preferences. The drab uniforms and grim grayness of Orwell's *1984* have been replaced by the iPhone 5c in its radiant pink, yellow, blue, and green. "Colorful through and through," its marketing slogan promises, and the desire for color-filled objects—for the sensual swoosh of a sent e-mail, the seductive click of the iPhone camera "shutter," and the "likes," clicks, and hearts that can be earned by sharing—seduce us into delivering ourselves to the surveillance technologies.

And as the monitoring and marketing of our private lives changes who we are, power circulates in a new way. Orwell depicted the perfect totalitarian society. Guy Debord described ours rather as a society of the spectacle, in which the image makers shape how we understand the world and ourselves. Michel Foucault spoke instead of "the punitive society" or what he called "panopticism," drawing on Jeremy Bentham's design of the panoptic prison. Gilles Deleuze went somewhat further and described what he called "societies of control." But in our digital age, total surveillance has become inextricably linked with pleasure. We live in a society of exposure and exhibition, an expository society.

It is precisely the pleasure and attractions, the seductions of the digital age that make us expose ourselves so willingly. And even those of us who do not partake in the rich world of social media, or hesitate to leave traces, end up sharing our intimate lives and political views digitally. It is practically impossible to have a social or family life without at least text messages, cell phones, and/or e-mail. It is almost impossible to live in today's world without searching the web, buying online, swiping an access card, retrieving money from an ATM. It is virtually impossible to have a professional life without filling out Doodles and SurveyMonkeys, or responding to Paperless Post.

Confronting the expository society requires looking both at and beyond the state to social media, corporate and retail interests, Silicon Valley, AT&T, and beyond these to ourselves, with our apparently insatiable and irresistible impulses, urges, and *jouissance* to exhibit ourselves. The problem today is not only the state; it is also all of *us*, we who give ourselves away to total surveillance. And not only us, but our gadgets as well: our smartphones that emit GPS data and allow Facebook to cull data from all other apps, or from virtual reality games like Pokémon GO. These devices have become powerful entry points into a treasure trove of personal information and interconnected geo-located data.

In August 2015, leaked documents revealed that the American telecommunications giant, AT&T, had willingly worked with the NSA as recently as 2013 to provide access "to billions of e-mails as they have flowed across its domestic networks." AT&T voluntarily installed cable-splicing equipment at its communications hubs in the United States. AT&T was particularly solicitous, the *New York Times* noted. "AT&T was the first partner to turn on a new collection capability that the NSA said amounted to a 'live' presence on the global net."[15]

Early on, AT&T's partnership fueled an intelligence program that, in a single month, captured and sent to the NSA four hundred billion Internet metadata records. On a daily basis, more than a million e-mails were processed through the keyword selection system at NSA's headquarters in Fort Meade, Maryland. According to the NSA's internal documents, which cover periods ranging from 2003 to 2013, AT&T's "corporate relationships provide unique accesses to other telecoms and I.S.P.s" as well. As the *New York Times* added, with a twist of irony, "One document reminds NSA officials to be polite when visiting AT&T facilities, noting, 'This is a partnership, not a contractual relationship.'"

These new revelations were a fitting capstone to the passage of the USA FREEDOM Act by the US Congress two months earlier in June 2015. The FREEDOM Act was Congress's attempt to redress the balance between privacy and security in the wake of the Edward Snowden leaks two years earlier. It targeted one and only one of the NSA's surveillance platforms, the Section 215 program of the USA PATRIOT Act, a provision that authorized the domestic bulk collection of telephony metadata in the United States.

President Obama heralded the FREEDOM Act as an important measure that would "strengthen civil liberty safeguards and provide greater public confidence in these programs."[16] The *Guardian* reported that "privacy and reform activists hailed the bill as a 'milestone' achievement, the first reform of surveillance programs in more than a decade."[17] In its most significant provision, the FREEDOM Act modified the Section 215 program so that, from now on, it would be the telecom companies, companies like AT&T, that will hold and maintain Americans' telephony metadata.

It is hard to miss the irony. It is now AT&T who protects us. The same telecom company that had gone out of its way to collaborate, often in illicit ways, for years if not decades, with US signal intelligence services to provide access to private telecommunications and personal data. The same company that, according to the newly leaked documents, enthusiastically and voluntarily cooperated with the NSA and "installed surveillance equipment in at least 17 of its Internet hubs on American soil."

And as if that were not enough, in the fine print of the landmark legislation, it turns out that we, American taxpayers, will compensate AT&T for holding their data. As Reuters reported, "The FREEDOM Act does contain a provision to compensate companies for costs they incur holding and turning over such data, which is something the carriers made clear they wanted in return for agreeing to store the data."[18] That arrangement was baked into the compromise early on. President Obama's advisers—a committee composed of an eclectic range of former officials and academics—had originally recommended this remunerative arrangement. In their report, *Liberty and Security in a Changing World*, Obama's advisers wrote that "it would be in the interests of the providers and the government to agree on a voluntary system that meets the needs of both"; but, they added, if such a mutually agreeable deal could not be worked out, "the government should reimburse the providers for the cost of retaining the data."[19]

And that's what happened: taxpayers would pay the telecoms to hold the data for the government. So, before, AT&T surreptitiously provided our private personal digital data to the intelligence services free of charge. Now, American taxpayers will pay them to collect and hold on to the data for when the intelligence services need them. A neoliberal win-win solution for everyone—except, of course, the ordinary, tax-paying citizen who wants a modicum of privacy or protection from the counterinsurgency.

We live in a new digital age that has fundamentally transformed every aspect of society and politics as we know it—and that will continue to. It is estimated that digital technologies and artificial intelligence will eliminate 40 to 50 percent of all jobs and employment over the next decades. These technologies have already radically transformed our leisure and punishment practices, and exposed us and our every whim to the watchful eyes of marketers, advertisers, social media, and intelligence services. The monitoring and marketing of our private lives here, on American soil, not only by the NSA, but also by Facebook, Google, Microsoft, Apple, etc., is stunning. The digital age has effectively inserted the surveillance capability into practically every daily routine.

In my previous book, however, I failed to fully grasp how our expository society fits with the other features of our contemporary political condition—from torture, to Guantánamo, to drone strikes, to digital propaganda. In part, I could not get past the sharp contrast between the fluidity of our digital surfing and surveillance on the one hand, and the physicality of our military interventions and use of torture on the other. To be sure, I recognized the deadly reach of metadata and reiterated those ominous words of General Michael Hayden, former director of both the NSA and the CIA: "We kill people based on metadata."[20] And I traced the haunting convergence of our digital existence and of correctional supervision: the way in which the Apple Watch begins to function like an electronic bracelet, seamlessly caging us into a steel mesh of digital traces. But I was incapable then of fully understanding the bond between digital exposure and analog torture.

It is now clear, though, that the expository society fits seamlessly within our new paradigm of governing. The expository society is precisely what allows the counterinsurgency strategies to be applied so impeccably "at home" to the very people who invented modern warfare. The advent of the expository society, as well as the specific NSA surveillance programs, makes domestic total information awareness possible, and in turn lays the groundwork for the other two prongs of counterinsurgency in the domestic context.

9

TARGETING AMERICANS

Having turned total surveillance onto the American population, the US government began targeting those Americans who came under suspicion. This step reflects counterinsurgency's strategy of isolating and eliminating the active minority—the second prong of the modern warfare paradigm. And it took myriad forms.

Shortly after 9/11, the federal government began compiling and enforcing a No Fly List that would include Americans. Many citizens found themselves grounded and unable to travel, unless they had enough political clout to challenge their inclusion on the list—as the late senator Ted Kennedy did after finding himself on the No Fly List and being prevented to board.[1] There were only sixteen people on the government's No Fly List in September 2001, but by 2006, that number had increased to about forty-four thousand, with an additional seventy-five thousand people on a separate list for additional security screening. It is estimated that hundreds of those were US citizens. After significant pruning in the late aughts, the number then increased dramatically under President Barack Obama, reaching 47,000 by 2013, 64,000 by 2014, and about 81,000 by 2016, of which, again, hundreds were American citizens. In 2016, another 28,000 people were listed for additional screening, of which about 1,700 were American citizens or permanent residents.[2]

The FBI also immediately cracked down on Muslim neighborhoods after 9/11. The FBI especially targeted Pakistani neighborhoods in New York City and arrested over 254 Pakistani immigrants over the course of the next year, despite the fact that not one of the 9/11 attackers was from Pakistan. Arrested on merely civil immigration charges, many of the detainees were placed in solitary confinement and detained in isolation for twenty-three hours per day, and many claimed to have suffered sleep deprivation and other abuses at Brooklyn's federal jail, the Metropolitan Detention Center (MDC). The FBI arrested more than five hundred other persons across the country—men and women who collectively became known as the "September 11 detainees"—in what amounted to one of the largest FBI interventions in history.[3]

In addition, in November 2002, the Department of Justice began implementing a new Special Registration Program that required all men over the age of fifteen, who held a US visa and were from Iraq, Iran, Syria, Libya, or Sudan, to register and be processed at an immigration office: fingerprinted, photographed, and interviewed under pain of perjury. Another 20 countries of origin would be added to the list over the following months: Afghanistan, Algeria, Bahrain, Bangladesh, Egypt, Eritrea, Indonesia, Jordan, Kuwait, Lebanon, Morocco, North Korea, Oman, Pakistan, Qatar, Saudi Arabia, Somalia, Tunisia, United Arab Emirates, and Yemen. With the exception of North Korea, these countries of origin could not more clearly have signaled that it was Muslim residents in America who were being targeted. As Jennifer Gonnerman reports, "By May, 2003, eighty-two thousand men had registered nationwide, and deportation proceedings had begun for more than thirteen thousand of them."[4]

The targeted surveillance of mosques and Muslim groups also fueled more aggressive federal and local prosecutions for material support of terrorism. Federal prosecutors started using communications eavesdropping under FISC warrants, with their lower threshold, as a basis for federal criminal prosecutions.[5] In his first months in office, President Donald Trump signed executive orders imposing travel restrictions on American Muslim residents. Meanwhile, in response to mounting protest, states and municipalities enacted or introduced more draconian laws aimed at restricting political protest, some with severe penalties under antiracketeering laws, for instance in Arizona, and others that carry prison terms.[6] These various federal and local measures implemented in the wake of 9/11 provide the context for a range of discrete incidents that reflect the particular ways in which the domestication of counterinsurgency strategies have played out. These ways are evident in a series of stories involving the militarized crackdown of police protesters and the targeting of Muslims at home by our government—stories of individuals like Izhar Khan or Ahmed Mohamed who became, unwittingly, part of a phantom active minority invented on American soil.

These incidents are not simply scattered instances of excessive repression against Muslims, African Americans, and other minorities in the United States since 9/11, but in fact reflect a broader impulse, rooted in counterinsurgency theory, to define, target, and eliminate an active minority—in effect, to invent an insurgency and then govern by it. There is an inextricable link between total information awareness at home and these incidents. The connection becomes evident the moment we see the larger picture of modern warfare. It is crucial, in effect, to place these incidents within the larger context of our new paradigm of government, in order to see how they reflect the domestication of the second prong of the counterinsurgency model.

Sending money home to family, friends, and institutions is not unusual among immigrants. Indeed, it is often one of the reasons that one emigrates to the United States or other advanced capitalist nations such as Germany, Sweden, or Saudi Arabia: to achieve some economic security and to give back to one's family and community of origin. It's almost expected.

But things are different if your family comes from the Swat Valley, a mountainous region in Pakistan near the border with Afghanistan. Then, any wire transfer becomes immediately suspect. And if your name is Izhar Khan and you are the twenty-four-year-old mufti of a large mosque called Jamaat Al-Mu'mineen in Margate, Florida, and you wear "a long black beard, a black cotton robe, and a skullcap," you are doubly suspect.[7] After 9/11, those elements made you suspect of being one of the active minority in favor of terrorism.

Suspicion fell on Izhar Khan primarily because of his father, Hafiz Khan, an elderly imam of one of Miami's oldest mosques, Masjid Miami. His father had immigrated to the United States in 1994 and was in his late seventies by 2011. Never having learned English, he had a propensity to spend all his time at the mosque on the phone with friends and family in the Swat Valley. According to FBI records, the agency collected thirty-five thousand telephone calls between February 2009 and October 2010—an average of about three or four calls an hour.[8]

Hafiz Khan's phone calls record his bad temper. "May God just make her dead," he said of his granddaughter when she would not stop crying. "May he be run over by a truck," he said of his son when his son left his wife at home to cook. According to Evan Osnos at the *New Yorker*, he "routinely described Pakistan's leaders as pimps, pigs, sons of donkeys, huge bastards, and dumb-asses," and begged God to "make them so scared that 'when they sit down to shit their guts start to spill out.'" He also called the Taliban leaders the "biggest bastards" and, according to Osnos, "wished that they would surrender." On another occasion, after hearing about injured civilians, he cursed, "May God destroy them whoever it is, whether they are mischievous or if they are the Taliban or if they are from the government."[9]

Hafiz Khan, the father, was by no means rich. He had never really adjusted to living in the United States. His belongings apparently fit in two plastic bags. He lived in a one-bedroom apartment across from the mosque with his wife. He was albino and his eyesight was bad.

But he did send money back to Pakistan, and told his children to do so as well—as Osnos suggests, "in the Muslim tradition of charity known as *zakat*." He was an imam, after all. And so, over the years, the father sent thousands of dollars back to Pakistan, possibly up to $50,000 in all, for the most part to help support a mosque and Islamic school, the Madrassa Arabia Ahya-al-Aloom in the Swat Valley. He had been instrumental in founding the school in 1971, and, according to Osnos, "He had ambitions to expand [the school], and when the complex needed repairs he told a friend that the school was 'dearer to me than my children.'"[10]

The money transfers raised the suspicions of the FBI, and a paid FBI informant, wearing a wire, began to befriend the father. He offered the father $5,000 to help repair the school he had founded in Swat. And then the informant did his best to get the father to say incriminating statements on surreptitious recordings. Apparently after much prodding, he did. He said some favorable things about the Taliban. As Osnos explains, though, "Away from the informant, Hafiz was recorded warning his grandson that Siddiqui [the informant] 'talks nonsense' and should be indulged only because he planned to give money to the school. 'He is a very nice person, but he is also stupid,' Hafiz said."[11]

Suspicion spread to Hafiz's son, Izhar Khan, and his brother, Irfan Khan, a thirty-seven-year-old software technician, because they too sent money to Pakistan. All three men were arrested and indicted, and Hafiz and Izhar Khan were prosecuted as conspirators materially supporting terrorism because of the wire transfers and statements about the Taliban.

Once arrested, the men were treated as dangerous insurgents. Both sons were detained for months in solitary confinement in Miami's federal jail, separated from each other and their families, locked down twenty-three hours a day by themselves in their cells in the special housing unit.[12] Irfan Khan spent more than ten months in isolation, Izhar Khan more than sixteen.

Both are free today. Irfan Khan, the older son, was abruptly released after all the charges were dropped. During his ten months in solitary confinement, it became apparent, for instance, that the money he had sent by Western Union to one "Akbar Hussein," a reputed Taliban commander in Kaboswatt, Pakistan, had actually been directed to "his wife's uncle, Akbar Hussain, a retired biology professor, who had taught at local universities."[13] The Western Union records listed the names and government ID number of Hussain. Hussein, Hussain—that small slip up was enough to take ten months of a man's life.

Izhar Khan, the younger son, was taken to trial, but the federal judge ruled favorably on a motion to acquit—practically unheard of in trial practice—because the evidence presented to the jury did not amount to anything. He was ultimately released after spending more than sixteen months in solitary confinement and four more months in general population.

Both sons' lives were ruined. Irfan Khan, the former software programmer, is driving a cab now, obsessively going over the wiretapped conversations. Izhar Khan is pretty much homeless, having sold his house and car to pay for his defense counsel. Of course, they cannot go back to Pakistan, because, having been detained for so long and ultimately released, they would be suspected back home of having cooperated with the feds—"they'll assume that you're working for either the CIA or the FBI." Plus, they would not want to leave their father behind. He was convicted of two counts of conspiracy and two counts of providing material support, and sentenced to a fixed term of twenty-five years without parole—which will extend to 2033 at which point he will be, if alive, ninety-eight years old.[14]

The case against the Khan brothers bore all of the indicia of counterinsurgency theory. It began, of course, with total information awareness, which in this case meant wiretapping their conversations and reviewing over thirty-five thousand calls. And then, it placed them in the category of that active minority of those who purportedly want to harm America. It eliminated the sons by placing them in solitary confinement and by destroying their lives. The arrests and prosecutions were also highly publicized, affording the rest of us the satisfaction of feeling safe and secure. Of showing us how well we are protected.

This first incident reflects how the counterinsurgency mindset produces black-and-white approaches to situations with a lot of gray. Lots of immigrants send money home, and it is not unheard of for some of it to end up in questionable hands. Yet only some people are looked at with deep suspicion and no presumption of innocence when they do so. A second incident shows how the counterinsurgency logic can be taken to more absurd extremes, outside the context of a conventional counterterrorism investigation, to the realm of school discipline—a much more quotidian sort of governance. But the impulses are revealingly similar.

Ahmed Mohamed was fourteen years old and lived with his parents in Irving, a small suburb of Dallas, Texas.[15] In 2015, he was a ninth-grader at the local school, MacArthur High School, and a model student. A science and technology buff, Ahmed spent his extracurricular time working on homemade science, robotics, and electronics projects in his bedroom. He was especially fond of NASA and space technology. He made lots of electronic gadgets, would repair his classmates' devices, and had earned the nickname "Inventor Kid" in middle school.

Born in Sudan and of Muslim faith, Ahmed had moved to the United States as a young boy. His father, Mohamed El-Hassan Mohamed, was well known in the community, having lived in the same house in Irving for thirty years. In 2015 and 2010, his father had unsuccessfully run to unseat the current president of Sudan, Omar al-Bashir.[16]

On Monday morning, September 14, 2015, Ahmed Mohamed took one of his inventions to school. This little LED clock that he had built in his bedroom consisted of an LED digital display mounted on a small metal case containing a circuit board. It was about the size of his extended hand. He was so proud that he wanted to show it to his engineering teacher.

At school, Ahmed showed the clock to his engineering teacher, who apparently praised him, during a morning class. Later that day, during his English class, the clock beeped, and when Ahmed took it out to silence it, his English teacher saw it and became concerned. Shortly thereafter, school officials notified the police.

Ahmed was forcibly detained and interrogated by four police officers—two school resource officers who were regularly assigned to the high school and their supervisor who arrived on the scene along with another police sergeant—for almost an hour, and was denied the opportunity to meet with his father. He was not allowed to have a parent present, or anyone else on his behalf. Ahmed was alone with four adult police officers.

Although the officers "quickly determined," in the words of Police Chief Larry Boyd of Irving, that they were not dealing with a bomb or incendiary device, Ahmed was arrested by the police and handcuffed.[17] There is a disturbing picture of the young boy, gangly and adolescent looking, wearing his NASA T-shirt, placed in handcuffs behind his back at the police station, looking dumbfounded and panicked.

He was transported to the nearest juvenile detention facility where he was booked; his fingerprints and a mug shot were taken.

He was immediately suspended from his high school for three days.

Following the event, many came to his defense, while others cast aspersions on him. Others, including President Obama, weighed in, not pointing fingers, but making the best of a bad situation. "Cool clock, Ahmed," President Obama's official Twitter account read. "Want to bring it to the White House? We should inspire more kids like you to like science. It's what makes America great."

The incident has been characterized, at one extreme, as an innocent mistake in a world where there is concern about school shootings and

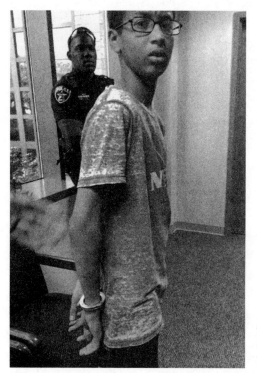

Ahmed Mohamed arrested at his high school, 2015. (@IStandWithAhmed, Twitter, September 17, 2015, retweet.)

other violence, and, at the other, as a clear case of racial profiling and Islamophobia. I would argue that it reflects the growing domestic influence of counterinsurgency thinking. In a dangerous world of supposed insurgents, Ahmed's name, color, and religion made him instantly suspect. He became potentially part of a small minority of insurgents at war with America. And for that reason, it became immediately necessary to isolate and contain him—to detain, handcuff, and send him to a juvenile facility.

Even as it became rapidly clear that Ahmed did not pose a threat, it nevertheless remained important to gather information about him. To get his fingerprints, his photograph. To book him. To place him in the system, so that we would have information on him the next time.

Ahmed's treatment reflected all three prongs of the counterinsurgency model: creating a member of an insurgent minority, containing him so that he did not contaminate the majority, and gathering intelligence so as to feed the larger project of total informa-tion awareness.

What might have been a legitimate effort to prevent actual terrorist attacks after 9/11 has fostered a counterinsurgency mindset that sees danger everywhere domestically and that, as a result, harshly targets Muslim people here in the United States, often notwithstanding their innocence.

While the first two incidents targeted particular individuals, turning them into an active minority that must be eliminated, two other ep-isodes construct an entire category of dangerous individuals out of whole cloth. The first involves protesters and, predominantly, African Americans in the context of social movements against police killings of unarmed civilians. The second, American Muslims as a whole.

"I can't breathe! I can't breathe!" Eric Garner repeated eleven times before dying of asphyxiation from a chokehold under the weight of several NYPD officers on the streets of Staten Island, New York, on July 17, 2014. A month later, August 9, 2014, an unarmed eighteen-year-old young man, Michael Brown, was shot dead in Ferguson, Missouri, by police officer Darren Wilson. The fatal encounter lasted about two minutes, and was witnessed by over a dozen witnesses who testified variously that Michael Brown was surrendering, falling, turn-ing around, walking back, or headed toward officer Wilson when he fired the twelfth, fatal shot. Two months later, on October 20, 2014, on the southwest side of Chicago, police officer Jason Van Dyke un-loaded sixteen rounds of his 9mm semiautomatic service weapon into seventeen-year-old Laquan McDonald. The shooting was captured by several dashcam videos, which show McDonald walking away from the officers as Van Dyke and his partner get out of their car with their guns drawn. Six or seven seconds later, Van Dyke starts firing. McDonald is fully spun around by the force of the bullets, and the video shows his body jerking and puffs of debris rising as officer Van Dyke continues to shoot him after he hit the ground. McDonald is fully on the ground, lying prone, for at least thirteen of the fifteen seconds the police officer is shooting.[18]

This epidemic of police shootings of unarmed civilians finally became visible as a result of a series of cellphone videos, dashcams, and surveillance footage that went viral on the Internet. The wave of police killings continued on and off camera, around the country, with the police shooting deaths of twenty-eight-year-old Akai Gurley in a Brooklyn stairwell on November 20, 2014; of twelve-year-old Tamir Rice in a Cleveland park on November 22, 2014; of fifty-year-old Walter Scott, shot in the back five times on April 4, 2015, in North Charleston, South Carolina; of thirty-two-year-old Philando Castile, pulled over in a suburb of Saint Paul, Minnesota, and shot seven times on July 6, 2016, while peacefully trying to explain his situation; of thirty-year-old Charleena Lyles, shot in front of her four children in Seattle, Washington, after calling the police on an attempted burglary on June 18, 2017; and the deaths in police custody of thirty-seven-year-old Tanisha Anderson in Cleveland, slammed on the pavement while being arrested, and of twenty-eight-year-old Sandra Bland, found hanging in her jail cell in Waller County, Texas, on July 13, 2015—all African American men and women.

A phenomenon that had been going on for years was finally exposed for everyone to see, over and over. Soon the *Guardian* and the *Washington Post* were keeping a tally of the police homicides reaching up to a thousand a year—police shootings that had fallen under the radar screen for years because of incompetent federal reporting requirements.

The wave of police killings was in itself evidence of the excessive lethality of policing in this country and of deep racial bias, both of which reflected elements of the domestication of military-style mentalities in law enforcement. But even more, the policing of the protests that accompanied the police killings fully reflected the deployment of counterinsurgency strategies at home.

In response to the police shootings, protesters around the country demonstrated in waves of marches, boycotts, Black Friday rallies, and die-ins. The protests, overwhelmingly peaceful, triggered a militarized police response the likes of which few could even have imagined. The shocking footage from Ferguson in the days following the police shooting of Michael Brown revealed the extreme degree to which our law-enforcement officials, now armed with military assault weapons, tanks, and armored vehicles, faced off against unarmed peaceful protesters as if they were insurgents.

The journalist Chris Hayes spent days broadcasting live the protests in Ferguson, and what he found there, essentially, was a military operation. "The police of Ferguson and St. Louis County mobilized as if for war," Hayes wrote: "flak jackets, masks, helmets, camouflage, assault weapons, and armored vehicles. Men pointed their long guns at civilians who assembled for peaceful protest." Hayes, who had reported from all around the country, said that he had never felt anywhere such a revolutionary atmosphere. Not because of the protesters, though. It was the way the *police* handled themselves that felt revolutionary, Hayes reported—or, I would say, *counterrevolutionary*. The police officers, Hayes observed, "fired tear gas canisters indiscriminately. Bands of armed cops in full combat gear chased unarmed peaceful protesters through the streets with guns raised."[19]

The police force in Ferguson deployed a full military arsenal, including military assault rifles, sniper equipment, and Mine Resistant Ambush Protected (MRAP) vehicles—all familiar to us from images of the war in Iraq and Afghanistan, and now deployed on Main Street USA. SWAT-team outfitted officers, dressed in marine pattern (MAR-PAT) camouflage, with their assault guns drawn, moved next to armored vehicles that looked like tanks with mounted high-caliber guns. Officers with the St. Louis County Police Department pointed their Mega AR-15 marksman and M4 rifles, their sniper Leupold long-range scopes, armored tactical vehicles, and acoustic riot-control devices at protesters. In their military helmets and goggles, with tear gas grenade launchers, twelve-gauge shotguns, long knives, and night-vision equipment, the police looked exactly like battlefield soldiers in the war on terror.[20]

The protesters were policed as if they were enemy insurgents in a war zone. Hayes recounts his days reporting from Ferguson: "At random I could take my microphone and offer it to a black Ferguson resident, young or old, who had a story of being harassed and humiliated." The citizens of Ferguson told of being targeted, hassled, wrongfully arrested, and wrongly treated—continuing a pattern that had been going on for several years. "At any given moment a black citizen of Ferguson might find himself shown up, dressed down, made to stoop and cower by the men with badges."[21]

During these and other protests around the country, all the excess equipment from Iraq and Afghanistan was on display—machine guns, ammunition magazines, camouflage, night-vision equipment, silencers, concussion grenades, armored cars, and even aircraft, giving the impression of a country under siege. Hayes recounted that elsewhere, in Cleveland, a large sign, displayed at a police station, designated the area as a "forward operating base"—a military term that refers to "a small, secured outpost used to support tactical operations in a war zone." As Hayes noted, that expression "captures the psychology of many police officers: they see themselves as combatants in a war zone, besieged and surrounded, operating in enemy territory, one wrong move away from sudden death."[22]

In his masterful account *A Colony in a Nation*, Hayes argues that the United States has created a colony within the nation—a colony comprised of the poverty-stricken minority neighborhoods in the country. Hayes traces our new style of policing in municipalities like Ferguson back to the revenue-seeking, heavy-handed policing of the English royalists in the American colonies. Hayes suggests that we have created in the very midst of our nation, in his words, "a territory that isn't actually free." It is a territory where policing takes on the character of an occupation. An occupation that requires constant vigilance. "The borders must be enforced without the benefit of actual walls and checkpoints. This requires an ungodly number of interactions between the sentries of the state and those the state views as the disorderly class."[23]

This idea of an occupied territory, of a colony within a nation, reso-nates perfectly with what we have witnessed in terms of the domestica-tion of the counterinsurgency. I would just push the logic further: we have not simply created an internal colony, we have turned the nation *itself* into a colony. We govern ourselves through modern counterinsur-gency warfare as if the entire United States was now a colonial domin-ion like Algeria, Malaya, or Vietnam.

While local police forces have been turning protesters and African American residents into insurgents, the federal government has been deliberately creating an active minority consisting of practically all American Muslims.

Only seven days into his presidency, President Donald Trump signed an executive order temporarily ending travel into the United States by nationals from seven predominantly Muslim countries. The executive order effectively banned many American residents of Muslim religion, living in the United States with a green card or a work or educational visa, from returning home to the states from abroad or from leaving the country since they no longer had permission to reenter. The exec-utive order was written in a broad manner that, on its face, applied to US green card holders as well from any of those seven predominantly Muslim countries. The executive order quickly became known as the "Muslim ban" because Trump, during his campaign, had expressly said he would ban Muslims from entering the United States.

Specifically, the executive order Trump signed on January 27, 2017, Executive Order 13769, banned outright for 90 days the entry into the country of any individual from Iraq, Iran, Libya, Somalia, Sudan, Syria, and Yemen—whether permanent residents of the United States, immi-grants, or nonimmigrants, such as those on work or educational visas.[24] The executive order also had a number of other provisions targeting refugees and Syrians especially. The order imposed a 120-day morato-rium on the entire US Refugee Admissions Program. And, proclaiming that "the entry of nationals of Syria as refugees is detrimental to the interests of the United States," the order also suspended indefinitely their entry into the country. The order also limited the number of refugees who could enter the country in 2017, down from 110,000 to 50,000, proclaiming that "the entry of more than 50,000 refugees in fiscal year 2017 would be detrimental to the interests" of the country.

Trump's Muslim ban effectively excluded from this country many American residents of Islamic faith who were legal residents in the United States and had lived here for years, but were traveling abroad at the time. It also detained and prevented many American Muslim residents from traveling outside the country since they could no longer reenter the states. It simultaneously created and targeted a supposed "active minority" of dangerous American residents. Dr. Amer Al Homssi, for instance, a young Syrian doctor on a residency at the University of Illinois in Chicago who had traveled to the United Arab Emirates to get married, saw his J-1 visa revoked and cancelled at the border and was excluded on January 29, 2017, from returning home to the United States.[25] Many others suffered the same plight, with more than 900 persons denied boarding, more than 200 denied entry once they landed, and, eventually, around 1,600 US green-card holders being granted waivers in the days immediately following the executive order.[26]

Trump had made very clear his intent: to ban and exclude Muslims from the United States. On December 7, 2015, at a very early time in his campaign, Trump issued a press release declaring:

> Donald J. Trump is calling for a total and complete shutdown of Muslims entering the United States until our country's representatives can figure out what is going on. According to Pew Research, among others, there is great hatred towards Americans by large segments of the Muslim population. Most recently, a poll from the Center for Security Policy released data showing "25% of those polled agreed that violence against Americans here in the United States is justified as a part of the global jihad" and 51% of

those polled, "agreed that Muslims in America should have the choice of being governed according to Shariah." Shariah authorizes such atrocities as murder against non-believers who won't convert, beheadings and more unthinkable acts that pose great harm to Americans, especially women.[27]

Shortly after making this campaign pledge, Trump drew a comparison between his proposed Muslim ban and the internment of Japanese Americans during World War II, stating that the president at the time, Franklin Delano Roosevelt, "is a president highly respected by all" and "did the same thing." When asked about his statements about the Muslim ban at the sixth Republican presidential debate on January 14, 2016, Trump responded that he would not take any of it back and stated, in a clear reference to Muslims: "Look, we have to stop with political correctness. We have to get down to creating a country that's not going to have the kind of problems that we've had with people flying planes into the World Trade Centers, with the—with the shootings in California, with all the problems all over the world." The following summer, on June 14, 2016, Trump again repeated his pledge to ban all Muslims entering the United States until "we as a nation are in a position to properly and perfectly screen those people coming into our country."[28]

As soon as he received the Republican nomination, Trump started to sanitize his language when discussing his anti-Muslim policies, but he continued in the same vein. He now said he would stop immigration "from any nation that has been compromised by terrorism," while admitting that this was pure veneer intended to avoid controversy. In an interview on NBC, Trump admitted, "People were so upset when I used the word Muslim. Oh, you can't use the word Muslim . . . And I'm OK with that, because I'm talking territory instead of Muslim." Immediately following the Republican National Convention, on July 24, 2016, Trump was asked whether he was "backing off" on his Muslim ban, and responded, "I actually don't think it's a pull-back. In fact, you could say it's an expansion."[29] In a speech a few days later on August 15, 2016, Trump spoke about the problem of screening immigrants because the United States admits "about 100,000 permanent immigrants from the Middle East every year," and he suggested a screening test to exclude any immigrants "who believe that Sharia law should supplant American law."[30]

The evidence is overwhelming: President Trump was targeting Muslims, including American residents. Not only had Trump proclaimed he would do as much during his campaign, but the original language in the order relating to the 120-day freeze was written in such a way as to privilege Christian over Muslim refugees from Muslim-majority countries. The order declared that, following the 120-day freeze on refugees, the secretary of state would "make changes, to the extent permitted by law, to prioritize refugee claims made by individuals on the basis of religious-based persecution, provided that the religion of the individual is a minority religion in the individual's country of nationality." And in fact, only hours before he signed the Muslim ban on January 27, 2017, Trump stated that his executive order was "going to help [persecuted Christians]."[31] The next day, former mayor Rudolph Giuliani, who was then being considered for an appointment in the Trump administration, admitted to the press that, after Trump had originally announced his Muslim ban, he, Giuliani, was asked to "show [Donald Trump] the right way to do [a Muslim ban] legally."[32] Giuliani then put together a team to achieve a ban without naming Muslims.

The Muslim ban formed part of a larger campaign to transform Muslims into an active minority. During his presidential campaign, President Trump also accused Muslims at home of not being sufficiently patriotic and failing to report threats to American law enforcement. As noted earlier, he also suggested that the government should monitor mosques and Muslim communities, and even possibly register American Muslims in a government database. He even suggested the possibility of issuing special identification cards for Muslims noting their religious faith.[33]

In effect, President Trump turned Muslims in the United States into a phantom insurgency. And he never let up. Confronted with adverse legal rulings, Trump first issued a revised Muslim ban in March 2017, then appealed to the United States Supreme Court, ultimately persuading the justices to allow the Muslim ban to go into effect with regard to individuals from six predominantly Muslim countries who have no close family or institutional ties to the United States and then revised the Muslim ban again in September 2017.[34] In the process, Trump laid the groundwork for the exclusion and stigmatization of Muslims—both Americans and foreigners.

These incidents—large and small, but all devastating for those targeted—also serve another objective of the domesticated counterinsurgency: to make the rest of us feel safe and secure, to allow us to continue our lives unaffected, to avoid disrupting our consumption and enjoyment. They serve to reassure, and also, in demonizing a phantom minority, to bring us all together against the specter of the frightening and dangerous other. It makes us believe that there would be, lurking in the quiet suburbs of Dallas or Miami, dangerous insurgents—were it not for our government. And these effects feed into the third prong of a domesticated counterinsurgency.

There are some counterinsurgency theorists today—I would describe them as proponents of a leaner antiterrorism approach—who advocate against the larger project of winning the hearts and minds of the general population. These proponents of leaner antiterrorism argue, against the more traditional counterinsurgency theorists, that we need to take a more limited approach that simply focuses on targeting suspected terrorists, like the Khan family. They prefer to avoid getting involved in social investment or hearts and minds—and favor, for instance, terrorism prosecutions at home or limited drone strikes abroad to eliminate identifiable terrorist suspects.[35]

We had seen earlier, within counterinsurgency theory, similar debates between population-centric and enemy-centric theorists. The enemy-centric approach tended to be the more brutal, but more focused. The population-centric favored the more legal and social-investment approaches. I argued then that they were just two facets of the same paradigm.

Here the debate is between population-and/or-enemy-centric theories versus individual-centric theory. But here too, I would argue, this is a false dichotomy. Again, these are just two facets of the same thing: a counterinsurgency paradigm of warfare with three core strategies. Like the population-and/or-enemy-centric theories, individual-centric theory naturally entails both incapacitating the individual terrorist or insurgent—eliminating him and all of the active minority—*and* preventing or deterring his substitution or replacement.

Originally, counterinsurgency and antiterrorism were hard to distinguish. During the Algerian War, the insurgents were in fact referred to as "terrorists." But gradually, as Grégoire Chamayou shows, with the growth of domestic terrorist groups in the West (like the Baader-Meinhof gang in Germany, the Red Brigades in Italy, or the Weather Underground in the United States), antiterrorism strategies began to look more and more like domestic policing. These tactics evolved toward the model of incapacitating individual actors. Antiterrorism became more closely aligned with policing and security, rather than the political and military. It oriented itself toward individuals who were seen as "dangerous," or even "mad," but not politically contagious. "With these new labels, the targets are no longer political adversaries to be opposed, but criminals to be apprehended or eliminated," Chamayou writes.[36]

As a result, domestic antiterrorism gravitated increasingly toward the imprisonment of criminal individuals. "Its policing logic individualizes the problem and reduces its objectives to neutralizing, on a case-by-case basis, as many suspects as possible," Chamayou explains.[37] So, whereas counterinsurgency is more population focused, the advocates of leaner antiterrorism argue, antiterrorist action should be more individual centered.

But rather than buy into this dichotomy of counterinsurgency and leaner antiterrorism, what history shows instead is a growing convergence of the two models in the United States since the 1960s. Counterinsurgency and domestic antiterrorism efforts, entwined from the start, have converged over time. The individual incapacitation strategy meshes perfectly into the counterinsurgency approach. And it leads seamlessly from the domestication of the second prong of counterinsurgency to the domestication of the third.

10

DISTRACTING AMERICANS

MANY OF US WILL NOT RECOGNIZE OURSELVES, OR AMERICA for that matter, in these dreadful episodes—in the waterboarding and targeted assassinations abroad or in the militarization of our police forces, in the infiltration of Muslim mosques and student groups or in the constant collection of our personal data at home. Many of us have no firsthand experience of these terrifying practices. Few of us actually read the full Senate torture report, and even fewer track drone strikes. Some of us do not even want to know of their existence. Most of us are blissfully ignorant—at least most of the time—of these counterinsurgency practices at home or abroad, and are consumed instead by the seductive distractions of our digital age.

And that's the way it is supposed to be. As counterinsurgency is domesticated, it is *our* hearts and minds that are daily being assuaged, numbed, pacified—and blissfully satisfied. We, the vast majority of us, are reassured daily: there are threats everywhere and color-coded terror alerts, but counterinsurgency strategies are protecting us. We are made to feel that everything's under control, that the threat is exterior, that we can continue with our daily existence. Even more, that these counterinsurgency strategies will prevail. That our government is stronger and better equipped, prepared to do everything necessary to win, and will win. That the guardians are protecting us.

The effort to win the hearts and minds of the passive American majority is the third aspect of the domestication of counterinsurgency practices—perhaps the most crucial component of all. And it is accomplished through a remarkable mixture of distraction, entertainment, pleasure, propaganda, and advertising—now rendered all so much more effective thanks to our rich digital world. In Rome, after the Republic, this was known as "bread and circus" for the masses. Today, it's more like Facebook and Pokémon GO.

We saw earlier how the expository society entices us to share all our personal data and how this feeds into the first prong of counterinsurgency—total information awareness. There is a flip side to this phenomenon: keeping us distracted. The exposure is so pleasurable and engaging that we are mostly kept content, with little need for a coordinated top-down effort to do so. We are entranced—absorbed in a fantastic world of digitally enhanced reality that is totally consuming, engrossing, and captivating. We are no longer being rendered docile in a disciplinarian way, as Michel Foucault argued in *Discipline and Punish*. We are past notions of docility. We are *actively* entranced—not passively, not in a docile way. We are actively clicking and swiping, jumping from one screen to another, checking one platform then another to find the next fix—Facebook, Instagram, Twitter, Google, YouTube, and on and on.

Winning over and assuaging the passive majority might be accomplished—indeed, has been accomplished in the past—through traditional propaganda, such as broadcast misinformation about the insurgent minority, and through the top-down provision of entertainment to keep us from thinking about politics. The new digital world we live in has rendered these older strategies obsolete. As the counterinsurgency's mandate to pacify the masses has been turned on the American people, the third prong of modern warfare looks and works differently than it did in previous times and in other places.

Things have changed. Just a few years ago, our politicians still had to tell us to go shopping and enjoy ourselves. "Get down to Disney World in Florida," President George W. Bush told the American people a few weeks after 9/11. "Take your families and enjoy life, the way we want it to be enjoyed."[1] A few years later, Bush would reiterate, after discussing the situation in Iraq, "I encourage you all to go shopping more."[2] Now, we no longer need our leaders to tell us that anymore. The entire digital world prompts us to do so.

Andrew Sullivan captures well this frenzied digital life we now lead. Sullivan recounts, in a brilliant article in *New York* magazine titled "Put Down Your Phone," his own journey through the digital age, starting with his gradual addiction, his eventual recovery in a rehab program, and his ultimate relapse:

> For a decade and a half, I'd been a web obsessive, publishing blog posts multiple times a day, seven days a week, and ultimately corralling a team that curated the web every 20 minutes during peak hours. Each morning began with a full immersion in the stream of internet consciousness and news, jumping from site to site, tweet to tweet, breaking news story to hottest take, scanning countless images and videos, catching up with multiple memes. Throughout the day, I'd cough up an insight or an argument or a joke about what had just occurred or what was happening right now. And at times, as events took over, I'd spend weeks manically grabbing every tiny scrap of a developing story in order to fuse them into a narrative in real time. I was in an unending dialogue with readers who were caviling, praising, booing, correcting. My

brain had never been so occupied so insistently by so many different subjects and in so public a way for so long.[3]

This is our new existence, fueled and enhanced by all the digital
media, apps, and devices. Not all of us are producers or creators like
Sullivan, but practically all of us are consumers. We participate actively. We read, click, like, share. We play. We interact. And we derive
extraordinary benefits and enjoyments from this. "The rewards," Andrew Sullivan notes, are "many": "a constant stream of things to annoy,
enlighten, or infuriate me; a niche in the nerve center of the exploding
global conversation; and a way to measure success—in big and beau-
tiful data—that was a constant dopamine bath for the writerly ego. If
you had to reinvent yourself as a writer in the internet age, I reassured
myself, then I was ahead of the curve."

To be sure, this frenzy may at times fuel political activity. Groups
of Facebook friends are politicizing each other every day, sharing sa-
tirical political commentary, forming new alliances on the web. Social
media can galvanize real-world protest. The Occupy Wall Street movement and the Arab Spring were, in part, facilitated by social media
and Internet networks—regardless of whether you ultimately believe,
with Evgeny Morozov, that the Internet does not effectively promote
democratic values.[4] Presidential candidates like Barack Obama, Bernie
Sanders, and Donald Trump have built entire political followings on
the Internet. There is no doubt that the digital age has important political dimensions and implications—not to be minimized.

But for the most part, the entertainment and the spectacle comes
first. Spectacle especially: the gladiator sport at which a politician like
Donald Trump excelled. President Trump's middle-of-the-night Twitter screeds drew our attention. His lewd words and extreme statements
on social media caused a frenzy. We were practically mesmerized.
For the younger generations, especially, the digital activity is primarily geared toward entertainment and pleasure: the YouTube videos,
Facebook news feeds, and snapchats. Selfies on Instagram. Dating

applications for all tastes, iPhone apps of all kinds.[5] Even meditation apps, like Sattva, Buddhify, or Headspace, to help us deal now with our digital addictions.

The paradigm of these new digital distractions—and of the myriad ways they then feed back into the surveillance apparatus—is Pokémon GO. An enhanced reality game, Pokémon GO went online at the start of summer 2016 and immediately went viral. For a few weeks or months, millions of young people around the globe started chasing virtual Pikachus in the streets and alleys, museums and national monuments, even in their own bedrooms across the world. Players became completely absorbed and obsessed with the game, spending all their free time—and even some class time, I noticed—trying to track down and catch Pokémons, or walking around or riding their bike slowly to make their Pokémon eggs hatch.

Pokémon GO became a viral obsession. A recurring image from the summer of 2016—one that I saw in New York, but also in Leiden and Paris—is of a young couple on a Vespa or motorcycle, the young man driving slowly and following the directions of the young woman, behind, both of her hands cradling an iPhone. She is looking back and forth, from one screen to the other, while giving driving instructions to her partner. They are meandering, perhaps waiting for a Pokémon to hatch or to appear on the screen to snatch. The couple stops every so often, discusses and conspires, looks at the screens, and then they take off again, cautiously at times, or fast enough to catch another—or catch them all!

Pokémon GO has already run its course, but that is to be expected. Another digital obsession will follow. These platforms are supposed to capture all of our attention for a while, to captivate us, to distract us—and simultaneously to make us expose ourselves and everything around us. This is the symbiosis between the third and first prongs of the domesticated counterinsurgency: while it pacifies us, a game like Pokémon GO taps into all our personal information and captures all our data. At first, the game required that players share all their personal contacts. Although that was eventually dropped, the game collects all our GPS locations, captures all the video of our surroundings in perfectly GPS-coded data, and tracks us wherever we are. Plus, even though it is free, many players are buying add-ons and in the process sharing their consumption and financial data. The more we play, the more we are distracted and pacified, and the more we reveal about ourselves.

A new powerful form of distraction—for many, an addiction—has taken hold of us, and in the process, fuels our own exposure and feeds the surveillance mechanisms of the NSA, Google, Facebook, etc. And what is so remarkable is how rapidly it has all emerged. There is a new temporality to the digital age, one that mimics the viral nature of memes. Like wildfire, these new addictions catch and spread at lightning speed. As Andrew Sullivan reminds us:

> We almost forget that ten years ago, there were no smartphones, and as recently as 2011, only a third of Americans owned one. Now nearly two-thirds do. That figure reaches 85 percent when you're only counting young adults. And 46 percent of Americans told Pew surveyors last year a simple but remarkable thing: They could not live without one. The device went from unknown to indispensable in less than a decade. The handful of spaces where it was once impossible to be connected—the airplane, the subway, the wilderness are dwindling fast. Even hiker backpacks now come fitted with battery power for smartphones. Perhaps the only "safe space" that still exists is the shower.[6]

The speed with which these new devices and applications are coming online, and the amount of time that we are spending on them, is stunning. A thorough study published in 2015 revealed that the young adults surveilled were spending at least five hours using their phones every day, with about eighty-five separate interactions per day. The individual interactions may be short, but added together, they represent about a third of these young adults' waking hours. What is also striking is that, according to the research, these young adults are not aware of the extent of their consumption: "Young adults use their smartphones roughly twice as much as they estimate that they do."[7]

The distractions are everywhere: e-mail notifications, texts, bings and pings, new snapchats and instagrams. The entertainment is everywhere as well: free Wi-Fi at Starbucks and McDonald's, and now on New York City streets, that allow us to stream music videos and watch YouTube videos. And of course, the advertising is everywhere, trying to make us consume more, buy online, subscribe, and *believe*. Believe not only that we need to buy the recommended book or watch the suggested Netflix, but also believe that we are secure and safe, protected by the most powerful intelligence agencies and most tenacious military force. Believe that we can continue to mind our own business—and remain distracted and absorbed in the digital world—because our government is watching out for us.

The fact is, the domestication of counterinsurgency has coincided with the explosion of this digital world and its distractions. There is a real qualitative difference between the immediate post–9/11 period and today. One that is feeding directly into the third strategy of modern warfare.

Meanwhile, for the more vulnerable—those who are more likely to veer astray and perhaps sympathize with the purported internal enemy—the same digital technologies target them for enhanced propaganda. The Global Engagement Center, or its equivalents, will profile them and send improved content from more moderate voices. The very same methods developed by the most tech-savvy retailers and digital advertisers—by Google and Amazon—are deployed to predict, identify, enhance, and target our own citizens.

The third stage of the domestication of counterinsurgency warfare piggybacks off these new digital technologies and distractions that render the vast majority of us docile consumers glued in front of the plasma screen. It is a connected life in which the privileged move from their iPhones to their iPads, wear their Apple Watches, text and snap-chat each other constantly, post selfies and narrate their thrilling, vi-brant lives, putting out of their minds the risk to their privacy and personal data. And when this new mode of existence is particularly threatened and directly attacked, it becomes even more sacrosanct. The Paris attacks made many young Westerners newly aware of the threat that terrorists pose to people like them. The Orlando attack similarly actualized the danger to the tolerant liberal way of life that now em-braces queer sexualities. With each such attack, this new way of living is under threat. And to protect this new mode of existence, many buy into the idea—subliminally or half-consciously—that a small minority of guardians must safeguard our security, while the rest of us must carry on, continue to shop, consume again as before, or even more.

My point is not that our fellow citizens are becoming *more* docile than they were before or that we are experiencing a waning of civil and political engagement. While I agree that the growing capacity of the state and corporations to monitor citizens may well threaten the private sphere, I am not convinced that this is producing new apathy or passiv-ity or docility among citizens, so much as a new form of entrancement. The point is, we were once kept apathetic through other means, but are now kept apathetic through digital distractions.

The voting patterns of American registered voters has remained constant—and apathetic—for at least fifty years. Even in the most im-portant presidential elections, voter turnout in this country over the past fifty years or more has pretty much fluctuated between 50 percent and 63 percent. By any measure, American democracy has been pretty docile for a long time. In fact, if you look over the longer term, turnout has been essentially constant since the 1920s and the extension of the suffrage to women. Of course, turnout to vote is not the only measure of democratic participation, but it is one quantifiable measure. And elec-toral voting is one of the more reliable longitudinal measures of civic participation. But our record, in the United States, is not impressive.

Elsewhere, I have argued that ours is not a democracy of voters, but of *potential* voters. It is not an actual democracy, so much as a potential or *virtual democracy*.[8] It has a potentiality, a capacity to democratic rule. And it is precisely through the democratic potentiality that the benefits of democracy are achieved. This is not new. But what *is* new is the method: rather than being rendered docile as we were in earlier times, in more disciplinarian societies, we are being *digitally entranced* by all the new technology. And this entrancement does not quash politics, it turns it into spectacle. If anything, there is growing interest in politics—but as entertainment. In fact, the first presidential debate of the 2016 election, the September 26, 2016, debate between Hillary Clinton and Donald Trump, set a record for TV viewership of presidential debates. As the *Los Angeles Times* reported, the debate drew the largest TV audience ever for a presidential debate, reaching up to eighty-four million according to Nielsen numbers.[9]

Why such numbers? Because Donald Trump turned the presidential election and subsequently his administration into a spectacle; because, in effect, Trump was a master of reality TV, then of digital media, and now of spectacle presidency—as, for instance, when he dealt with an international diplomatic crisis in public, on the dining-room terrace of his Mar-a-Lago resort alongside the prime minister of Japan, Shinzo Abe, with club members taking snapshots and posting them on social media. Trump succeeded in drawing attention precisely because he became one of social media's great communicators. The cable news network CNN captured this best in a pithy lead to a story titled "Trump: The Social Media President?": "FDR was the first 'radio' president. JFK emerged as the first 'television' president. Barack Obama broke through as the first 'Internet' president. Next up? Prepare to meet Donald Trump, possibly the first 'social media' and 'reality TV' president."[10]

Trump's presidential campaign was unique in this sense and his success was directly related to his command of reality TV—his commanding performances on *The Apprentice* and *Celebrity Apprentice*, and other entertainment venues. Trump became such a social-media phenomenon that even when he did not participate in one of the Republican primary debates, that very night he dominated the other candidates in terms of searches on the Internet and social-media postings.[11]

This is not to suggest that this new digital entrancement is mere spectacle or simply innocuous. Much of it is based on despicable forms of hatred. Trump's comments about not letting any Muslims into the country—and his subsequent executive orders prohibiting entry from particular Muslim-majority countries—as well as his derogatory remarks about Mexican immigrants (suggesting that they are rapists and murderers) and women all play on racial and gender prejudice, religious bias, and ethnic hatred. And similarly, a lot of the attention on the Internet is "gawker" interest: the curiosity of the freak show, of the extreme position. In February 2016, Trump was caught unwittingly retweeting a quote from Benito Mussolini—it was a ruse set up by the website Gawker intended to trap Trump. Trump himself, however, did not miss a beat, and when asked by a news network whether he wanted to be associated with Mussolini, Trump responded: "No, I want to be associated with interesting quotes."[12] According to the report, Trump then added that "he does 'interesting things' on his social-media accounts, which have racked up 'almost fourteen million' followers combined, and, 'Hey, it got your attention, didn't it?'"

"It got your attention": that is the modus operandi of a *social* media, and it reflects how citizens consume politics today. Van Jones at CNN captured this phenomenon most succinctly in these words: "The Trump phenomenon flabbergasts pundits like me. We thought the billionaire was leaving the world of Entertainment, climbing over a wall and joining us in the sober domain of Politics. But in fact, the opposite happened. 'Trump, The Entertainer' stayed exactly where he was. Instead, he pulled the political establishment over the wall and into HIS domain. The political class is now lost in the world of reality television and social media."[13] And not only that. It was also lost—or captured—by people who were earnestly moved by racial or other forms of hatred, as well as people who enjoyed being shocked by other people's hatred or radicalism.

This new mode of existence and digital consumption pleases and distracts the majority of Americans. The old-fashioned TV has now been enhanced and augmented, displaced by social media on digital devices of all sorts and sizes—from the Apple Watch and tablet, through the MacBook Air and Mac Pro, to the giant screen TV and even the Jumbotron. And all of it serves to pacify the masses and ensure that they do not have the time or attention span to question the domestication of the counterinsurgency.

And, then, it all feeds back into total information awareness. Hand in hand, government agencies, social media, Silicon Valley, and large retailers and corporations have created a mesmerizing new digital age that simultaneously makes us expose ourselves and everything we do to government surveillance and that serves to distract and entertain us. All kinds of social media and reality TV consume and divert our attention, making us give our data away for free. A profusion of addictive digital platforms—from Gmail, Facebook, and Twitter, to YouTube and Netflix, Amazon Prime, Instagram, and Snapchat, and now Pokémon GO—distract us into exposing all our most private information, in order to feed the new algorithms of commerce and intelligence services: to profile us for both watch lists and commercial advertising.

To understand how the American population is being pacified in this new digital age, it is important to analyze more closely how the information and data shape us so deeply and unconsciously. The fact is, whether it is the attention-grabbing brashness of Donald Trump or the pleasure of Pokémon GO, these new forms of entertainment mold our thoughts and emotions. They shape our deeper selves in profound ways—ways that render us entranced, gullible, and submissive. These new obsessions blunt our criticality.

A good illustration of how these new digital distractions shape us, almost surreptitiously, was the Internet phenomenon "Damn, Daniel!" You may already have forgotten about it—that is the singularity of these fleeting viral episodes. They consume all our attention and then vanish and are forgotten, under the spell of the next one. "Damn, Daniel!" exploded on the scene in February 2016 and rapidly went viral. The video, made on an iPhone using Snapchat, was that of a young man, Daniel Lara (age fourteen), caught on camera on successive days, showing off his stylish shoes. It had an overlaid voice, each day and each time, saying, "Damn, Daniel!" with a swagger. On particular snippets, when Daniel was wearing particular shoes—white slip-on Vans—the voiceover said "Damn, Daniel! Back at it again with those white Vans!"

The short video, only thirty seconds long, was made public on February 15, 2016, and went viral in a matter of days. It had over forty-five million views by the time the two boys—Daniel Lara and Joshua Holtz (age fifteen)—were invited on *The Ellen Degeneres Show* on February 24, 2016.[14] The boys became overnight celebrities because of the supposed catchiness of the meme "Damn, Daniel!" (You can still watch the video.[15]) Within days, songs and remixes were being written and produced using the meme. Rappers Little, Teej, and LeBlanc created a track using the meme, raising issues of race and white privilege.[16] Another artist, Suhmeduh, made a more popular techno remix as well.[17] Celebrities as far and wide as Justin Bieber, Kanye West, and Kim Kardashian began sporting white Vans, riffing off the meme.[18] On February 25, 2016, the *New York Times*—yes, the *Times* began writing about it— referred to the video as "the latest Internet sensation," and reported that "Daniel said that he can't even go to the mall or a swim meet without being asked for photos with his fans or getting marriage proposals."[19]

Only twelve days after the video had been released, on February 27, 2016, it was hard to keep up with all of the fallout from the meme— positive (Ellen gave Daniel a lifetime supply of Vans) and negative (Joshua Holtz, for instance, got swatted).[20] Although easily dismissed as just "entertaining nonsense"—that's how the *New York Times* starts its article about the Internet phenomenon, describing it as "a meme ris[ing] up from the wondrous bog of entertaining nonsense that is the Internet"—a lot was going on with the "Damn, Daniel!" meme.

For instance, the video itself valorized consumption. In the video, Daniel sported a different pair of new shoes practically every day, with the climax being his white Vans. It's unclear whether the shoe company, Vans, was in on the phenomenon, according to the *Times*; but they certainly benefited commercially. They could not have produced a more effective commercial. The whole phenomenon centered on consumption and the commercialization of those white Vans, masquerading under the surface of a popular joke.

There was also a clear racial dimension to the meme. It was filmed by white boys at a white high school in Riverside, California, and had all the trappings of white privilege: sunny, monied, fashionable, blond-haired white boys. The rappers Little, Teej & LeBlanc made the racial dimensions clear in their take, suggesting that black kids might not so easily get away with the same things, and they rapped about the racial-sexual innuendos surrounding the phenomenon. "Back at it again with the white Vans. Back at it again with the black Vans [. . .] Black canvas with the black stiches and the white slit." The white vans symbolized, for these rappers, white privilege. "Vans on, they are Mr. Clean."[21]

But notice that all of these racial and consumerist political dimensions were buried in the entertainment, hidden, though at the same time internalized by us all through a process of addictive web surfing, clicking, and downloading. As of February 22, 2016, seven days in, the video had 260,000 retweets and 330,000 "likes" on Twitter. The official YouTube version had almost 1.5 million views by February 27, 2016, with 13,617 "likes." The meme—with all its hidden messaging and politics—surreptitiously shaped viewers through a process that included hundreds of thousands of "likes" and tens of millions of "shares," "follows," and "clicks." It spread contagiously and simultaneously turned into a mode of existence. A style of life. The pool. The white Vans. The swim team. The girls.

And what is not in the picture? The political economy surrounding how those white Vans were produced and made their way to the poolside at Riverside High School, or the differential treatment that young black teenagers received at their high school. Or the forms of wealth inequality and residential segregation that produced all-white public high schools. Or the contrast to the daily lived experience in an inner-city school. All of the politics were elided behind the pleasure and catchiness of the meme.

This third aspect of counterinsurgency's domestication is perhaps the most important, because it targets the most prized military and political objective: the general masses. And today, in the expository society, the new algorithms and digital-advertising methods have propelled the manipulation and propaganda to new heights. We are being encouraged by government and enticed by multination corporations and social media to expose and express ourselves as much as possible, leaving digital traces that permit both government and corporations to profile us and then try to shape us accordingly. To make model citizens out of us all—which means docile, entranced consumers. The governing paradigm here is to frenetically encourage digital activity—which in one sense is the opposite of docility—in order to then channel that activity in the right direction: consumption, political passivity, and avoiding the radical extremes.

What we are witnessing is a new form of digital entrancement that shapes us as subjects, blunts our criticality, distracts us, and pacifies us. We spend so much time on our phones and devices, we barely have any time left for school or work, let alone political activism. In the end, the proper way to think about this all is not through the lens of docility, but through the framework of entrancement. It is crucial to understand this in the proper way, because breaking this very entrancement is key to seeing how counterinsurgency governance operates more broadly. Also, because the focus on docility—along an older register of discipline—is likely to lead us into an outdated focus on top-down propaganda. We need to think of domesticated counterinsurgency as not simply something done to us, but something in which we are also choosing to participate—and could choose not to.

We could have foreseen the domestication of counterinsurgency. The French officers who developed modern warfare in the 1950s and 1960s, in fact, realized quickly that the principles and doctrines could have wider application than just the colonial conflict. Roger Trinquier identified, early on, the domestic implications of insurgent warfare. "Tried out in Indochina and brought to perfection in Algeria, [the *guerre révolutionnaire*] can lead to any boldness, even a direct attack on metropolitan France," Trinquier warned. He even suggested that the French Communist Party might facilitate domestic terrorism, leading to the possibility that a "few organized and well-trained men of action will carry out a reign of terror in the big cities" of France. The countryside and the "hilly regions such as the Massif Central, the Alps, or Brittany" would be even more susceptible to insurgency. And "with terrorism in the cities and guerrillas in the countryside, the war will have begun," Trinquier warned his French compatriots. "This is the simple mechanism, now well known, which can at any instant be unleashed against us."[22] Modern warfare, it seemed, could flow seamlessly from the colonies to the homeland—and thus counterinsurgency needed to as well.

The historian Peter Paret also anticipated the domestication of the counterinsurgency paradigm. In 1964, he admonished his readers "not to ignore the theses of *guerre révolutionnaire*, nor their implications in fields other than the purely military"—a clear reference to the political and the domestic. In fact, in the very next sentence, Paret referred to the fact that the new strategies had impacts "across military and political France."[23]

At about the same time Paret was writing on counterinsurgency, Michel Foucault advanced the idea in his 1971–1972 lectures, "Penal Theories and Institutions," that domestic law enforcement and, more generally, relations of power in civil society could be mapped on the model of civil war. Taking the historical example of the brutal repression of the 1639 peasant uprisings in Normandy by Cardinal Richelieu and his appointed agent, the Chancelier Séguier, Foucault demonstrated how there emerged at that time a repressive model of power, or what he called a repressive judicial state apparatus. Neither purely military, nor purely fiscal—as had been the state apparatuses of the Middle Ages—the repressive strategies of Richelieu and Séguier gave way to a new law-enforcement mechanism that combined the military and the civil. This repressive judicial state apparatus appropriated the military right to give orders and the civilian right to mete out punishments. And it infringed all boundaries between military and civilian, placing itself above both simultaneously.

That new repressive form of governing, Foucault suggested, had to be understood through the lens of the domestication and extension of civil war. Foucault's embrace of a war matrix was influenced by his engagements with the Maoist movement, the *Gauche prolétarienne*. In dialogue with Maoist insurgency theory, Foucault would invert Clausewitz's famous dictum. It is not so much that war is the continuation of politics by other means, but that politics is the continuation of war by other means. At practically the same time, Peter Paret argued, "A full understanding of Clausewitz' famous dictum on the interaction of war and politics is the key to successful modern guerrilla operations. The guerrillas' motive for fighting is at least partly political—or, to put it differently, ideological."[24]

The domestication of the counterinsurgency is the marriage of warfare and politics. That union is what we now face in the United States. A few months after he proclaimed a national emergency in the wake of 9/11, President George W. Bush declared that "the war against terrorism ushers in a new paradigm."[25] At the time, the new paradigm was framed in military terms. It has, however, far exceeded the laws of war. Over time, it has matured into a full-blown paradigm of governing.

PART IV

FROM COUNTERINSURGENCY TO THE COUNTERREVOLUTION

11

THE COUNTERREVOLUTION IS BORN

EVER SINCE THE EARLY DAYS OF MODERN WARFARE IN THE 1960s, there were instances of the domestic use of counterinsurgency strategies on American soil. But in the years since 9/11, counterinsurgency has reached a crescendo in terms of its systematic and pervasive deployment at home. The paradigm was refined and systematized, and has now reached a new stage: the complete and systematic domestication of counterinsurgency against a home population *where there is no real insurgency or active minority.* This new stage is what I call "The Counterrevolution."

The Counterrevolution is a new paradigm of governing our own citizens at home, modeled on colonial counterinsurgency warfare, despite the absence of any domestic uprising. It is aimed not against a rebel minority—since none really exists in the United States—but instead it creates the illusion of an active minority which it can then deploy to target particular groups and communities, and govern the entire American population on the basis of a counterinsurgency warfare model. It operates through the three main strategies at the heart of modern warfare, which, as applied to the American people, can be recapitulated as follows:

1. *Total information awareness of the entire American population . . . :* An elite group in the United States collects, monitors, and data-mines all our personal communications and information. These self-appointed leaders—high-ranking officials at the White House and Pentagon; heads of intelligence agencies and of police departments; members of the national security apparatus and of congressional intelligence committees; high-level CEOs at social media, private security, and tech companies like Google, Microsoft, or Facebook—could be called the "counterrevolutionary minority." Assuming the role of guardians, they put in place, through programs such as PRISM and UPSTREAM, Section 215 and mosque surveillance, social media and data collection, a system of total information awareness of the entire American population. They have acquired the ability to know everything about everyone and every device by gathering and analyzing all foreign and domestic digital traces.

2. *. . . in order to extract an active minority at home . . . :* In addition to targeting suspected enemies in Afghanistan, Iraq, Yemen, and elsewhere abroad, this self-appointed counterrevolutionary minority tries to identify and target an active minority in the United States. In the process, it fabricates out of whole cloth an amorphous, ill-defined active minority, whose boundaries shift depending on the perceived threat, but that generally includes American Muslims and Mexicans, police protesters, African American and Latino social activists, and other communities predominantly of color. These supposed internal enemies are then targeted for containment and possible elimination by the most efficient means possible: hypermilitarized policing, surveillance of mosques and Muslim communities, infiltration of protests and

student groups, arrests and preventive custody, solitary confinement, juvenile detention, imprisonment, and deportation.

3. *. . . and win the hearts and minds of Americans*: Meanwhile, the counterrevolutionary minority works to pacify and assuage the general population in order to ensure that the vast majority of Americans remain just that: ordinary consuming Americans. They encourage and promote a rich new digital environment filled with YouTube, Netflix, Amazon Prime, tweets, Facebook posts, instagrams, snapchats, and reality TV that consume attention while digitally gathering personal data—and at times, pushing enhanced content. They direct digital propaganda to susceptible users. And they shock and awe the masses with their willingness to torture suspected terrorists or kill their own citizens abroad. In the end, entertaining, distracting, entrancing, and assuaging the general population is the key to success—our new form of bread and circus.

These three key strategies now guide governance at home, as they do military and foreign affairs abroad. What has emerged today is a new and different art of governing. It forms a coherent whole with, at its center, a security apparatus composed of White House, Pentagon, and intelligence officials, high-ranking congressional members, FISC judges, security and Internet leaders, police intelligence divisions, social-media companies, Silicon Valley executives, and multinational corporations. This loose network, which collaborates at times and competes at others, exerts control by collecting and mining our digital data. Data control has become the primary battlefield, and data, the primary resource—perhaps the most important primary resource in the United States today.

This security apparatus thrives on learning everything about each and every one of us, and draws us in through our own desires, distractions, and indulgences. And it executes a set of simple instructions: total surveillance to achieve full and perfect knowledge; solitary confinement, juvenile detention, militarized policing, and robot bombs to eliminate a radical minority—and all of it geared toward making the American population feel safe and secure to ensure that we consume rather than sympathize with those who are targeted.

Pulsing through this new form of governing are reflections and echoes of that inherited tension, from early counterinsurgency theory, between brutality and legality: between the administration of water-boarding and the legalistic torture memos, between the targeted assassination of American citizens abroad and the lengthy forty-one-page memorandum justifying such killings; between human mapping of Muslim neighborhoods and court-approved guidelines for the investigation of political activity; between the surreptitious cable-splicing of underground communications networks and the Foreign Intelligence Surveillance Court. This inherited tension still beats through our new style of governing, even though it has essentially been resolved today by means of the legalization of brutality, which ends up producing not a temporary state of exception, but rather variations on the counterinsurgency theme.

The "new paradigm" that President George W. Bush first announced shortly after 9/11 has come to fruition. It patiently burrowed, and has now returned home. Today, it constitutes a new art of governing one's own citizens. Defying all predictions, rebutting progressive histories, it has come alive and broken through the crust of the earth like that old mole of history, who only makes his appearance when he is finally ready to overthrow the old regime.[1] This new mode of governing has no time horizon. It has no sunset provision. And it is marked by a tyrannous logic of violence. There is the widely televised violence of the most extreme faction abroad—the beheadings by ISIS. There are selective videos of riots and looting by the purportedly active minority at home—whether it is in Baltimore, Milwaukee, Ferguson, or London or the Paris *banlieus*. There are the targeted drone strikes and special operations, torturous interrogations, and the violence and militarized response of the police and state at home. That violence is not exceptional or aberrational. It is part and parcel of the new paradigm of governing that reconciles brutality with legality.

To be clear, episodes involving the domestic use of counterinsurgency techniques occurred in the 1960s, with the application of modern-warfare methods against the Black Panther Party; in the 1970s, in the context of prison uprisings; and in the 1980s and 1990s, against various resistance movements such as MOVE and the Branch Davidians. But what makes The Counterrevolution new and unique today is that the methods have been refined, systematized, applied across the country, and, most importantly, have become dominant at a time when there is not even a semblance of a domestic insurgency or revolution going on in this country. When you add to that the new digital technologies that make possible so much more powerful forms of surveillance and long-distance remote-controlled military force, as well as the systematicity and pervasiveness of counterinsurgency logics—when you put this all together, it is clear that there is a difference of kind, not just degree. We govern ourselves differently in the United States now: no longer through sweeping social programs like the New Deal or the War on Poverty, but through surgical counterinsurgency strategies against a phantom opponent. The intensity of the domestication now is unprecedented.

To be sure, when ISIS broadcasts beheadings of innocent hostages abroad or takes credit for attacks in Paris, Beirut, and Istanbul or when Al Qaeda attacks the Twin Towers causing the deaths of almost three thousand innocent victims, counterinsurgency methods seem more necessary than ever. It felt perhaps different when the counterinsurgency strategies were targeted at individuals like Dr. Martin Luther King Jr. or organizations like Students for a Democratic Society (SDS) or the National Lawyers Guild—people and organizations that so many admired. In those cases, the idea of a domestic counterinsurgency simply seemed inappropriate, and that itself justified criticism. But things may seem different today. Don't the beheadings alone call for more aggressive counterinsurgency interventions?

The answer is that the existence of enemies *abroad*—foreign enemies intent on brutally killing United States citizens, Westerners, and others—simply does not justify creating out of whole cloth an active minority in this country. It does not warrant fabricating an internal enemy. Even the few men and women on American soil who wreak terroristic damage do not form an insurgency. (By terroristic, I am referring to attacks that the media refer to as domestic terrorism by contrast to the more ordinary multiple-victim shootings that involve four or more victims and occur on average every day in America).[2] For the most past, the men and women who wreak terroristic damage on American soil are unstable individuals who gravitate to radical forms of Islam—or radical forms of Christianity, or the KKK for that matter—because those ideas and organizations represent the most cutting-edge and threatening fringe. In effect, certain extremely violent individuals are expressing their violent acts in the language of radical Islam (and radical Christianity) because that language gains the most attention and plays on the greatest fears of the public. But there is an important distinction between a handful of unstable, lone-wolf, extremely violent individuals and an active minority. A few individuals are, of course, in a literal sense a minority; however, they do not necessarily compose— as counterinsurgency theory envisions them—an organized group with a shared goal. The attempt to define them as an insurgency or active minority is imposing a coherence that does not exist—at a dangerous political cost.

Counterinsurgency, with its tripartite scheme (active minority, passive masses, counterrevolutionary minority) and its tripartite strategy (total awareness, eliminate the active minority, pacify the masses) is a deeply counterproductive self-fulfilling prophecy that radicalizes individuals against the United States. This is especially the case for its more brutal manifestations, such as the Muslim ban, waterboarding, or indefinite detention at Guantánamo Bay. The images from Abu Ghraib, the drone casualties, the torture of Muslims during interrogation: these actions have all contributed to the radicalization of many abroad and the alienation of many at home. This fact does not excuse terroristic acts or beheadings in any way, but surely it should compel us to take a different approach, informed by the inescapable reality that each one of us is inevitably implicated in producing the present political situation we live in.

Counterinsurgency strategies sow the seeds of conflict. As Richard Stengel, a former undersecretary of state, explains in the pages of the *New York Times,* "The Islamic State is not just a terrorist group, it is an idea. Its rallying cry is that the West is hostile to Islam and that every good Muslim has a duty to join the caliphate."[3] Strategies that feed into that perception of American hostility to Islam are therefore deeply counterproductive. In order to combat extremists abroad and to prevent an insurgency at home, the exact opposite is necessary. Americans need to show who they really are: a nation predominantly of immigrants, slaves, and natives that thrives on tolerance and acceptance, and is deeply connected, through its immigrant populations, to every country, creed, and religion of the world. This approach is not only ethically proper, it also serves foreign policy. As Stengel writes, "To defeat radical Islamic extremism, we need our Islamic allies—the Jordanians, the Emiratis, the Egyptians, the Saudis—and they believe that [the idea of "radical Islamic terrorism"] unfairly vilified a whole religion."

It is true, of course, that the 9/11 attacks were carried out by Muslim individuals who came to and lived within the United States. Several of them had been identified and were being tracked (though the intelligence about them was not being properly shared). These facts alone call for extreme vigilance of any person suspected of terrorist links. But they certainly do not call for turning all Muslims—abroad and on American soil—into a potential active minority. Domesticating the counterinsurgency turns millions of ordinary Americans into potential enemies. It ill-treats our fellow citizens and neighbors. It alienates people, instead of healing wounds. It is the wrong response. The Counterrevolution sees an active minority where there simply isn't one.

These difficult and delicate issues demand careful thought. The fact is, there are people who try and succeed in carrying out terror attacks both on American soil and abroad. The effort to stop these attacks is of vital importance and entirely legitimate. But it surely must not involve governing ourselves and large swaths of the rest of the world with a counterinsurgency logic that has proven to cause more harm than good. The fact is, counterinsurgency's track record has been simply abysmal— it failed everywhere: In Indochina. In Algeria. In Malaya. In Vietnam. And in Iraq and Afghanistan, where we were constantly reminded that any small gains rarely extended beyond the momentary surge in ground troops. The United States poured more than $1 trillion and lost almost 5,000 of its own citizens in a war and counterinsurgency effort in Iraq that caused more than 125,000 direct casualties and more than 650,000 excess deaths: it was a failed counterinsurgency that has, at the end of the day, only benefited Iran and private contractors.[4] Counterinsurgency produces its own effects of radicalizing minorities, of perpetuating brutality, and of creating social divisions that make it a perilous mode of governing. Historically, counterinsurgency warfare has been strategically ineffective, politically destructive, and ethically dreadful. This does not mean we do not need to be vigilant and protect against terrorist attacks. It does mean that we must resist the counterinsurgency approach to foreign affairs and The Counterrevolution at home.

The attack on the World Trade Center and ISIS beheadings were unconscionable. But it is precisely when we feel so self-righteous—and properly so—that we are at greatest risk of overreaching and embracing simplistic solutions with devastating effects. It is when we feel so morally certain that things get out of hand, that we ignore the collateral damage to innocent men, women, and children, and turn entire communities into internal enemies. These modern warfare strategies have fueled the enemies abroad that they seek to eliminate and created the illusory specter of a rebellion at home that is harming and alienating millions of Americans.[5] The Counterrevolution must end.

Instead, we are moving in the exact opposite direction. With the election of President Trump, the United States embraced the most brutal version of counterinsurgency warfare. On the campaign trail, Donald Trump vowed to worsen the torture, increase domestic surveillance, and target Muslims, Mexicans, and minorities in this country—in sum, to accelerate and amplify the counterinsurgency abroad and at home.

In just his first months in office, President Trump ratcheted up and accelerated The Counterrevolution on every front. With his executive order banning travel of American residents from Muslim-majority countries, his promise to build the wall on the southern border, and his pledge to refill Guantánamo, including with American suspects, President Trump threw fuel on the flames. The Muslim ban was particularly egregious and counterproductive because it fed right into the recruitment strategy of ISIS. As Richard Stengel quickly reported, "The Islamic State has called it 'the blessed ban' because it supports the Islamic State's position that America hates Islam. The clause in the order that gives Christians preferential treatment will be seen as confirming the Islamic State's apocalyptic narrative that Islam is in a fight to the death against the Christian crusaders. The images of Muslim visitors being turned away at American airports will only inflame those who seek to do us harm."[6]

While the Muslim travel ban represented Trump's determination to cast Muslims as an active minority, the president quickly loaded his cabinet with counterinsurgency warriors. Trump appointed as his secretary of defense General James Norman Mattis, who was a close collaborator and contributor to General Petraeus's counterinsurgency field manual. Petraeus had reached out to Mattis early on, during the time they overlapped in Iraq in the early aughts. Mattis's wealth of experience with counterinsurgency as a Marine Corps commander, after having led the invasion of Iraq in 2003, was of great influence on Petraeus.[7] On February 20, 2017, Trump appointed another counterinsurgency champion as his national security adviser: Lieutenant General H. R. McMaster, a respected military strategist with a particular expertise in modern warfare.[8] McMaster was responsible for what was claimed to be one of the great counterinsurgency successes of the Iraq war, the 2005 effort to secure the city of Tal Afar in northern Iraq, discussed earlier and described at length in General Petraeus's field manual. In fact, that particular counterinsurgency success weighed heavily on Petraeus, who would draw on it both theoretically, to develop his style of modern warfare, and practically, when he took command in Iraq in 2007. General McMaster published his PhD under the title *Dereliction of Duty: Lyndon Johnson, Robert McNamara, the Joint Chiefs of Staff, and the Lies that Led to Vietnam*, a devastating criticism of the failures of the joint chiefs of staff to stand up against President Johnson and Robert McNamara during the Vietnam War. He was also a critic of the manner that President George W. Bush fought the war in Iraq, stating that the administration had not planned for "a sustainable political outcome that would be consistent with our vital interests," which "complicated both of those wars."[9] The political rather than the military dimensions were key for McMaster, a classic reflection of the counterinsurgency paradigm. And on July 28, 2017, President Trump elevated another counterinsurgency warrior, former general John Kelly, who had served for months as secretary of homeland security, to chief of staff. A tried and true counterinsurgency practitioner was running all White House operations.

President Trump's first budget proposal virtually enacted counterinsurgency strategy, combining a sharp increase in unconventional military spending and funding for a southern wall with dramatic reductions in refugee and social spending—effectively, to provide "essential services" only. Trump proposed to increase defense spending by $54 billion, or 10 percent, for 2018 and budgeted $469 billion in discretionary monies for defense over the next decade. In his own words, he sought to achieve "one of the largest increases in national defense spending in American history." His proposed budget also included $2.6 billion to enhance border security, to begin building a wall on the border with Mexico, and to keep immigrants out. Trump proposed slashing social programs, such as Medicaid and health-care services (down 23.3 percent over the next ten years), supplemental food assistance, formerly known as the Food Stamp Program (down 25.3 percent), and refugee programs (down 74.2 percent); and eliminated wholesale other programs, such as national service programs like AmeriCorps, Senior Corps, and Vista—in effect, cutting social programs and essential services to their bare essentials.[10]

The Muslim ban, the counterinsurgency cabinet, the budget proposals—as well as the promises of a wall on our southern border, of American detainees at Guantánamo, and of more surveillance of mosques—fit perfectly in The Counterrevolution framework. These measures serve, first, to produce a fictitious active minority in the United States consisting of resident nationals from those Muslim-majority countries (despite the fact that no single terrorist attack on United States soil has to date been conducted by a national from those countries) and our southern neighbors. Having created an active minority and instilled fear in the general population, second, these measures seek to eradicate and eliminate the minority by excluding it from the country. Finally, the measures also serve to demonstrate who is in charge, who is willing to and able to protect best, and who is looking out for the American people. It is the perfect counterinsurgency strategy—except that it rests on a phantom enemy at home and fuels real enemies abroad.

One of the greatest tragedies—and the most worrisome—is that so many Americans knowingly embraced The Counterrevolution when they cast their ballots for Trump in November 2016. During his presidential campaign, Trump had pledged to do exactly what he did in the first days of his administration—and worse. Yet despite that, he was elected president.

During the campaign, Trump explicitly stated that he was prepared to resume torture. "I would bring back waterboarding and I'd bring back a hell of a lot worse than waterboarding," Trump pledged. He expressed his intention to fill Guantánamo Bay prison again, and for a while claimed he would torture the family members of suspected terrorists to get information from them if necessary. He embraced torture not only because it "works," he said, but because even "if it doesn't work, they deserve it anyway."[11] He even said he would send American terrorism suspects to Guantánamo for military prosecutions.

"I have made it clear in my campaign that I would support and endorse the use of enhanced interrogation techniques if the use of these methods would enhance the protection and safety of the nation," Trump wrote in *USA Today*. "Though the effectiveness of many of these methods may be in dispute, nothing should be taken off the table when American lives are at stake. The enemy is cutting off the heads of Christians and drowning them in cages, and yet we are too politically correct to respond in kind [. . .] I will do whatever it takes to protect and defend this nation and its people [. . .] With their support, we will make America great again."[12]

During his campaign, Trump identified an active minority in the United States that effectively included not only all Muslims, but also undocumented residents, especially those with criminal records, and large segments of the African American community, especially those who have participated in Black Lives Matter protests. Muslims in America, he said, need to inform on each other, and the influx of any more Muslims must be stopped. As for Mexicans, Trump equated them with rapists: "When Mexico sends its people, they're not sending their best [. . .] They're sending people that have lots of problems, and they're bringing those problems with us. They're bringing drugs. They're bringing crime. They're rapists. And some, I assume, are good people." He vowed to deport eleven million undocumented residents, and then said he would start with the two to three million undocumented persons with criminal records. He also vowed to put back in place law-and-order measures that target minorities. He lent all his support to even more NSA surveillance. He called for targeted surveillance of mosques in America.[13]

Trump warned Americans explicitly that "we're going to have to do things that we never did before." In an interview during the campaign, he emphasized: "Some people are going to be upset about it . . . Certain things will be done that we never thought would happen in this country in terms of information and learning about the enemy," he said. "We're going to have to do things that were frankly unthinkable a year ago."[14]

In effect, Trump threatened to up the ante on each and every counterinsurgency maxim: more information awareness, harsher treatment of minorities, and more tweets and misinformation for the people. He did everything possible to delegitimize the mainstream media, to spin factless claims, and to help circulate false information. He embraced the language of brutality against a phantom minority. He adopted the political logic, if not the explicit theory, of the counterinsurgency paradigm. Donald Trump even reenacted, in the most vulgar terms, the link between brutality and masculinity discussed earlier in the context of the hidden functions of terror. Trump infamously was caught on tape making derogatory and violent comments about women, saying, "When you're a star, they let you do it. You can do anything. Grab them by the pussy. You can do anything." In another incident, he blended misogyny with homophobia when he mocked Arianna Huffington, saying that she was "unattractive both inside and out. I fully understand why her former husband left her for a man—he made a good decision."[15] The traditional masculine tropes laced his campaign rhetoric.

Despite all this, over 62 million people voted for Donald Trump, resulting in his Electoral College victory. And it was by no means an unusual election. Voter turnout in 2016 was typical for this country. About 60.2 percent of the approximately 231 million eligible voters turned out to vote, representing about 139 million votes case. That number is consonant with historical turnout in this country, almost squarely between voter turnout in 2012 (58.6 percent) and in 2008 (61.6

percent), but still above most presidential election year turnouts since 1972.[16] In all categories of white voters, Trump prevailed.

Embracing The Counterrevolution, Donald Trump was knowingly elected president, which painfully brings to mind Hannah Arendt's haunting words from *The Origins of Totalitarianism*: "It is quite obvious that mass support for totalitarianism comes neither from ignorance nor from brainwashing."[17]

The totalization and domestication of counterinsurgency in the United States today—at a time when there is not even a semblance of a domestic insurgency—deserves its new label: The Counterrevolution. It is all the more worrisome because it appears to be without end, as the legal historian Samuel Moyn warns us.[18] We are headed not, as Kant would have it, toward perpetual peace, but instead, sounding the refrain of Nietzsche's eternal return, toward an endless state of counterinsurgency warfare.

Now that it's clear that The Counterrevolution has arrived and is likely only to grow more brutal, we need to examine it more closely to understand fully how it functions and how to resist it.

12

A STATE OF
LEGALITY

MANY COMMENTATORS ARGUE THAT WE NOW LIVE, IN THE United States and in the West more broadly, in a "state of exception" characterized by suspended legality. In this view, our political leaders have placed a temporary hold on the rule of law, with the tacit understanding that they will resume their adherence to liberal legal values when the political situation stabilizes. Some commentators go further, arguing that we have now entered a "permanent state of exception."

This view, however, misperceives one particular tactic of counterinsurgency—namely, the state of emergency—for the broader rationality of our new political regime. It fails to capture the larger ambition of our new mode of governing. The fact is, our government does everything possible to *legalize* its counterinsurgency measures and to place them solidly within the rule of law—through endless consultations with government lawyers, hypertechnical legal arguments, and lengthy legal memos. The idea is not to put law on hold, not even temporarily. It is not to create an exception, literally or figuratively. On the contrary, the central animating idea is to turn the counterinsurgency model into a fully legal strategy. So, the governing paradigm is not one of exceptionality, but of counterinsurgency *and* legality.

To be sure, legal devices such as states of emergency are actively deployed and play an important role in the counterinsurgency model. Crises and emergencies justify modern-warfare practices. President George W. Bush declared a formal state of emergency right after 9/11, and President François Hollande triggered a formal state of emergency under French law after the November 2015 terrorist attacks in Paris. Less formally, but more metaphorically, the US Homeland Security Advisory System, with its orange high risk and red severe risk levels of terrorist threat; the "if you see something, say something" public campaigns; the recorded warnings in subway and train stations; the militarized patrols with fully automatic machine guns at train stations or at airports—all of these function importantly as emergency measures.

But it is important to distinguish these specific exceptional measures from the larger, fully coherent rationality that constitutes The Counterrevolution. The logic of that framework is not one of rules and exception, whether permanent or temporary. It is not a binary logic. It is, instead, a model that *legalizes* counterinsurgency practices, *legitimates* them, and thereby produces a fully coherent *legal system*— all grounded in notions of legality. The counterinsurgency paradigm is fully ensconced in a web of legal advisory memos, Office of Legal Counsel briefs, quasi and real judicial review, and top lawyers. Rather than resting on a binary logic of norm and exception, it depends on rendering all these "exceptional tactics" fully legal. It rests not on exceptional *illegality*, but rather on recurring forms of what we might call *legalizations*, or even *legalities*—a term I will come back to.

One could, of course, contend that a fully legalized Counterrevolution produces a "permanent state of exception," but that has little meaning— since the exception requires the rule—and it fails to capture the overarching *logic* of our new governing paradigm. The logic today is based on a model of counterinsurgency warfare with, at its heart, the resolution of that central tension between brutality and legality. The counterrevolutionary model has resolved the inherited tension and legalized the brutality. It is vital that we properly identify and understand the logic of this new paradigm; otherwise, it will be impossible to resist it.

The term "state of exception" is wide-ranging and covers a variety of different legal mechanisms including, among others, a state of emergency or a state of siege, the imposition of martial law, cases of necessity, and national security or *raison d'État* justifications. What all these different legal forms have in common is that they represent a rupture from the more ordinary legal process, a temporary lifting of the conventional liberal paradigm. And they generally require, in a liberal democracy, the suspension of certain legal rules.

So, for instance, just three days after 9/11, President George W. Bush proclaimed a national emergency, issuing Proclamation 7463 titled "Declaration of National Emergency by Reason of Certain Terrorist Attacks." The proclamation authorized, under the National Emergencies Act, the calling up of reserves to active duty and it made easier bureaucratic tasks regarding the deployment of armed forces personnel.[1] Similarly, President François Hollande of France immediately called a state of emergency following the Paris attacks of November 13, 2015, thereby lifting ordinary warrant restrictions on police searches, seizures, and arrests. Whereas ordinarily searches of homes or house arrest would require a prior magistrate's approval, in the state of emergency these practices can be ordered by the minister of the interior. The French Assembly extended the state of emergency for months on end, doing so again after the Nice attack on July 14, 2016. France remained in a state of emergency for almost two years, until President Emmanuel Macron integrated the exceptional measures into ordinary common law.

The argument that we have entered a new political paradigm characterized by the state of exception, though, goes beyond these strictly legal devices. The argument suggests that our form of governing itself has been fundamentally altered and rendered exceptional—outside the realm of ordinary law. As applied to the post–9/11 era, the argument is that we have begun to accept, as a nation, that the special circumstances of the threat presented by nonstate networks of enemies such as Al Qaeda, the Taliban, other terrorist organizations, and now ISIS, demand a temporary interruption of legal normality. This interruption would allow the United States and its allies to deploy exceptional military and political measures in order to reestablish order and, eventually, return to the ordinary rule of law.

Now there is, of course, some evidence to support this view. As noted earlier, a few months after President Bush declared a limited national emergency, he created a new category of "enemy combatants" not recognized by law, declaring on February 7, 2002, that "the war against terrorism ushers in a new paradigm."[2] This extralegal category of "enemy combatants" surely suggested something important, as does the idea of a new paradigm. But, I would argue, it is far broader and far-reaching than the mere framework of the exception. That would be too reductionist, too simplistic. Rather, President Bush's notion of a "new paradigm" prefigured something more complex, coherent, and systematic. It presaged the larger paradigm of modern warfare and The Counterrevolution.

Carl Schmitt, the German political theorist, is most closely associated with the notion of the state of exception, and his writings have most influenced both the defenders and the critics of the idea. Schmitt himself was a leading advocate of a strong executive and of the assertion of emergency measures to respond to crisis situations. Schmitt argued for and justified President von Hindenburg's assertion of emergency powers under Article 48 of the Weimar Constitution in September 1930—an exercise of emergency powers that triggered the immediate election of the Nazi party to the Reichstag. After Schmitt joined the Nazi party in April 1933, he defended the legality of the purge of July

30, 1934—what is known as the Night of the Long Knives, when Hitler had hundreds of his political opponents murdered.[3] Drawing on his defense of emergency powers, as well as his writings on the concept of "the political" and on dictatorship, Schmitt famously—or infamously—declared: "The Führer protects the law from its worst abuse when in the moment of danger he, by his domain as Führer and as the supreme judicial authority, directly creates law."[4]

In his 1922 book *Political Theology*, Schmitt defined the *sovereign* as "he who decides on the exception,"[5] placing the ability to call a state of exception as the *sine qua non* of sovereign political power. The seeds of Schmitt's defense of the executive assertion of emergency powers could be found in his penchant for dictatorship and his antagonistic conception of the political—that is, his view that the defining element of the political relation is discerning friends from enemies and doing whatever is necessary in order to both advance one's political interests and simultaneously defend oneself against one's enemies.[6] The critical distinction between friend and foe—or more precisely, the ability to keep that opposition in view, to fully appreciate it, to be guided by it—stands at the very heart of Schmitt's defense of emergency powers. It would lead him, for instance, to drive out his rival and colleague, the legal theorist Hans Kelsen, from the University of Cologne and to write in the pages of Cologne's Nazi paper of new regulations forbidding non-Aryans from certain occupations: "We are once again learning to discriminate. Above all, we are learning to discriminate between friend and foe."[7]

In his writings, especially *State of Exception* published in 2003, the philosopher Giorgio Agamben traced a genealogy of the concept of the state of exception, linking it back to sovereign power as "the dominant paradigm of government in contemporary politics," but also relating it to many other concepts of necessity. The variants of the wide-ranging notion of exception all relate to the Latin maxim *necessitas legem non habet* ("necessity has no law"); but they do so in a somewhat confusing or imprecise manner. To help disentangle them, Agamben linked the German terms "state of exception" (*Ausnahmezustand*) and "state of necessity" (*Notstand*) to the French and Italian legal categories of "emergency decrees" and "real" or "fictitious state of siege," and the American and English categories of "martial law" or "emergency powers," as well as the suspension of the American constitution's provision of habeas corpus. By means of this genealogy, Agamben emphasized that "the state of exception has today reached its maximum worldwide deployment." His analysis then focused on the question of the legal regulation of the state of exception—whether the latter can ever be said to be subject to rules, given that it, by definition, is outside the rule of law. "If the state of exception's characteristic property is a (total or partial) suspension of the juridical order," he asks, "how can such a suspension still be contained within it?"[8]

Agamben underscored the pressing and urgent nature of the problem. He emphasized "the urgency of the state of exception 'in which we live.'" And he characterized the military order signed by President George W. Bush on November 13, 2001 (allowing for indefinite detention of suspected terrorists), and the USA PATRIOT Act as examples of a state of exception in which the detained enemy combatants were placed in the same "legal situation of the Jews in the Nazi *Lager* ["camps"], who, along with their citizenship, had lost every legal identity, but at least retained their identity as Jews."[9] In an earlier volume of *Homo Sacer*, Agamben interpreted the use of camps—such as Guantánamo Bay—and torture as an instance of the logic of the state of exception. Agamben suggested that this state of exception traced much further back in time, far before 9/11, and that it may well define the long-term history of Western civilization. For Agamben, this history revealed a paradox: the model of the exception had become the rule, and we now live in a permanent state of exception that forms the very foundation of Western political thought.

Schmitt and Agamben's writings have unleashed an outpouring of interest in the state of exception, and many contemporary thinkers have embraced the idea that it constitutes our new paradigm of governing post 9/11. The concept has practically come to dominate debates among contemporary political theorists on both sides of the question. "The state of exception has become permanent and general," Antonio Negri and Michael Hardt wrote in their book *Multitude* in 2005: "the exception has become the rule, pervading both foreign relations and the homeland."[10] Already in 2002, Judith Butler characterized the Guantánamo detention camp as "the exception," arguing that "when [Secretary of Defense Donald] Rumsfeld says that this is no regular situation, [. . .] he implies that the extraordinary character of terror justifies the suspension of law in the very act of responding to terror."[11] Similarly, Slavoj Žižek warned in 2002 that "we are entering a time in which a state of peace can at the same time be a state of emergency." Žižek too characterized the rhetoric of liberal-democratic societies post 9/11 as "that of a global emergency in the fight against terrorism, legitimizing more and more suspensions of legal and other rights." Žižek introduced some ambiguity to the notion of emergency, but nevertheless remained closest to Schmitt and the idea of emergency powers: "Our pluralistic and tolerant liberal democracies remain deeply Schmittean: they continue to rely on political *Einbildungskraft* to provide them with the appropriate figure to render visible the invisible Enemy."[12]

Other critics have also used the concept of the state of exception as a way to challenge features of our current political condition—at times, very productively. The Guantánamo lawyer and social critic Thomas Anthony Durkin, who has had a front-row seat on the war on terror as a pro bono lawyer for several detainees and other defendants charged with domestic terrorism, also embraced the exception as the right framework for our times. In Durkin's view, we are building a two-tiered system of justice in federal court based on a state-of-exception logic that goes back to the wars on drugs and crime, and now on terror. There has been a gradual increase in the use of emergency powers, under the guise of predator dangerousness, starting with the Bail Reform Act of 1984, which for the first time acknowledged pretrial detention in the federal system. This emerging two-tiered system, Durkin argued, is designed for intelligence gathering, originally about crime and drugs but now filtered through national security—and it is becoming a permanent fixture of federal procedure. Similarly, the sociologist Kim Lane Scheppele argued, "Since 9/11, the Bush administration has repeatedly invoked its ability to make exceptions to normal legality to cope with the terroristic threat in domestic policy through increasing invocation of military rationales for its actions." She identified the practices of preventive detention, the new guidelines for surveillance and investigation for terrorism-related activities, and the Bush administration's attempt to bypass Congress and the courts by "trying to bring the war on terrorism entirely within the executive branch," as departures from normal operating procedures in domestic policy.[13]

At the other end of the political spectrum, those who have come to the defense of practices such as enhanced interrogations, indefinite detention, Guantánamo Bay, or unbounded executive power, such as legal scholars Eric Posner and Adrian Vermeule, also drew extensively on the writings of Carl Schmitt and his notions of political exceptionalism. John Yoo, professor at Berkeley and author of some of the torture memos, similarly justified the aggrandizement of executive power by invoking notions of exception and turned to the idea of the "emergency situation" to justify practices that others described as torture.[14]

And in between these poles, some liberal thinkers as well embraced the concept of the state of exception, though they mainly sought to rein it in. Legal and political theorist Bruce Ackerman, for instance, called for a constitutional regime that "allows short-term emergency measures, but draws the line against permanent restrictions." Ackerman noted, "The state of emergency enables the government to take extraordinary measures in its life-and-death struggle for survival." He argued that "we must rescue the concept" of emergency powers "from fascist thinkers like Carl Schmitt" and "view the state of emergency as a crucial tool enabling public reassurance in the short term without creating long-run damage to foundational commitments to freedom and the rule of law."[15]

The state of exception has dominated the theoretical conversation and has seeped into the broader public conversation as well. Fareed Zakaria, the popular host of CNN's *GPS* and a public intellectual in his own right, stressed in the *Washington Post* in 2012: "For 11 years, the United States has been operating under emergency wartime powers granted under the 2001 Authorization for Use of Military Force." He added, "That is a longer period than the country spent fighting the Civil War, World War I and World War II combined."[16] Scott Horton, who writes for *Harper's Magazine*, argued in an article titled "State of Exception: Bush's War on the Rule of Law," that "the experience of America in the period after 9/11 bears some noteworthy parallels to the Schmitt-Benjamin dialogue" and that "the American executive in this period [made] clever use of Schmittian theories."[17] Horton was referring to the fact that the critic Walter Benjamin, in his own essay *On the Concept of History* in 1940, attempted to recuperate the notion of the state of emergency as a means for emancipatory revolution. He too, like Agamben, argued that "the 'state of emergency' in which we live is not the exception but the rule," but explicitly argued against Schmitt that the exception be used *against* Nazism: "It is our task to bring about a real state of emergency" in "the struggle against fascism," Benjamin wrote. This Benjaminian reversal can be felt in the work of Ackerman. Others as well have deployed the concept of the exception as the main framework to analyze our contemporary times.[18]

Interpreted through the lens of the state of exception, the extreme practices of total surveillance, drone strikes including against American citizens, and torture and solitary confinement must be justified (or not) as *exceptional but necessary* means at this particular historical juncture. They are proper (or not) because of their *necessary but temporary* nature. But they are expected eventually to recede, allowing the United States to return to more ordinary practices of liberal democracy.[19] Agamben's idea of a *permanent* state of exception pushes this further, but simultaneously undermines the defining element of the exception, since it becomes the rule. For the most part, though, the state of exception is presented as aberrational but *temporary*. The lifting of ordinary warrant requirements for police searches, seizures, or house arrest in France, for instance, is justified as a necessary departure from the rule of law, essential to reestablishing order and ordinary civil liberties—or alternatively, as measures that will eventually integrate the rule of law. Most often, the practices represent a temporary exception to liberal democratic rule-of-law norms. It is unclear, in this view, how long the war on terrorism, on Al Qaeda, on ISIS, and more generally on violent extremism will need to extend before the country can return to normal; but what justifies the exceptional use of NSA surveillance, solitary confinement, or remote targeted assassinations is the fact that these are provisional measures necessary to end a state of siege that began with the 9/11 attacks. The long-term practices of the United States, in this view, are consonant with liberal legalism and the rule of law. And those who theoretically embrace but practically oppose the state-of-exception framework essentially disagree with the claim of necessity, or argue that any temporary window should close more quickly, if not immediately.

The problem with the state-of-exception view is that it mistakes tactics for the overarching logic of our new paradigm of governing and, in the process, fails to see the broader framework of The Counterrevolution. The state-of-exception framework rests on an illusory dichotomy between rule and exception, a myth that idealizes and reifies the rule of law. The point is, the use of torture at CIA black sites and the bulk collection of American telephony metadata were not exceptions to the rule of law, but were rendered fully legalized and regulated practices—firmly embedded in a web of legal memos, preauthorized formalities, and judicial or quasi-judicial oversight. In this sense, hardly anything that occurred was outside or exceptional to the law, or could not be brought back in. The Counterrevolution, unlike the state of exception, does not function on a binary logic of rule and exception, but on a fully coherent systematic logic of counterinsurgency that is pervasive, expansive, and permanent. It does not have limits or boundaries. It does not exist in a space outside the rule of law. It is all encompassing, systematic, and legalized.

Of course, the rhetoric of "exception" is extremely useful to The Counterrevolution. "States of emergency" are often deployed to seize control over a crisis and to accelerate the three prongs of counter-insurgency. In France, the state of emergency allowed for *perquisitions*—"searches and seizures"—without advance judicial approval or oversight. It allowed for administrative house arrest decreed by the minister of the interior alone. It almost made possible the stripping of the nationality of dual nationals suspected of terrorism. The state of emergency was a rapid and effective way to recalibrate relations of power. In the United States as well, President Bush declared an emergency in order to mobilize police powers and resources. During the Algerian conflict, the French declared martial law in the Casbah, which allowed for military control of entry and exit, as well as extensive searches and seizures. Following the war in Iraq, the entire country of Iraq was under an effective state of emergency and a protectorate government. And one could easily imagine a full-blown state of emergency being called in the United States today *within* the counterinsurgency paradigm.

But it is important to distinguish strategic maneuvers like these from the overall paradigm of governing. For the overarching logic and dominant theoretical rationality of The Counterrevolution is not that of the state of exception. To the contrary, the counterinsurgency-warfare paradigm forms a coherent, permanent, and systematic approach that now applies *at all times*. As Galula wrote, counterinsurgency theory is the "basic tenet of the exercise of political power" and it applies "*in any situation, whatever the cause,*" a phrase repeated in General Petraeus's field manual.[20]

The dichotomy of law versus exception simply does not hold today. All of the strategies of The Counterrevolution are formalized and legalized. From the infamous torture memos, to domestic surveillance, to the forty-one-page legal brief permitting the execution of American citizens abroad, everything fits within a legal framework—or is made to fit.

In his 1973 lectures on what he would call "the punitive society," Michel Foucault coined a concept that he referred to as "*illégalismes*." The term was often translated into English as "illegalities," but that misses its thrust—namely, that so much of the negotiation of relations of power in society takes the form of pushing the boundaries of law, of playing in a space that is neither clearly legal nor clearly illegal. A better, albeit awkward, translation would be "illegalisms." The ultimate exercise of power, Foucault argued, is precisely to transform ambiguities about illegalisms into conduct that is "illegal." Translating *illégalismes* as "illegalities" would draw the conclusion prematurely, and miss the struggle that is at the heart of social relations: a play for the line drawing of the law itself. The idea of illegalisms is that the law itself is a struggle, a negotiation, an agonistic combat, a competition over the very question of defining the line of illegality—the line that divides deviations, disorderliness, rule-breaking, rule-interpretation, from illegality and the punitive sanction.

In those 1973 lectures, Foucault demonstrates how, during the early nineteenth century, social conflict expressed itself through the privileged classes converting popular illegalisms—drinking, carnivals and festivities, pleasure, leisure, debaucheries—into illegalities. Being able to turn legally ambiguous acts into legal violations, Foucault argues, represented the ultimate force of the law. In a detailed historical analysis, Foucault documents a political shift in the treatment of illegalisms.

During the *ancien régime*, Foucault argues, the popular and the privileged classes worked together to evade royal regulations, fees, and impositions. Illegalisms were widespread throughout the eighteenth century and well distributed across the different strata of society: there were not only popular illegalisms—the illegalisms of the popular classes—but illegalisms of merchants and men of commerce, even illegalisms of the privileged and powerful—of *the lieutenant de police,* of the *commissaires,* etc. And for the most part, the privileged tolerated popular illegalisms because they also practiced their own forms of deviance against the monarchy, and the relationship "worked" in a certain way. They collaborated to get around the administrative rules. For example, in the practices of weavers in the 1750s, even the police and representatives of the local government would participate in illegalisms to evade royal levies. Or in the London ports, workers and local residents would collaborate to circumvent strict laws regulating commerce. The model of law here was that of a fluid medium. "There was a whole interplay between popular illegalisms and the law," Foucault explains. "It could almost be said that respect for legality was only a strategy in this game of illegalism."[21]

As wealth became increasingly mobile after the French Revolution, new forms of wealth accumulation—of moveable goods, stocks, and supplies as opposed to landed wealth—exposed massive amounts of chattel property to the workers who came in direct contact with this new commercial wealth. The accumulation of wealth began to make popular illegalisms less useful—even dangerous—to the interests of the privileged. The commercial class seized the mechanisms of criminal justice to put an end to these popular illegalisms—not only the depredation of material property and private wealth, but also the "dissipation" of their own time and bodies, of the strength of the workers themselves, of their human capital (dissipation that took precisely the form of absenteeism, or delay, or laziness). The privileged seized the administrative and police apparatus of the late eighteenth century to crack down on popular illegalisms.

The propertied classes, in this way, took charge of the judicial institutions in order to discipline and to regulate the popular classes through legal enforcement against their illegalisms. They effectively turned popular illegalisms into *illegalities,* and, in the process, created the notion of the criminal as social enemy—Foucault even talks here of creating an "internal enemy."[22] In doing so, they turned to the penitentiary and the prison-form, which was not so much a model of confinement for violations of a statute so much as imprisonment for irregular behavior. The process of seizing judicial power rested, in this model, on the concept of illegalisms.

In The Counterrevolution—by contrast to the bourgeois revolutions of the early nineteenth century—the process is turned on its head. Illegalisms and illegalities are inverted. Rather than the privileged turning popular illegalisms into illegalities, the guardians are turning their own illegalisms into *legalities*. The Counterrevolution, with its total surveillance, detentions, and drone strikes, functions precisely by means of turning the gaps and ambiguities of the law surrounding the right to eavesdrop, the right of self-defense, or even the definition of torture into *legally* approved practices, or *legalities*. The strategy here is to paper one's way into the legal realm through elaborate memorandums and advice letters that justify the use of enhanced interrogation or the assassination of American citizens abroad. This strategy is evident not only in the dozens of legal memos that served to legally justify counterinsurgency excesses, but also in books such as Ganesh Sitaraman's fascinating *The Counterinsurgent's Constitution: Law in the Age of Small Wars*, or Appendix D to General Petraeus's field manual, "Legal Considerations," both of which sketch the proper legal framework for counterinsurgency practices.

The Counterrevolution turns illegalisms into legalities. It smothers potentially problematic situations under a mound of memos and briefs and procedures. It creates legalities through formalism and bureacracy. David Barron's forty-one-page memorandum justifying the targeted killing of American citizens abroad is the perfect illustration. The memo reads like a law school exam question: all the facts have to be assumed in order to isolate a discrete legal issue that must be narrowly answered. Would the assassination of an American citizen abroad violate Title 18, section 1119 of the US Code? Would it fall within the justification of public authority? Would it violate any other federal prohibitions on murder, or the prohibition against war crimes? Would it violate constitutional due process?

In a puzzling exercise of legal reasoning *qua* rationalization, Barron's memo uses the federal criminal code to imply justifications that are not explicitly articulated there, creating new legal norms for when those now-implied justifications are in fact met. The memo is hyperlegalistic and technical. Its skilled words and phrases are minutely pulled together to justify an outcome and create a "legality." The memo is the perfect illustration of this *legalization* process, in all its bureaucratic and judicious glory.

On the one hand, there is a strict division of responsibilities: the intelligence agencies and the military determine all the facts outside the scope of the legal memorandum. The facts are assumed to be true. Barron's memo must only decide the narrow legal issues. Everything is compartmentalized. The law is separate from the facts. But the facts, it turns out, are so extreme that they justify the law. Nevertheless, the facts are not reviewed or questioned. They are not disturbed, for fear of disabling them. Each party has its function. The lawyers are just deciding the narrow legal question presented.

On the other hand, the memo authorizes: it allows the political authority to function within the bounds of the law. It sanitizes the political decision. It cleans the hands of the military and political leaders. It produces *legalities*. Because of the extreme facts, it even renders the decision to kill morally compelling. It is an act that will save many lives. A justified homicide, one that does not run counter to the legal order. Given the facts, we are almost obligated to kill. If it is going to prevent future deaths, then the targeted assassination here is practically morally required.[23]

A few months after Barron wrote his memo, in December 2010, Judge John D. Bates, a federal judge on the US District Court for the District of Columbia, went out of his way to rule that there could be no judicial review of these types of decisions because such decisions are entrusted to the political branch: "There are circumstances in which the Executive's unilateral decision to kill a US citizen overseas is 'constitutionally committed to the political branches' and judicially unreviewable." The case of al-Awlaki, the federal court declared, "squarely presents such a circumstance."[24] The forty-one-page memo had so fully legalized killing US citizens overseas that the drone strikes became judicially unreviewable.

Law, we know, can serve as a crutch. Robert Cover demonstrated this elegantly in the case of abolitionist judges in the antebellum period who upheld the Fugitive Slave Act of 1850.[25] Robert Weisberg showed it well in the context of the death penalty.[26] Similarly, in the context of The Counterrevolution, we have witnessed that legal crutch in painful ways—a lengthy legal memo, intricate, bureaucratized, judicious, that served to cleanse and legalize the political decision to kill a US citizen without trial or due process. A legal undertaking to make possible the unimaginable: to "mark for death" a fellow citizen without the semblance of a trial.

Any exceptionalism of The Counterrevolution, in this regard, is not that it is prepared to kill a citizen abroad. Many nations are prepared to do that—and have. What is unique and exceptional is the *legalistic* and procedural dimensions, and the effort we are prepared to expend in order to make these acts justified, defensible, and legal—and to protect our political leaders from the possible consequences of later criminal or human-rights prosecutions. We are even prepared to produce these *legalities* through notions of the exception—as when the lawyers relied in part on the principle of necessity to justify torture or targeted assassination. Recall that legal counsel at CIA was originally pushing a necessity defense as a potentially "novel" legal defense for officers who engaged in torture.[27] They ultimately did not need it because the White House lawyers redefined torture, but it too would have fit within the formal legalistic framework. Anything does, in fact, so long as it renders the counterinsurgency paradigm *legal*.

In her fascinating and meticulous account of the legal battles over the "war on terror" in the Bush and Obama administrations, the historian

Karen Greenberg argues that most of the Bush and many of the Obama administration decisions ultimately deviated from what we would consider to be our due-process tradition. We have not "hew[ed] to the rule of law and the constitutional principles that it embodies," Greenberg writes. Instead, we have allowed those constitutional principles to be watered down and muddied. "The institutions of justice, caught up in the war on terror," Greenberg concludes, "have gone rogue."[28]

What the history reveals, though, is not so much that we departed from the rule of law, but that the lawyers in the presidential administrations and in Congress did everything in their power to make the counterinsurgency strategies conform to law, and in the process made the law conform to counterinsurgency. Their legalizations reshaped due process by means of the very rules of due process.

The first example that Greenberg provides is illustrative. When President Obama took office, his new attorney general, Eric Holder, announced that he was determined to try Khalid Sheikh Mohammed and the other four 9/11 coconspirators in federal court in New York. Holder was adamant that they should be tried in a civil courtroom, rather than be subject to a special military commission. This would have been significant. It would have amounted to a fundamental shift in the way that the US government dealt with the 9/11 conspirators—through a criminal law, rather than war paradigm. But Congress got in the way. In the annual authorization for the armed services, the National Defense Authorization Act (NDAA), Congress inserted a few paragraphs that expressly prohibited the use of Defense Department money to "transfer, release, or assist in the transfer or release to or within the United States, its territories, or possessions of Khalid Sheikh Mohammed or any other detainee."[29] Congress passed that version of the NDAA in December 2011. Obama signed it the following month.[30]

One might argue that the prohibition on trying Mohammed in federal court does not conform to our ideal of due process and the rule of law.[31] I find the prohibition appalling and agree entirely with Holder that Congress took "one of the nation's most tested counterterrorism tools off the table" and in the process prevented the government from "adhering to the bedrock traditions and values of our laws."[32] But President Obama nevertheless signed the legislation, making it the law of the land. In effect, the rule of law triumphed: a properly passed bill, signed by the president of the United States, became law and has been followed. None of this violates the rule of law or transgresses the boundaries of legal liberalism. Instead, the change was rendered "legal." If this feels circular, it is because *it is*: there is a constant feedback effect in play here. The counterinsurgency practices were rendered legal, and simultaneously justice was made to conform to the counterinsurgency paradigm. The result of the feedback loop was constantly new and evolving meanings of due process. And however rogue they may feel, they had gone through the correct procedural steps of due process to render them fully lawful and fully compliant with the rule of law.

Legality, like terror, serves many masters. It serves to distance the commander-in-chief from the act of killing. It functions as well to strip decision-makers of responsibility by legally justifying, if not morally mandating, their actions. This *de-responsibilization* purifies the political decisions. It cleans everyone's hands. The lawyers certainly never bear the weight of their decision. They are just applying law, technically. The intelligence operatives are absolved as well, because the legal decision is taken elsewhere. The drones and missiles do all the killing: unmanned, and remotely guided. It is almost as if, at the post, everyone thinks that they are the one with the blank in the rifle: everyone is allowed to believe that they are not responsible. Just doing their little task that does not amount to much. Meanwhile the US Supreme Court perpetuates these myths with its quasi-immunity doctrines and hyperformalism. So, for instance, the militarized police officer cannot be held responsible for excessive force or violating civil rights because there was no prior decision from the Supreme Court explicitly covering that situation—it is a Catch–22 that serves to shield the police. Here too, the hyperlegalism and proceduralism allow the Supreme Court itself to keep distance from issues of excessive use of force that are wreaking havoc across the country.

This de-responsibilization is what makes possible such a seamless transition from a Bush administration to an Obama administration, and to a Trump administration—despite their policy differences. Charlie Savage, the national security columnist at the *New York Times*, persuasively argued that the contradictions between President Obama's rhetoric during the 2008 campaign about scaling back the Bush administration's counterterrorism program and Obama's retention of most aspects of that program while in office could only be reconciled by understanding the Obama administration as lawyerly through and through.[33] Obama not only retained the substance of Bush's counterterrorism measures, but also added memos to legalize other practices.

Karen Greenberg noted that the Bush memos stand "for the right to implement 'Counter-Resistance Strategies.'" One such memo, dated October 25, 2002, and authored by James T. Hill, specifically stated that the Bush administration had been "trying to identify counterresistant techniques that we can lawfully employ."[34] There is a close connection between counterinsurgency theory and these "counterresistance techniques." Brutal methods became necessary, in this rationale, because of the strategic actions of the resisting minority. The legal memos themselves stated as much. For example, Diane E. Beaver, a staff judge advocate at Guantánamo Bay, specifically noted that the traditional methods commonly approved by the Geneva Conventions were not working on the detainees "because detainees have been able to communicate among themselves and debrief each other about their respective interrogations." Beaver stressed that their "interrogation resistance strategies have become more sophisticated."[35] Their resistance required the development and use of counterresistance techniques. And it eventually justified the *legalities* of The Counterrevolution. As Ganesh Sitaraman notes, law itself is "inevitably an instrument of counterinsurgency—as are military, political, economic, social, and other operations."[36]

Legal gaps and ambiguities can be generative. A breach between different legal or political logics can give birth to new paradigms. In his lectures, "Abnormal," in 1975, Foucault explored how the clash between the juridical power to punish and the psychiatric thirst for knowledge produced new medical diagnoses that then did work. He showed how the psychiatric category of *monomania* in the nineteenth century—a mental disease that effectively corresponded to the occurrence of a violent crime without any motive or explanation—served to fill a gap in the law and to justify punishment. In his 1978 lecture on the invention of the notion of *dangerousness* in French psychiatry, Foucault showed how the idea of future dangerousness emerged from the gaps and tensions in nineteenth-century law.[37]

There are surely gaps here too in The Counterrevolution—tensions between rule-boundedness on the one hand and a violent warfare model on the other. Those tensions give momentum to the pendulum swings of brutality that are then resolved by bureaucratic legal memos. Today, these legal documents justify the act of killing one's own fellow citizen without the semblance of a trial or adjudication. The single greatest violation of due process: that, indeed, would require a well-crafted legal memo by our most talented lawyers. Killing others in war is far easier. It is natural. But killing one's own without a trial is a different matter. Marking one's own for death is radical. In Great Britain and the United States, it is precisely what motivated habeas corpus and gave birth to the due process clause. At the Office of Legal Counsel, in our best and brightest lawyers' most able hands, it is precisely what was turned into a *legality*. There is, in the end, no need to govern through the exception when The Counterrevolution has been fully legalized.

13

A NEW SYSTEM

NEITHER EXCEPTIONAL NOR TEMPORARY, THE COUNTER-
revolution is also not piecemeal or chaotic. It is not makeshift, but
systematic and fully coherent. The counterinsurgency approach draws
on a rigorous method, what is known as "systems analysis," and as
a result, The Counterrevolution is characterized by a tight logic that
rationally harmonizes seemingly discordant strategies in pursuit of a
precise objective.

The manifestations of counterinsurgency often appear at first glance
improvised, somewhat disorganized, not properly thought-out—for example, the acts of torture during the Bush years or the rollout of the
Muslim ban in the first months of the Trump presidency. But what may
appear at first as random tactics at odds with each other are in truth a
coherent set of policies filtered through a systems-analytic approach.
The Counterrevolution, in effect, is a fully integrated, coordinated, and
systematic approach to governing.

The RAND Corporation played a seminal role in the development of
counterinsurgency practices in the United States and championed for
decades—and still does—a systems-analytic approach that has come to
dominate military strategy. Under its influence, The Counterrevolution

has evolved into a logical and coherent system that regulates and adjusts itself, a fully reasoned and comprehensive approach. Understanding systems analysis and its underlying logic is crucial to understanding the systemic nature of The Counterrevolution—and to resisting it.

The systems-analytic approach grew out of Operations Research (OR), a field developed during World War II as a way to extend quantitative analysis to military decision-making with the goal of optimizing the operation of weapons systems. Famous early applications of OR included studies of the placement of aircraft-detection radar devices to optimize antiaircraft effectiveness and of the use of depth-charge explosions to maximize antisubmarine efficacy in the early phases of World War II.[1] The "distinctive approach" of OR, according to a report by the Operational Research Society of Great Britain in the early 1960s, was "to develop a scientific model of the system, incorporating measurements of factors such as change and risk, with which to predict and compare the outcomes of alternative decisions, strategies or controls."[2]

Eventually, OR would apply the same mathematical algorithms and models to larger management problems, such as the determination of efficient transportation delivery routes or warehouse stock control. From this larger perspective, OR was understood, again in the words of the Operational Research Society of Great Britain, as "the attack of modern science on complex problems arising in the direction and management of large systems of men, machines, materials and money in industry, business, government and defense . . . The purpose is to help management determine its policy and actions scientifically."[3] The question it tackled was how to optimize efficiency where the measure of efficiency is clearly defined, or, as Edward S. Quade of the RAND Corporation explained in 1966, how "to increase the efficiency of a man-machine system in a situation where it is clear what 'more efficient' means."[4]

During the 1950s, Quade, Alain Enthoven, Charles Hitch, and others at the RAND Corporation extended this method of analysis from the narrow field of OR to defense strategy more broadly—from deciding, for instance, the optimal altitude for a bombing mission to determining broader nuclear engagement policies. The broader application would become known as systems analysis or SA. Systems analysis was often confused with OR, but it was distinct in several regards. OR tended to have more elaborate mathematical models and solved lower-level problems; in systems analysis, by contrast, the pure mathematical computation was generally applied only to subparts of the overall problem. Moreover, SA took on larger strategic questions that implicated choices between major policy options. In this sense, SA was, from its inception, in the words of one study, "less quantitative in method and more oriented toward the analysis of broad strategic and policy questions, [. . .] particularly [. . .] seeking to clarify choice under conditions of great uncertainty."[5]

The emerging logic of systems analysis was simple. It involved an analytic decision-making method that privileged quantification, modeling, statistical analysis, and a cost-benefit approach. The decision-maker first had to identify a particular problem to address within a particular social sphere—or "system"—and to have a clear idea of the system's objectives. For instance, a policy maker involved in the administration of public housing might identify crime as a problem, and might set as a goal affordable crime reduction, given that the overall objective of a public-housing system is to provide safe and affordable housing. With a clear objective in mind, the decision-maker would then set the proper criteria to evaluate different promising policy alternatives. So, for instance, in our example, the evaluation metrics might involve crime rates and the cost associated with any policy. Then, the systems-analytic process would proceed in five steps:

Step one, the input, was the set of promising policy alternatives, each of which could possibly advance the objectives of the system. Each alternative policy was then filtered in step two through a set of models to assess, for example, its maintenance costs, manpower requirements, communication capabilities, etc. This produced in step three each policy's level of effectiveness and cost, which could then be compared in step four using a metric, "the criterion." This comparison of each promising policy alternative along the chosen criterion would produce, as the output, the relative rank of each policy compared to the others. The output, at step five, would be the correct ordinal ranking of the policy alternatives.[6]

This five-step process was depicted in a RAND model, Figure 1 of Edward Quade's RAND Report P-3322 on "Systems Analysis Techniques for Planning-Programming-Budgeting" from March 1966. Quade's graphics captured well the five key steps of the analytic decision-making method called *systems analysis* developed in the 1950s and 1960s.

In order to perfect this method, the operation could be reiterated, testing for sensitivity, questioning assumptions, reexamining objectives, exploring new alternatives, and tweaking the model again and again. This reiterative process could also be visualized in Quade's report at Figure 2.[7]

Presenting this model to federal bureaucrats in 1966, Quade offered this concise definition of systems analysis:

> A systems analysis is an analytic study designed to help a decision maker identify a preferred choice among possible alternatives. It is characterized by a systematic and rational approach, with assumptions made explicit, objectives and criteria clearly defined, and alternative courses of action compared in the light of their possible consequences. An effort is made to use quantitative methods but computers are not essential. What is essential is a model that enables expert intuition and judgment to be applied efficiently.[8]

As this definition made clear, there were two meanings of the term *system* in systems analysis: first, there was the idea that the world is made up of systems, with internal objectives, that need to be analyzed

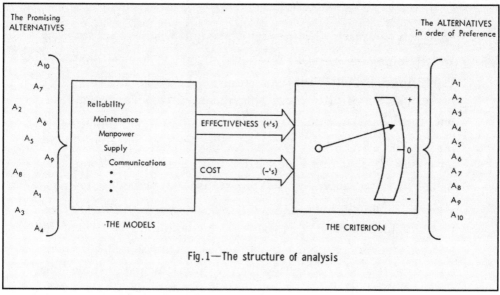

Fig.1—The structure of analysis

Figure 1 from Edward Quade's RAND Report P-3322.

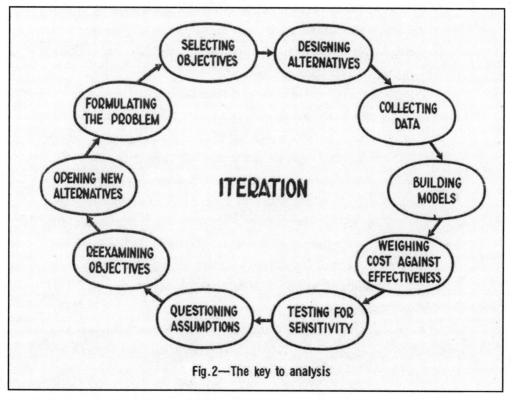

Fig.2—The key to analysis

Figure 2 from Edward Quade's RAND Report P-3322.

separately from each other in order to maximize their efficiency. Along this first meaning, the analysis would focus on a particular figurative or metaphorical system—such as a weapons system, a social system, or, in the case of early counterinsurgency, a colonial system. Second, there was the notion of systematicity that involved a particular type of method—one that began by collecting a set of promising alternatives, constructing a model, and using a defined criterion. This method involved the systematic comparative analysis of different policies, using quantification, algorithms, and metrics. Though they could be distinguished, these two meanings were both integral parts of the systems-analytic approach: the central idea was to systematically select and compare a set of policies to improve a system, and to choose the one that would maximize the functionality of that system.

This method of systems analysis became influential in government and eventually began to dominate governmental logics starting in 1961 when Robert McNamara acceded to the Pentagon under President John F. Kennedy. McNamara's own personal background had included statistical analysis—as a young statistical control officer in the US Air Force during the war in the Pacific and then as an advocate of systems analysis as he rose to the top of the Ford Corporation—and he took it upon himself to propel systems logics at the Pentagon. Systems analysis would be the progenitor of a broader kind of cost-benefit analysis that is today widespread throughout the American administrative state.[9]

Immediately upon taking office in 1961, McNamara imposed systems analysis on military procurement and defense strategy under the name "Planning-Programming-Budgeting System (PPBS) analysis." This first round of expansion—from narrow OR on weapons systems to broader applications of systems analysis to defense strategy—generated a lot of resistance within the military establishment, much of it targeted primarily at the controversial figure of McNamara himself. But, in Quade's opinion, by 1966 "there ha[d] been substantial progress, and the years since 1961 have seen a marked increase in the extent to which analysis of policy and strategy have influenced decisionmakers on the broadest issues of national defense."[10]

President Johnson expanded the reach of systems analysis even further, announcing in a statement to members of his cabinet and heads of federal executive agencies in 1965 that he had directed his budget director, Charles Schultze, to implement the new PPBS method throughout all federal agencies. Johnson emphasized that the new method would "identify national goals with precision and on a continuing basis," help "search for alternative means of reaching those goals most effectively at the least cost," and accurately "measure the performance of programs to insure a dollar's worth of service for each dollar spent." And to make it all work, President Johnson emphasized, would "take good people, the best you now have and the best you can find."[11] (These men came to be known as "the best and the brightest.")

This second round of expansion of systems analysis—from defense strategy to all governmental decision-making—carried the possibility of major repercussions, or, in Edward Quade's words, was "possibly even more radical" than the earlier developments.[12] According to its proponents, systems analysis would allow policy makers to put aside partisan politics, personal preferences, and subjective values. It would pave the way to objectivity and truth. As RAND expert and future secretary of defense James R. Schlesinger explained: "[Systems analysis] eliminates the purely subjective approach on the part of devotees of a program and forces them to change their lines of argument. They must talk about reality rather than morality."[13] With systems analysis, Schlesinger argued, there was no longer any need for politics or value judgments. The right answer would emerge from the machine-model that independently evaluated cost and effectiveness. All that was needed was a narrow and precise objective and good criteria. The model would then spit out the most effective strategy.

The influence of systems analysis has persisted in federal policy making ever since, now often in the guise of what are called "economic impact analyses." A decade after President Johnson embraced PPBS for his entire administration, President Carter's Executive Order 12044 tasked all executive agencies with the duty to conduct economic impact studies of all major government regulations. President Reagan's Executive Order 12291 assigned the responsibility to the Office of Management and Budget, which now oversees and coordinates the economic impact analyses.[14] President Bill Clinton continued in this tradition with his executive order requiring impact analyses of all significant regulations, Executive Order 12866.[15] The recent independent commission report on NSA surveillance, submitted to former president Obama, succinctly recounts the subsequent history of cost-benefit analyses to the present.[16] As the report makes clear, systems analysis continues to influence public policy, even as the method itself is continuously revised.

Counterinsurgency theory blossomed at precisely the moment that systems analysis was, with RAND's backing, gaining influence in the Pentagon and at the White House. The historian Peter Paret pinpoints this moment, in fact, to the very first year of the Kennedy administration: "In 1961, the Cuban revolution combined with the deteriorating Western position in Southeast Asia to shift attention to what was variously called guerrilla, subversive, sublimated, brushfire, and unconventional warfare."[17] Two days before assuming the presidency, on January 18, 1961, Kennedy had already set up a new Special Group, Counterinsurgency (SGCI) to push the military toward modern warfare.[18] In April 1961, Paret tells us, McNamara "asked for a '150 per cent increase in the size of antiguerrilla forces.'" Kennedy would emphasize the new orientation toward unconventional warfare and would soon appoint a dedicated general for special warfare. A newly revised and expanded edition of the field manual for unconventional warfare was issued in 1961. In Paret's words, "a new weapon system was in the making"— and that weapons system was counterinsurgency.[19] A frenzy of activity surrounding counterinsurgency would ensue under the Kennedy administration.

    RAND, of course, was developing all kinds of different military strategies—including nuclear-weapons strategy and policy, and ordinary operations research. But it got in the business of counterinsurgency early and would be one of its greatest advocates. It convened, as mentioned earlier, the seminal counterinsurgency symposium in April 1962, where RAND analysts discovered David Galula and commissioned him to write his memoirs. RAND would publish his memoirs as a confidential classified report in 1963 under the title *Pacification in Algeria 1956–1958*.[20] (RAND would republish the memoirs for the public in 2006—the report was only declassified in 2005[21]—to coincide with the publication of General Petraeus's field manual.) Martin Lee and Bruce Shlain document in their book *Acid Dreams* the important role that RAND played alongside the CIA in developing counterinsurgency tactics, including the "strategies for counterrevolution and pacification that were implemented in Vietnam."[22]

Incidentally, RAND continues to shape counterinsurgency theory with ongoing research and reports, such as for instance RAND analysts David Gompert and John Gordon's 2008 report on *War by Other Means: Building Complete and Balanced Capabilities for Counterinsurgency*. That 518-page report, commissioned by the secretary of defense, was a comprehensive study that drew, in its own words, "on a dozen RAND research papers on specific cases, issues, and aspects of insurgency and COIN" and "included an examination of 89 insurgencies since World War II to learn why and how insurgencies begin, grow, and are resolved."[23] The research is sponsored by the Department of Defense and conducted within the International Security and Defense Policy (ISDP) Center of the RAND National Defense Research Institute, which is described as "a federally funded research and development center sponsored by the Office of the Secretary of Defense, the Joint Staff, the Unified Combatant Commands, the Department of the Navy, the Marine Corps, the defense agencies, and the defense Intelligence Community."[24] (It should come as no surprise that some critics of RAND perceive it as an arm of the Pentagon or the CIA.[25])

Counterinsurgency theory—itself largely incubated at RAND—drew directly on the central insights of the systems-analytic approach. As a result, the synergies remain clear today. General Petraeus's field manual, for instance, made systems analysis one of the main considerations for the design of a successful operation. The manual described the systems-analytic considerations in the following terms:

> *Systems thinking* involves developing an understanding of the relationships within the insurgency and the environment. It also concerns the relationships of actions within the various logical lines of operations. This element is based on the perspective of the systems sciences that seeks to understand the interconnectedness, complexity, and wholeness of the elements of systems in relation to one another.[26]

The key design considerations in the field manual included "model making" and "continuous assessment," both core elements of systems analysis represented in the figures from Edward Quade's RAND Report. The field manual described them in SA terms:[27]

> In *model making,* the model . . . includes operational terms of reference and concepts that shape the language governing the conduct (planning, preparation, execution, and assessment) of the operation.
>
> *Continuous assessment* is essential as an operation unfolds because of the inherent complexity of COIN operations. No design or model completely matches reality. The Object of continuous assessment is to identify where and how the design is working or failing and to consider adjustments to the design and operation.[28]

Drawing on these design considerations, the counterinsurgency model views different strategies as fungible substitutes that need to be evaluated and compared in order to choose rationally the most effective. Monitoring mosques, collecting American telephony metadata, or enhanced interrogations become simply a set of promising alternatives whose effectiveness and costs need to be modeled and assessed against common criteria to determine preferences from among the range of options. Counterinsurgency theory views societies abroad or the population at home as coherent systems and posits their security as the purported objective. Different counterinsurgency strategies—from robot-bombs to digital propaganda—then become the promising alternatives that can be filtered through the systems analysis.

In the counterinsurgency view, the security objective is subdivided into several more defined goals, such as military operations to secure the civilian population, civil services to promote economic development, policing, or intelligence gathering. Each one of these goals then serves as a basis for the systematic comparison of tactics. These tactics might include the deployment of a SWAT team, or a sniper, or the use of a robot-bomb; undersea cable splicing or partnerships with telecoms; or special-operations forces or a drone strike. The tactics are interchangeable, and need to be evaluated and compared based on the criterion of cost, casualties, collateral damage, and reputation, among other things. Everything is evaluated through a systematic lens, and then reevaluated for purposes of continual assessment.

Once again, the figures are telling. The design and iterative process that General Petraeus's field manual set out is actually a mirror image of the RAND systems-analysis model depicted earlier. It simply combined the two graphs—Figures 1 and 2 above—into one visual, Figure 4-2 of the field manual (see Figure on next page).

It is here that we can locate the central logic of counterinsurgency: it is a systems-analytic approach. It is an integrated coherent system. It is neither piecemeal, nor improvised—nor, as we saw in the last chapter, based on a binary model of rule and exception. It is fully *legalized* and *systematized*.

Much of the operational logic of counterinsurgency is classified, and as a result, often difficult to document. However, one gets a strong sense of the systematic approach any time there is leaked information about counterinsurgency strategizing. One recent episode regarding

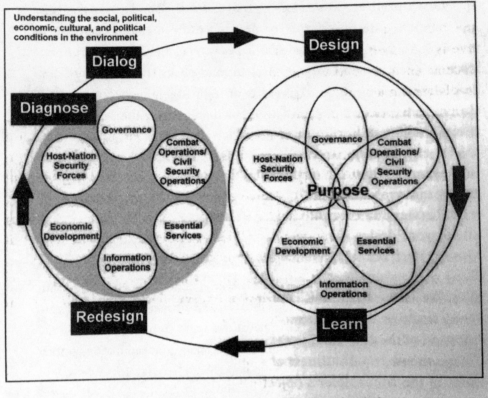

FIGURE 4-2. Iterative counterinsurgency campaign design

Figure 4-2 from General Petraeus's *Counterinsurgency Field Manual.*

interrogation methods is telling. It involved the evaluation of different tactics to obtain information from informants, ranging from truth serums to sensory overload to torture. These alternatives were apparently compared and evaluated using a SA approach at a workshop convened by RAND, the CIA, and the American Psychological Association (APA). Again, the details are difficult to ascertain fully, but the approach seemed highly systems-analytic.

What we know about the workshop comes predominantly from a RAND policy analyst named Scott Gerwehr, who was a behavioral scientist specializing in "deception detection" at RAND, in other words, the study of when people are lying. Gerwehr was also working in some capacity for the CIA.[29] In July 2003, Gerwehr helped organize, along with the CIA and the APA's senior scientist and director of science policy, a series of workshops on "The Science of Deception" sponsored by the three organizations. According to one source, the workshops analyzed different strategies to elicit information, including pharmacological agents "known to affect apparent truth-telling behavior," the "use of 'sensory overloads' to 'overwhelm the senses and see how it affects deceptive behaviors,'" and different forms of torture.[30]

More specifically, according to this source, the workshops probed and compared different strategies to elicit information. The systems-analytic approach is reflected by the set of questions that the participants addressed: How important are differential power and status between witness and officer? What pharmacological agents are known to affect apparent truth-telling behavior? What are sensory overloads on the maintenance of deceptive behaviors? How might we overload the system or overwhelm the senses and see how it affects deceptive behaviors? These questions were approached from a range of disciplines. The workshops were attended by "research psychologists, psychiatrists, neurologists who study various aspects of deception and representatives from the CIA, FBI and Department of Defense with interests in intelligence operations. In addition, representatives from the White House Office of Science and Technology Policy and the Science and Technology Directorate of the Department of Homeland Security were present."[31]

And in effect, from a counterinsurgency perspective, these various tactics—truth serums, sensory overloads, torture—are simply promising alternatives that need to be studied, modeled, and compared to determine which ones are superior at achieving the objective of the security system. Nothing is off limits. Everything is fungible. The only question is systematic effectiveness. This is the systems-analytic approach: not piecemeal, but systematic.

Incidentally, a few years later, Gerwehr apparently went to Guantánamo, but refused to participate in any interrogation because the CIA was not using video cameras to record the interrogations. Following that, in the fall of 2006 and in 2007, Gerwehr made several calls to human-rights advocacy groups and reporters to discuss what he knew. A few months later, in 2008, Gerwehr died of a motorcycle accident on Sunset Boulevard.[32] He was forty years old.

It is, in the end, difficult to document, but what is clear is that systems analysis has had a direct and significant influence on the development of The Counterrevolution.[33]

Counterinsurgency was born of a systems-analytic approach, and as it has been refined, extended, and domesticated, now forms a closed, coherent system. The logic of systems analysis pervades the practices and rhetoric, and has come to infuse, almost subconsciously, much of what has been written about the experience on the ground—for instance, by military officers and soldiers in Iraq and Afghanistan who frequently include offhanded references to "systems," to "military social systems," or simply to "the system."[34]

Even the violence that we might find aberrational—the waterboarding, the drone strikes, the monitoring of mosques—fits neatly within the systems-analytic logic. The counterinsurgency method sanctions any effective strategy—any promising alternative—that achieves the political objective. A comparative analysis of promising strategies was there from the inception. Sometimes, depending on the practitioner, the analysis favored torture or summary execution; at other times, it leaned toward more "decent" tactics. But these variations must now be understood as *internal* to the system. Under President Bush's administration, the emphasis was on torture, indefinite detention, and illicit eavesdropping; under President Obama's, it was on drone strikes and total surveillance; in the first months of the Trump presidency, on special operations, drones, the Muslim ban, and building the wall. What unites these different strategies is counterinsurgency's coherence as a system—a system in which brutal violence is heart and center. That violence is not aberrational or rogue. It is to be expected. It is *internal* to the system. Even torture and assassination are merely variations of the counterinsurgency logic.

Counterinsurgency abroad and at home has been legalized and systematized. It has become our governing paradigm "in any situation," and today "simply expresses the basic tenet of the exercise of political power." It has no sunset provision. It is ruthless, game theoretic, systematic—and legal. And with all of the possible tactics at the government's disposal—from total surveillance to indefinite detention and solitary confinement, to drones and robot-bombs, even to states of exception and emergency powers—this new mode of governing has never been more dangerous.

In sum, The Counterrevolution is our new form of tyranny.

OCKHAM'S RAZOR, OR, RESISTING THE COUNTERREVOLUTION

AT THE HEIGHT OF THE PAPAL INQUISITION IN 1318, THE Franciscan friar William of Ockham was summoned to the papal enclave at Avignon to account for certain theological and political ideas contained in his writings. Suspected of heretical thought, Ockham traveled, as a mendicant, from England to Avignon to face the accusations—at grave risk to himself. He was absolved of those charges, but became embroiled a few years later in another papal quarrel over Franciscan poverty. Ockham ultimately sought refuge in the court of Louis IV of Bavaria, and there penned a short treatise in response to the overreaching, inquisitorial, sovereign power of the Avignon Papacy—but not before writing, in staccato form, while still in Avignon, undaunted and in an insolent rhetoric reminiscent of the Cynics of antiquity, that the series of papal bulls on poverty and Church property were chock full of "*haereticalia, erronea, stulta, ridiculosa, fantastica, insana et diffamatoria*"—"heresies, errors, stupidities, ridiculousness, fantasies, insanities et defamations."[1]

In the short treatise on tyrannical government that ensued—the *Breviloquium de principatu tyrannico*—Ockham fearlessly spoke against the absolute powers that the popes claimed over both theological and secular matters. Boldly, in a frank but insolent tone once again reminiscent of the cynical *parrhesiasts*, the Franciscan declares that "subjects should be warned not to be subjugated more than is strictly necessary."[2] To accept the plenipotentiary power of the pope over temporal matters, Ockham protests, would amount to a form of servitude that would be "truly dreadful and incomparably greater than under ancient law." To fail to actively resist, Ockham declares—at the risk of his very life— would produce not "a realm of freedom," but instead, *the rule of intolerable servitude*."[3]

Not to be governed in this tyrannical fashion. Not to be subjected to a regime of intolerable servitude. That was precisely the reason to reject ancient laws and embrace a new path, which, Ockham adamantly maintained, "represents not a greater servitude, but precisely a lesser servitude" than the earlier regime. "It is evident," Ockham wrote, "that it would simply be wrong to impose a yoke as heavy to bear, or found a bondage as constraining as the laws of our ancestors."[4]

Ockham called, courageously, for less tyrannical subjection: for a political realm in which forms of sovereign power—inevitable though they may be, necessary in certain domains, eternally recurring—would be contained and limited, chastened as much as possible. He called not for a world devoid of subjection—that would not be possible—but one in which the reach of the tyrannical is restricted, limited to the greatest extent possible. Not, as Michel Foucault would remind us more than five hundred years later, a world without government, but one in which we are "not governed *like this*"—referring precisely to those elements of political tyranny, repression, and domination that Foucault witnessed in French president Georges Pompidou's security measures of the early 1970s and analyzed in Cardinal Richelieu's suppression of the *Nu-pieds* peasant rebellions of 1639.[5] And the first step in that direction is to understand, as Ockham underscored, that "subjects cannot be on guard against excessive subjection unless they know what kind and how much power is being exercised on them."[6]

The eternal recurrence of new forms of intolerable servitude, and with them new forms of resistance, reveals that human history—rather than a progressive march toward absolute knowledge, the withering of the state, or the end of history—is a constant struggle over our own subjection, a recurring battle over the making of our own subjectivity, of ourselves as subjects. Once we recognize the perpetual recurrence of this struggle, then and only then will we know our task, for today and for the future: to resist the always encroaching forms of tyrannical power, those violent desires for subjection, the constant and recurring attempts to govern through fear, through terror, through absolute domination.

Today, it is not the inquisitorial theocratic tyranny of Ockham's time that we face, even though the inquisitorial dimensions are not entirely absent. No, what we face today in the West—in the United States and some of its allies—is a new form of governing rooted in a military paradigm of counterrevolutionary war. The very methods and strategies that we developed to contain the colonized other have come back to inflect the way that our government now governs us. We in the West now live, at home, shoulder to shoulder with the insurgent other—*ourselves*—and have started to govern ourselves, at home and abroad, as we brutally and mistakenly learned to govern the colonized others.

Brutal excesses, terror, and tyrannical power dominate the wider political and social realm—whether in the form of sexual humiliation at Abu Ghraib, indefinite detention at Guantánamo Bay, solitary confinement in prisons, surveillance of American mosques, or the fact that our precision drone strikes have, as of April 2017, killed upwards of 200 innocent children outside war zones.[7] The fact that US drones have killed more civilians than high-profile targets and that our policing at home has now become hypermilitarized is precisely the rule of a despotic power. When sitting presidents condone this kind of terrorizing "collateral damage," when our highest public officials justify and legal-ize it, when presidential candidates up the ante—seemingly without consequences—by literally calling for the violent torture of innocent family members of suspected terrorists or the outright ban of Muslims, we need to take heed. Just as we must when some people strap bombs on themselves or mercilessly kill innocent civilians in Beirut, Paris, Istanbul, Orlando, or Baghdad.

This contemporary form of terrorizing tyrannical power is not ex-ceptional, as we know from the tragic history of totalitarianism in the twentieth century, the ghastly record of slavery in the nineteenth, the brutal *supplices* of the eighteenth, and forms of inquisition before then. Just as torture was legislated and legally regulated during the Inquisi-tion, ordeals during the *ancien régime*, and pogroms during the twen-tieth century, The Counterrevolution is firmly within the structure of a rule of law. We simply fail to recognize how manipulable the rule of law can be—we fail to acknowledge the dark side of legality.

In the end, though, the fact that we are not facing an utterly ex-ceptional, but rather a fully coherent and systematic paradigm should neither render us complacent nor resigned, but rather, on the contrary, like William of Ockham, intolerably insolent.

Neither resigned, of course, but not too ambitious or arrogant on the other hand: not too confident or superior to believe that we could re-verse the facticity of social conflict—that we, mere mortals, could here and now end the phenomenon of violence that has marked all known human existence and all known human history. No, we would just as much fail by overreaching.

Another battle in an endless struggle—that is what we face.

William of Ockham understood this well. And so would a long line of women and men who followed in his footsteps, over the ages, and resisted new tyrannous forms of government. Women and men who contested the rule of intolerable servitude, whether in the form of the Inquisition or chattel slavery, of fascism or mass incarceration, of colonialism or of the counterinsurgency practices of torture, summary executions, and total information awareness.

Women and men during the Algerian war like Simone de Beauvoir, Frantz Fanon, Ahmed Ben Bella, or countless others who put themselves at risk to denounce the terror and disappearances—as de Beauvoir reminded us, "The most scandalous part of scandal is the getting used to it."[8] Scholars and historians like Pierre Vidal-Naquet who took his pen and pulpit to denounce counterrevolutionary methods.[9] Conservative thinkers like François Mauriac, Nobel laureate of literature, who famously decried the inquisitorial tactics of the French army.[10] Even government officials such as General Jacques Pâris de Bollardière (himself a torture victim at the hands of the Gestapo) who demanded that he be relieved of his duties in the French army in Algeria in March 1957 when he became aware of the use of torture, and for which he would serve sixty days in prison; or Paul Teitgen, secretary general of the police in Algiers, who resigned his post in September 1957 in protest over the three thousand disappearances.[11]

Women and men in this country like Angela Davis, James Baldwin, Daniel Ellsberg, and countless others who, with great courage and risk to themselves, challenged counterinsurgency practices abroad and their domestication at home. Many Americans before us contested COINTELPRO, the brutal repression of the Black Panthers, the violent excesses at Attica and elsewhere. And many today continue to challenge the excess of counterinsurgency warfare and the domestication of the counterinsurgency—women and men like Linda Sarsour, Alicia Garza, Rachel Herzing, Edward Snowden, Laura Poitras, Glenn Greenwald, and so many others—so many unnamed others—and collectivities, who defy these new forms of tyranny.

There is ongoing resistance. The Black Lives Matter movement, Black Youth Project 100, Critical Resistance, and other groups have challenged the militarization and lethality of the police. United We Dream, the New Sanctuary Coalition NYC, metropolitan cities, and even the state of California have actively challenged the demonization of undocumented residents. The Council on American-Islamic Relations, the American Civil Liberties Union, again even states, such as Washington and Hawaii, have challenged the Muslim ban.

But it is time to see the larger arc of what we are facing. It is critical to understand what exactly we are up against. The militarized policing, the demonization of Muslims and Mexicans, total information awareness—these are all interlocking pieces of a larger phenomenon: The Counterrevolution. We now need to visualize the whole, to see the governing paradigm, in order to translate our activism into a truly effective mobilization.

And in resisting The Counterrevolution, my only hope is that we, and our children too, will be mindful of the words and the courage, and will heed the parrhesia of the friar Ockham.

ACKNOWLEDGMENTS

This book has been enriched and inspired by conversations and exchanges with friends and colleagues, and my only hope is that I will be able to express in person my deep gratitude and the extent of my appreciation. Mia Ruyter has been my constant and treasured interlocutor. Jesús R. Velasco, a brilliant intellectual camarade and critic. Seyla Benhabib, an inspiring and generous mentor. Didier Fassin, an extraordinary critical companion. François Ewald, a constant intellectual force. Steve Bright, a moral compass. And Tom Durkin, an unbending partner.

It has been a privilege to work so closely with Brian Distelberg at Basic Books on this project. Brian has been my most remarkable reader and critic, and has offered superb guidance and advice throughout, for which I am deeply grateful. I also was privileged to receive such generous counsel, feedback, and suggestions from Edward Kastenmeier, for which I am also extremely grateful.

I had the privilege to be at the Institute for Advanced Study (IAS) at Princeton for the 2016–2017 academic year and to discuss these ideas all year long. It was for me a luxury to think about this project with Didier Fassin, Joan Scott, Michael Waltzer, Malcolm Bull, Andrew Dilts, Thomas Dodman, Karen Engle, Peter Goddard, Juan Obarrio, Massimiliano Tomba, Linda Zerilli, and the many other brilliant members from a memorable year at the institute, including Lori Allen, Fadi Bardawil, Nick Cheesman, Marcello Di Bello, Allegra McLeod, Reuben

Miller, Amr Shalakany, and our other friends and colleagues. I also have been extremely fortunate to be so well supported and encouraged at two other exceptional institutions while I worked on this project: Columbia University in New York City and the École des hautes études en sciences sociales (EHESS) in Paris. I am deeply grateful to everyone there who so warmly and generously supported my work, especially Lee Bollinger, Pierre-Cyrille Hautcoeur, Gillian Lester, and David Madigan.

My colleagues at Columbia University, especially David Pozen, Jeremy Kessler, Nadia Urbinati, Sarah Knuckey, Patricia Williams, Rosalind Morris, Jessica Bulman-Pozen, Jameel Jaffer, Sarah Cleveland, Liz Emens, Jeff Fagan, Katherine Franke, Carol Sanger, and Kendall Thomas have been a source of inspiration and guidance, as have my other wonderful colleagues around campus and everyone who attended and critiqued an early sketch at the faculty retreat in September 2015. The students in Jesús Velasco's and my seminar at Columbia University, "From the Inquisition to Guantánamo," especially Kalinka Alvarez, Raphaëlle Burns, Clava Brodsky, Alexandra Cook, Gilles Gressani, Joseph Lawless, Matthew Mautarelli, David Ragazzoni, and many others, also deeply enriched my thinking, for which I am deeply indebted. I would like to extend a special thanks to Joseph Lawless and Anna Krauthamer for all their collaboration and support, especially as the manuscript came together. It has been an honor and a privilege to work with you both on this project.

I have placed this work in the memory of an inspiring teacher, brilliant critical thinker, and exceptional mentor, who inspired me to pursue my theoretical interests and guided me at an early stage of my intellectual journey—Sheldon S. Wolin, an extraordinary man, an inspiring professor, and a deeply generous adviser who encouraged me, early on, to *dire vrai*. I would also like to place this work under the sign of the many women and men with whom I have had the privilege of struggling over the years to resist forms of excess, especially Bryan Stevenson, George Kendall, Randy Susskind, LaJuana Davis,

Brett Dignam, Ruth Friedman, Jim Liebman, Cathleen Price, Azim Ramelize, and our many colleagues; of the many intellectual comrades over the years as well, especially of late Etienne Balibar, Patricia Dailey, Daniel Defert, Bob Gooding-Williams, Daniele Lorenzini, W. J. T. Mitchell, John Rajchman, Judith Revel, Ann Stoler, Michael Taussig, Brandon Terry, and Adam Tooze; and of the wonderful students whose dedication to public service has been, for me, a true inspiration, including most recently Laura Baron, Nika Cohen, Michael Cassel, Maria Teresa LaGumina, Patricio Martinez-Llompart, Jindu Obiofuma, Egon Von Conway, Phoebe Wolfe, and many more.

I dedicate this book to my real teachers, mentors, and heroes, Isadora Ruyter-Harcourt and Léonard Ruyter-Harcourt, with my sincere confidence that you and your generation are now and will continue to heed the call of Ockham's parrhesia.

"The antidote to repression is, simply put, *more resistance.*"
—Kristian Williams,
Life During Wartime: Resisting Counterinsurgency (2013)

NOTES

THE BIRTH OF THE COUNTERREVOLUTION

1. Senate Select Committee on Intelligence, *Committee Study of the Central Intelligence Agency's Detention and Interrogation Program*, approved December 13, 2012, updated for release April 3, 2014, declassification revisions December 3, 2014 (hereafter "Senate Report"), pp. 85 and 87.

2. Senate Report, pp. 90, 40, 42, and 43–44 of "Executive Summary." Regarding the last incident, by the sixth day of the torture, the CIA interrogators believed the detainee had no useful information and none was obtained. Senate Report, pp. 42 and 45–46 of "Executive Summary."

3. Senate Report, pp. 3, 4, 10, 19n4 of "Findings and Conclusions," and pp. 44 and 56 of "Executive Summary"; and see Anthony Lewis, introduction to *The Torture Papers: The Road to Abu Ghraib*, eds. Karen J. Greenberg and Joshua L. Dratel (New York: Cambridge University Press, 2005), xiii–xvi.

4. The Bureau of Investigative Journalism, "YEM178, December 6, 2014," https://www.thebureauinvestigates.com/2014/01/06/yemen-reported-us-covert-actions-2014/#YEM178; and see embedded video here: https://www.thebureauinvestigates.com/2014/01/06/yemen-reported-us-covert-actions-2014/#YEM178.

5. Charlie Savage and Scott Shane, "US Reveals Death Toll from Airstrikes Outside War Zones," *New York Times*, July 1, 2016, http://www.nytimes.com/interactive/2016/07/01/world/document-airstrike-death-toll-executive-order.html; for a full archive surrounding the drone wars, see *The Drone Memos: Targeted Killing, Secrecy, and the Law*, ed. Jameel Jaffer (New York: The New Press, 2016); for theoretical perspectives on drones and air power, see Derek Gregory, "From a View to a Kill: Drones and Late Modern War," *Theory, Culture, and Society* 28, no. 7–8 (2011): 188–215; and Sven Lindqvist, *A History of Bombing*, trans. Linda Haverty Rugg (New York: The New Press, 2001); and for drone-victim statistics as per the Bureau of Investigative Journalism on April

23, 2015, see https://www.thebureauinvestigates.com/2015/04/23/hostage-deaths-mean-38-westerners-killed-us-drone-strikes/.

6. The Bureau of Investigative Journalism, "Drone Warfare," accessed April 23, 2017, https://www.thebureauinvestigates.com/projects/drone-war.

7. Grégoire Chamayou, *A Theory of the Drone*, trans. Janet Lloyd (New York: The New Press, 2015), 14.

8. John Ribeiro, "Secret Court Extends NSA Surveillance Rules with No Changes," *IDG News Service,* December 9, 2014, http://www.pcworld.com/article/2857352/us-court-extends-nsa-surveillance-rules-in-current-form.html; and Office of the Director of National Intelligence, "Joint Statement from the Office of the Director of National Intelligence and the Office of the Attorney General on the Declassification of Renewal of Collection Under Section 501 of the Foreign Intelligence Surveillance Act," IC on the Record, December 8, 2014, http://icontherecord.tumblr.com/post/104686605978/joint-statement-from-the-office-of-the-director-of.

9. Klayman v. Obama, 957 F.Supp.2d 1, at p. 33 (DDC 2013), reversed in Obama v. Klayman, 800 F.3d 559 (DC Cir. 2015).

10. For the most part, these NSA surveillance programs continue unabated. The Section 215 bulk-collection program itself was amended in June 2015 under the USA FREEDOM Act so that the telecommunication companies, rather than the NSA, would hold our personal data and make it available to the government on request. For quotations in paragraph, see Glenn Greenwald, "XKeyscore: NSA Tool Collects 'Nearly Everything a User Does on the Internet,'" *Guardian*, July 31, 2013, http://www.theguardian.com/world/2013/jul/31/nsa-top-secret-program-online-data; Glenn Greenwald and Ewen MacAskill, "NSA Prism Program Taps into User Data of Apple, Google and Others," *Guardian*, June 6, 2013, http://www.theguardian.com/world/2013/jun/06/us-tech-giants-nsa-data; and Glenn Greenwald, *No Place to Hide: Edward Snowden, the NSA, and the U.S. Surveillance State* (New York: Henry Holt, 2014), 153–157.

11. DOI's Inspector General for NYPD, "An Investigation of NYPD's Compliance with Rules Governing Investigations of Political Activity—August 23, 2016," http://www1.nyc.gov/site/oignypd/reports/reports.page.

12. Matt Apuzzo and Adam Goldman, "With CIA Help, NYPD Moves Covertly in Muslim Areas," Associated Press, August 23, 2011, https://web.archive.org/web/20120309020234/https://www.ap.org/pages/about/whatsnew/wn_082511a.html; and "Highlights of AP's Pulitzer Prize–Winning Probe into NYPD Intelligence Operations," Associated Press (with links to stories and documents), https://www.ap.org/about/awards-and-recognition/highlights-of-aps-pulitzer-prize-winning-probe-into-nypd-intelligence-operations.

13. Intelligence Division, Demographics Unit, "Newark, New Jersey Demographics Report," http://hosted.ap.org/specials/interactives/documents/nypd/nypd_newark.pdf.

14. As Ganesh Sitaraman opens his book, *The Counterinsurgent's Constitution: Law in the Age of Small Wars* (New York: Oxford University Press, 2013), 3: "We live in an age of small wars. Around the world, warfare is no longer characterized by amassed armies on pitched battlefields or even by tank battalions maneuvering to break through enemy lines. Rather, insurgents hibernate in the shadows, emerging only when ready for devastating attack."

15. See generally Joshua Bloom and Waldo E. Martin Jr., *Black Against Empire: The History and Politics of the Black Panther Party* (Berkeley: University of California Press, 2014); and Richard Wolin, *The Wind from the East: French Intellectuals, the Cultural Revolution, and the Legacy of the 1960s* (Princeton: Princeton University Press, 2010), 318–321.

16. James Baldwin, quoted in Imani Perry, "*From the War on Poverty to the War on Crime* by Elizabeth Hinton," *New York Times Book Review*, May 27, 2016, http://www.nytimes.com/2016/05/29/books/review/from-the-war-on -poverty-to-the-war-on-crime-by-elizabeth-hinton.html.

17. Sharon Lafraniere, Sarah Cohen, and Richard A. Oppel Jr., "How Often Do Mass Shootings Occur? On Average, Every Day, Records Show," *New York Times*, December 2, 2015, https://www.nytimes.com/2015/12/03/us/how-often -do-mass-shootings-occur-on-average-every-day-records-show.html; Sharon Lafraniere, Daniela Porat, and Agustin Armendariz, "A Drumbeat of Multiple Shootings, but America Isn't Listening," *New York Times*, May 22, 2016, https:// www.nytimes.com/2016/05/23/us/americas-overlooked-gun-violence.html.

18. Philip Rucker, "Trump Touts Recent Immigration Raids, Calls Them a 'Military Operation,'" *Washington Post*, February 23, 2017, https://www .washingtonpost.com/news/post-politics/wp/2017/02/23/trump-touts-recent -immigration-raids-calls-them-a-military-operation/?utm_term= .f99a5615801e.

PART I: THE RISE OF MODERN WARFARE

1. See generally Fred Kaplan, *The Wizards of Armagedon: This Is Their Untold Story* (New York: Simon and Schuster, 1983); S. M. Amadae, *Rationalizing Capitalist Democracy: The Cold War Origins of Rational Choice Liberalism* (Chicago: University of Chicago Press, 2003); Jennifer S. Light, *From Warfare to Welfare: Defense Intellectuals and Urban Problems in Cold War America* (Baltimore: Johns Hopkins University Press, 2003); and Bruce L. R. Smith, *The RAND Corporation: Case Study of a Nonprofit Advisory Corporation* (Cambridge: Harvard University Press, 1966).

2. Roger Trinquier, *Modern Warfare: A French View of Counterinsurgency*, trans. Daniel Lee (New York: Frederick A. Praeger, 1964); and Peter Paret, *French Revolutionary Warfare from Indochina to Algeria: The Analysis of a Political and Military Doctrine*, vol. 6, Princeton Studies in World Politics (New York: Frederick A. Praeger, 1964), 5.

3. See Gérard Chaliand, *Guerrilla Strategies: An Historical Anthology from the Long March to Afghanistan* (Berkeley: University of California Press, 1982), 7 (arguing that Mao was the theorist who essentially invented revolutionary war: "The point is that *guerrilla warfare is a military tactic aimed at harassing an adversary, whereas revolutionary war is a military means whereby to overthrow a political regime*"); and Ann Marlowe, *David Galula: His Life and Intellectual Context*, SSI Monograph, August 2010, p. 27, http://www.strategicstudies institute.army.mil/pubs/display.cfm?pubID=1016. "Mao is crucial for the history of COIN theory," she writes or, more simply, "Mao begot COIN as theory."

4. Richard Stevenson, "President Makes It Clear: Phrase Is 'War on Terror,'" *New York Times*, August 4, 2005, http://www.nytimes.com/2005/08/04/politics /president-makes-it-clear-phrase-is-war-on-terror.html.

1. COUNTERINSURGENCY IS POLITICAL

1. Ganesh Sitaraman *The Counterinsurgent's Constitution: Law in the Age of Small Wars* (New York: Oxford University Press, 2013), 3, 165; and Chaliand, *Guerrilla Strategies*, 1.

2. Peter Paret, "The French Army and *La Guerre Révolutionnaire*," *Journal of the Royal United Service Institution*, February 1, 1959, 59–69; and Peter Paret, *French Revolutionary Warfare*, v.

3. Paret, *French Revolutionary Warfare*, 7; Marnia Lazreg, *Torture and the Twilight of Empire: From Algiers to Baghdad* (Princeton: Princeton University Press, 2008), 19; Marlowe, *David Galula*, 1. For an in-depth analysis of the reception of Mao among French commanders at the time, see Grey Anderson, "Revolutionary Warfare after 1945: Prospects for an Intellectual History," paper presented at the CHESS-ISS Conference, "War and Its Consequences," at Yale University, February 13, 2015 (working paper in author's possession, June 19, 2015).

4. Paret, *French Revolutionary Warfare*, 7.

5. S. M. Chiu, "Chinese Communist Revolutionary Strategy, 1945–1949: Extracts from Volume IV of Mao Tse-tung's *Selected Works*," Center of International Studies, Research Monograph 13, December 15, 1961, p. 45.

6. Ibid., 46.

7. Paret, *French Revolutionary Warfare*, 7.

8. Peter Paret and John W. Shy, *Guerrillas in the 1960's*, vol. 1, Princeton Studies in World Politics, rev. ed. (New York: Frederick A. Praeger, 1962), 39.

9. Paret, *French Revolutionary Warfare*, 10 and 11.

10. Ibid., 12.

11. Paret and Shy, *Guerrillas in the 1960's*, 6–15, 17, and 24n9, referring to T. E. Lawrence, "The Evolution of a Revolt," *The Army Quarterly* 41 (October 1920); and Peter Paret, "Internal War and Pacification: The Vendée, 1789–1796," Research Monograph 12, Center for International Studies, Princeton University, 1961.

12. Paret and Shy, *Guerrillas in the 1960's*, 40–41.

13. Ibid., 41 and 51.

14. Ibid., 45 and 49.

15. See Jean-Jacques Servan-Schreiber, *Lieutenant en Algérie* (Paris: Julliard, 1957); Antoine Argoud, "La guerre psychologique," *Revue de defense nationale* (March/April 1948); and Jean Nemo, "Réflexions sur la guerre subversive," December 30, 1958; cf. Grégor Mathias, *Galula in Algeria: Counterinsurgency Practice versus Theory*, trans. Neal Durando (Santa Barbara, CA: Praeger, 2011), 25–27. On Argoud, see Lazreg, *Torture and the Twilight of Empire*, 88–93.

16. Bernard F. Fall, "A Portrait of the 'Centurion,'" in Trinquier, *Modern Warfare*, xiii and vii; Anderson, "Revolutionary Warfare after 1945."

17. Trinquier, *Modern Warfare*, 6, 4, 35; (emphasis added in final quoted excerpt).

18. For biographical details on David Galula, see Marlowe, *David Galula*; Mathias, *Galula in Algeria*; and A. A. Cohen, *Galula: The Life and Writings of the French Officer Who Defined the Art of Counterinsurgency* (Santa Barbara, CA: Praeger, 2012).

19. David Galula, introduction in *Counterinsurgency Warfare: Theory and Practice* (New York: Frederick A. Praeger, 1964), x; Mathias, *Galula in Algeria*, 7; and Marlowe, *David Galula*, 27.

20. Galula, *Counterinsurgency Warfare*, 56.

21. US Department of the Army, *Counterinsurgency*, Field Manual 3-24 (Washington, DC: US Department of the Army: December 2006) (hereafter "FM"), 35. As his biographer Paula Broadwell writes in *All In: The Education of General David Petraeus*, General Petraeus produced the field manual in 2006 while he was at Fort Leavenworth between tours of duty in Iraq. His field manual would be dubbed "King David's Bible." Paula Broadwell, *All In: The Education of General David Petraeus* (New York: Penguin Press, 2012), 54 and 59. See, generally, Fred Kaplan, *The Insurgents: David Petraeus and the Plot to Change the American Way of War* (New York: Simon & Schuster, 2014).

22. FM, 36.

23. For General Petraeus's twenty-four-point memorandum, which provided guidance to his field manual, see Broadwell, *All In*, 59; and David Galula, *Pacification in Algeria 1956–1958* (1963; repr. Santa Monica: RAND, 2006), 246. See also Galula, *Counterinsurgency Warfare*, 58.

24. Galula, *Pacification in Algeria*, 69; FM, 51; see also FM, 35 ("It is usually not enough for counterinsurgents to get 51 percent of popular support; a solid majority is often essential. However, a passive populace may be all that is necessary for a well-supported insurgency to seize political power"); and David C. Gompert and John Gordon., *War by Other Means: Building Complete and Balanced Capabilities for Counterinsurgency* (Santa Monica: RAND, 2008), 76 ("The people will decide whether the state or the insurgents offer a better future, and to a large extent which of the two will be given the chance").

25. Quoted in Broadwell, *All In,* 59.

26. FM, 41.

27. FM, 39–40, citing Galula, *Counterinsurgency Warfare,* 89 (emphasis added).

28. FM, 53 (quoting Galula, *Counterinsurgency Warfare,* 89) and 68; and FM, 150 (quoting from Sir Robert Thompson, *Defeating Communist Insurgency,* 171). In the University of Chicago Press edition from 2006, the acknowledgements come after the signature and short preface; in the online version, there is the table of contents between them.

29. John A. Nagl, foreword to *The U.S. Army/Marine Corps Counterinsurgency Field Manual* (Chicago: University of Chicago Press, 2007), xix; and Sarah Sewell, introduction to *The U.S. Army/Marine Corps Counterinsurgency Field Manual,* xxiv. Petraeus's field manual "incorporates insight from French counterinsurgency guru David Galula" (Mathias, *Galula in Algeria,* xiii).

30. Petraeus's development of this evaluation is contained in the foreword to the 2008 French translation of Galula's *Counterinsurgency Warfare.* David Petraeus and John Nagl, foreword to *Contre-insurrection: théorie et pratique,* trans. Philippe de Montenon (Paris: Economica, 2008). For further analysis, see Mathias, *Galula in Algeria,* xiii; and A. A. Cohen, *Galula,* xviii–xviii. Many counterinsurgency practitioners and theorists today agree with General Petraeus's assessment of the importance and influence of Galula, including General Stanley A. McChrystal, who commanded all US and NATO forces in Afghanistan from 2009 to 2010; the French general Ollivier, head of the strategic nerve-center of the French army (*Centre de doctrine d'emploi des forces* or CDEF); and the American counterinsurgency expert David H. Ucko. See Mathias, *Galula in Algeria,* xiii and 111n2; Bertrand Valeyre and Alexandre Guérin, "De Galula à Petraeus, l'héritage français dans la pensée américaine de la contre-insurrection," *Cahier de la recherché doctrinale* (June 2009); and David H. Ucko, foreword to *Galula in Algeria* by Grégor Mathias, xi.

31. One would think one was reading the intellectual historian Richard Wolin's book *The Wind from the East: French Intellectuals, the Cultural Revolution, and the Legacy of the 1960s,* tracing the influence of Mao's thought on French intellectuals such as Michel Foucault, Jean-Paul Sartre, Julia Kristeva, Phillipe Sollers, and Jean-Luc Godard. Perhaps we should add to that list General David Petraeus.

32. FM, 7, 11–13, 13, 14, 11, 159, and 258.

33. Mao Zedong letter, August 26, 1945, in *Mao Tse Tung Hsuan Chi* vol. 4 (Peking: Jen Min Chu Pan She, 1960), 1151–154, reproduced in S. M. Chiu, "Chinese Communist Revolutionary Strategy, 1945–1949: Extracts from Volume IV of Mao Tse-tung's *Selected Works,*" Center for International Studies, Research Monograph 13, December 15, 1961, p. 10–11. See also Mao Zedong,

"Questions of Tactics in the Present Anti-Japanese United Front," *Selected Works*, vol. 3 (London: Lawrence & Wishart, Ltd, 1954), 193–203.

34. Chiu, "Chinese Communist Revolutionary Strategy, 1945–1949," 29 and 31.

2. A JANUS-FACED PARADIGM

1. Roger Trinquier, *La guerre moderne* (Paris: La Table Ronde, 1961); Roger Trinquier, *Modern Warfare*; Fall, "A Portrait of the 'Centurion,'" ix; and Machiavelli, *The Prince*, eds. Quentin Skinner and Russell Price (Cambridge: Cambridge University Press, 1988), 59 (modified translation).

2. Trinquier, *Modern Warfare*, 8–9.

3. Ibid., 113 and 115.

4. Ibid., 43, 2 –22, and 23.

5. Fall, "A Portrait of the 'Centurion,'" xv.

6. Général Paul Aussaresses, *Services Spéciaux. Algérie 1955-1957* (Paris: Perrin, 2001); General Paul Aussaresses, *The Battle of the Casbah: Terrorism and Counter-Terrorism in Algeria 1955– 1957* (New York: Enigma Books, 2004); and see also Chaliand, *Guerrilla Strategies*, 29 (emphasis added).

7. Aussaresses, *The Battle of the Casbah*, 13; and Aussaresses, *Services Spéciaux*, 26.

8. Aussaresses, *The Battle of the Casbah*, 128; and Aussaresses, *Services Spéciaux*, 155.

9. Aussaresses, *The Battle of the Casbah*, 19–20; and Aussaresses, *Services Spéciaux*, 34. The following block quote is at 128 (155–156 in original).

10. Benjamin Stora, *Algeria 1830-2000: A Short History*, trans. Jane Marie Todd (Ithaca, NY: Cornell University Press, 2001), 50. Marnia Lazreg, in her meticulously researched book *Torture and the Twilight of Empire*, offers perhaps the most detailed and haunting account of the full ethnography of torture in Algeria. See Lazreg, *Torture and the Twilight of Empire*, 111–169. General Jacques Massu, *The Real Battle of Algiers*, quoted in Michael T. Kaufman, "The World: Film Studies; What Does the Pentagon See in 'Battle of Algiers'?," *New York Times*, September 7, 2003.

11. Aussaresses, *The Battle of the Casbah*, 128; and Aussaresses, *Services Spéciaux*, 155.

12. Aussaresses, *The Battle of the Casbah*, 124 and 126; and Aussaresses, *Services Spéciaux*, 151 and 153.

13. Aussaresses, *The Battle of the Casbah*, 126; and Aussaresses, *Services Spéciaux*, 153.

14. Benjamin Stora, *Algeria 1830-2000*, 50; and see also George Armstrong Kelly, *Lost Soldiers: The French Army and Empire in Crisis, 1947-1962* (Cambridge, MA: MIT Press, 1965), 196–205. For further discussion of torture and

summary executions, see Lazreg, *Torture and the Twilight of Empire*, 53–55; and Richard Wolin, *The Wind from the East*.

15. Aussaresses, *The Battle of the Casbah*, 129 and 130; Aussaresses, *Services Spéciaux*.

16. "Colonel Roger Trinquier : la bataille d'Alger," INA, June 12, 1970, http://www.ina.fr/video/CAF86015674, and on YouTube, https://www.youtube.com/watch?v=JLy_MjvaYhw. Special thanks to Raphaëlle Jean Burns for bringing this to my attention.

17. The leading source to consult here would be Alistair Horne's *A Savage War of Peace—Algeria 1954–62* (New York: New York Review books Classics, 2006). See also Kelly, *Lost Soldiers,* p. 196 and following.

18. Henri Alleg, *The Question*, trans. John Calder (Lincoln, NE: University of Nebraska Press, 2006), 84.

19. Jean-Paul Sartre, preface to *The Question*, by Henri Alleg, xliv.

20. Ibid., xxviii.

21. Geoff Demarest, "Let's Take the French Experience in Algeria Out of US Counterinsurgency Doctrine," *Military Review* (July/August 2010), 24n7, quoting Galula, *Pacification in Algeria*, 183.

22. Galula, *Pacification in Algeria*, 118–119. On p. 118 of the text, it is noted that "Bakouch locked Amar in one of the ovens in the bakery and told him that if he did not talk, he would light a fire under the oven. Within ten minutes Amar was screaming to be let out, and he says he's ready to talk now." On p. 119, Galula writes that, after inspecting the oven, he finds the system "miraculous" and intends to use it; he requests that any persons using the oven should check with him first (not because he had an ethical concern—he explains that he required it so that he could remain in control).

23. Galula, quoted in Mathias, *Galula in Algeria*, 62.

24. Galula, *Pacification in Algeria*, 77 and 103.

25. Demarest, "Let's Take the French Experience," 21, quoting Galula, *Pacification in Algeria*, 262 and 268; and Galula, *Pacification in Algeria*, 258–261. This includes an appendix in Galula's text that contains a meditation on why Galula's efforts had not been as successful as he had predicted, where he discusses his control over the population's movements and his system for rewarding proof of complete loyalty and punishing evidence of disloyalty. Trinquier, *Modern Warfare*, 113.

26. See Gompert and Gordon, *War by Other Means*, 90n8.

27. Fall, "A Portrait of the 'Centurion,'" xiii; Aussaresses, *The Battle of the Casbah*, 164; Aussaresses, *Services Spéciaux*, 196; and Marlowe, *David Galula*, 41 and 42. See also Mathias, *Galula in Algeria*, 99. Aussaresses, Galula, and the academic Bernard Fall lectured at Fort Bragg.

28. Kaufman, "The World: Film Studies."

29. Marlowe, *David Galula*, 7–9 and 14–15; and Stephen T. Hosmer and Sibylle O. Crane, *Counterinsurgency: A Symposium, April 16–20, 1962* (Santa Monica: RAND Corporation, November 1962), xx.

30. Galula, *Counterinsurgency Warfare*. Galula wrote that book while a research associate at the Center for International Affairs at Harvard University between 1962 and 1964. It was published by Frederick A. Praeger, which published over a dozen other monographs on counterinsurgency theory in the early 1960s. Praeger published the Princeton Studies in World Politics series for the Center of International Studies at Princeton University. Peter Paret was a research associate at the Princeton Center for International Studies starting in 1960, and published both *Guerrillas in the 1960's* (with John W. Shy) and *French Revolutionary Warfare from Indochina to Algeria* in the series.

Galula's relationship with RAND continues to the present. In 2006, the RAND Corporation finally openly published Galula's 1963 book, *Pacification in Algeria*, as well as a new edition of the 1962 symposium. See Hosmer and Crane, *Counterinsurgency: A Symposium*. RAND continues to highlight the work of Galula in its own continuing research on counterinsurgency, such as David Gompert and John Gordon's 2008 comprehensive 519-page RAND report, *War by Other Means*.

31. See Mathias, *Galula in Algeria*, 103, discussing Galula's influence in Vietnam, including on Operation PHOENIX. Marlowe reports that "Tennenbaum notes that one of the architects of the Phoenix Program in Vietnam, Nelson Brickham, was 'very taken' by Galula's Counterinsurgency Warfare and carted it all over Vietnam with him" (Marlowe, *David Galula*, 15). However, Marlowe sees less of an influence overall. See Marlowe, *David Galula*, 14.

32. Paret, *French Revolutionary Warfare*, 66–76.

33. Paret and Shy, *Guerrillas in the 1960's*, 47.

34. Paret, *French Revolutionary Warfare*, 73 and 74.

35. FM, 252.

36. Broadwell, *All In*, 204 and 205.

37. Demarest, "Let's Take the French Experience," 19.

38. US Department of the Army, *Insurgencies and Countering Insurgency*, Field Manual 3-24, MCWP 3-33.5 (Washington, DC: US Department of the Army: May 2014); and Anderson, "Revolutionary Warfare after 1945," 22.

PART II: A TRIUMPH IN FOREIGN POLICY

1. Andy Müller-Maguhn et al., "Treasure Map: The NSA Breach of Telekom and Other German Firms," *Der Spiegel*, September 14, 2014, http://www.spiegel .de/international/world/snowden-documents-indicate-nsa-has-breached -deutsche-telekom-a-991503.html.

2. FM, 41.

3. As many commentators note, counterinsurgency theory is often divided into "enemy-centric" and "population-centric" approaches. See, for example, Sitaraman, *The Counterinsurgent's Constitution*, 5. I argue that both are dimensions of counterinsurgency theory.

4. FM, 41; and Sitaraman, *The Counterinsurgent's Constitution*, 5 and 149.

5. FM, 49.

6. As the historian Edgar O'Ballance writes of the war in Algeria, "one can say briefly that from a military point of view the war in Algeria was lost by the insurgents, but that they won it by political and diplomatic means," Edgar O'Ballance, *The Algerian Insurrection, 1954–62* (Hamden, CT: Archon Books, 1967), 220.

7. FM, 37 and 39.

8. Michael Hayden, *Playing to the Edge: American Intelligence in the Age of Terror* (New York: Penguin Books, 2016).

9. FM, 51.

3. TOTAL INFORMATION AWARENESS

1. See generally National Commission on Terrorist Attacks Upon the United States, *The 9/11 Commission Report* (2004), https://www.9-11commission.gov/report/911Report.pdf; and Richard Posner, *Preventing Surprise Attacks: Intelligence Reform in the Wake of 9/11* (Lanham, MD: Rowman & Littlefield, 2005).

2. James Bamford, *The Shadow Factory: The NSA from 9/11 to the Eavesdropping on America* (New York: Anchor Books, 2009), 102; and Daniel Solove, *Nothing to Hide: The False Tradeoff Between Privacy and Security* (New Haven: Yale University Press, 2011), 183–185.

3. David Cole, "Can the NSA Be Controlled?" *The New York Review of Books*, June 19, 2014, 17, http://www.nybooks.com/articles/archives/2014/jun/19/can-nsa-be-controlled.

4. Dan Eggen and Paul Kane, "Gonzales Hospital Episode Detailed," *Washington Post*, May 16, 2007, http://www.washingtonpost.com/wp-dyn/content/article/2007/05/15/AR2007051500864.html; and Bernard E. Harcourt, *Exposed: Desire and Disobedience in the Digital Age* (Cambridge, MA: Harvard University Press, 2015).

5. Gompert and Gordon, *War by Other Means*, 137 and 137n25. For a fascinating early instance of a RAND and Pentagon project to obtain total information awareness about a population, listen to Malcolm Gladwell, "Saigon 1965," *Revisionist History* (podcast), season 1, episode 2, http://revisionisthistory.com/seasons.

6. Anthony Lewis, introduction to *The Torture Papers*, xiii–xvi.

7. Senate Report, 53, 54, and 69.

8. Senate Report, 77.

9. Marie-Monique Robin, *Escadrons de la mort, l'école française* (Paris: La Découverte, 2004), 55.

10. Senate Report, 77, 30–31, and 33.

11. Ibid., 35.

12. Ibid.

13. Ibid., 18.

14. Ibid., 18, 22, and 23.

15. Ibid., 36, 36–37 (emphasis added), and 38.

16. Ibid., 118.

17. Ibid., 69–70 (gun and drill incidents resulted in the CIA officer and chief of base being disciplined, see Senate Report, 70), 117 ("placing a broom handle behind the knees of a detainee while that detained was in a stress position" resulting in decertification of interrogator), 76 (interrogation plan for Ramzi bin al-Shibh, which becomes template), and 81–82 (interrogation plan for Khalid Sheikh Muhammad).

18. Ibid., 115–116.

19. Karen J. Greenberg and Joshua L. Dratel, eds., *The Torture Papers: The Road to Abu Ghraib* (New York: Cambridge University Press, 2005), 134–135 and 122.

20. Ibid., 119–120.

21. Ibid., 122 and 222.

22. Ibid., 213–214 (emphasis added).

23. Ibid., 227–228, 237, and 360–361.

24. Though these metaphors of ticking time-bombs are themselves so misleading and mask the reality of torture. See generally Michelle Farrell, *The Prohibition of Torture in Exceptional Circumstances* (Cambridge, UK: Cambridge University Press, 2013).

25. Reproduced in Lu Ann Homza, *The Spanish Inquisition, 1478–1614: An Anthology of Sources* (Indianapolis: Hackett Publishing Company, 2006), 45–46. See also the notary's description of the use of the rack and water torture in the case against María González in Toledo in 1513, reproduced in Homza, *The Spanish Inquisition*, 56–57.

26. See, for example, Greenberg and Dratel, eds., *The Torture Papers*, 229.

27. See, for example, Gompert and Gordon, *War by Other Means*, 6 and following; and Sitaraman, *The Counterinsurgent's Constitution*, 35–38.

28. However, I do not go as far as Marnia Lazreg who suggests, in her book *Torture and the Twilight of Empire*, that torture is the *direct and necessary* outcome of modern warfare theory or that it "could not be implemented successfully without its [torture's] use." Marnia Lazreg, *Torture and the Twilight of Empire*, 15; see also p. 3. Under certain variations of counterinsurgency theory, torture can be avoided and replaced by substitutes such as psychological methods or drone strikes. That does not, however, redeem counterinsurgency theory. It merely represents different styles of modern warfare.

29. Laleh Khalili, *Time in the Shadows: Confinement in Counterinsurgencies* (Stanford: Stanford University Press, 2013).

4. INDEFINITE DETENTION AND DRONE KILLINGS

1. Mohamedou Ould Slahi, *Guantánamo Diary*, ed. Larry Siems (New York: Back Bay Books, 2015), 29–30.

2. Ibid.

3. Ibid.

4. Slahi, *Guantánamo Diary*, 31–32.

5. The continuities in the treatment of detained suspects throughout the history of counterinsurgencies is analyzed in depth in Khalili, *Time in the Shadows*.

6. Giorgio Agamben, *Homo Sacer: Sovereign Power and Bare Life*, trans. Daniel Heller-Roazen (Stanford: Stanford University Press, 1998) 114.

7. Jenifer Fenton, "Freed Guantanamo Detainees: Where are they now?" *Aljazeera*, January 11, 2016, http://www.aljazeera.com/indepth/features/2016/01/released-guantanamo-bay-detainees-160110094618370.html; and Noah Rayman, Where Are All Those Freed Guantanamo Detainees Now?" *Time*, December 8, 2014, http://time.com/3624445/guantanamo-detainees-uruguay/.

8. Andrew Taylor, "Speaker: Legal Steps to Stop Obama from Closing Guantánamo," *US News & World Report*, February 24, 2016, https://www.usnews.com/news/politics/articles/2016-02-24/speaker-legal-steps-to-stop-obama-from-closing-guantanamo.

9. Tom Kludt, "Gitmo Diary Cracks Amazon's Top-Sellers List," CNN: Media, January 21, 2015, http://money.cnn.com/2015/01/20/media/guantanamo-diary-mohamedou-ould-slahi-aclu/; "*Guantánamo Diary*," Little, Brown and Company, accessed May 10, 2017, http://www.littlebrown.com/guantanamo.html; "Zero Dark Thirty," Box Office Mojo, accessed May 10, 2017, http://www.boxofficemojo.com/movies/?id=binladen.htm. The film has grossed over $132,800,000 in box-office revenues, which, at an average movie ticket of $8.15 (the national average at the time) would mean more than sixteen million tickets sold.

10. Slavoj Žižek, "Zero Dark Thirty: Hollywood's Gift to American Power," *Guardian*, January 25, 2013, https://www.theguardian.com/commentisfree/2013/jan/25/zero-dark-thirty-normalises-torture-unjustifiable.

11. Chamayou, *A Theory of the Drone*, 46.

12. The Bureau of Investigative Journalism, "Drone Warfare," accessed April 23, 2017, https://www.thebureauinvestigates.com/projects/drone-war.

13. Ken Dilanian, Courtney Kube, and William M. Arkin, "US Launches Airstrikes in Yemen," NBC News, March 2, 2017, http://www.nbcnews.com/news/us-news/u-s-launches-air-strikes-yemen-n728186.

14. Murtaza Hussain, "US Has Only Acknowledged a Fifth of Its Lethal Strikes, New Study Finds," *The Intercept*, June 13, 2017, https://theintercept.com/2017/06/13/drone-strikes-columbia-law-human-rights-yemen/; Alex Moorehead and Waleed Alhariri, "US Secrecy and Transparency in the Use of Lethal Force," *Just Security*, June 13, 2017, https://www.justsecurity.org/42059/u-s-secrecy-transparency-lethal-force/.

15. Chamayou, *A Theory of the Drone*, 64.

16. David Kilcullen and Andrew McDonald Exum, "Death from Above, Outrage Down Below," *New York Times*, May 16, 2009, http://www.nytimes.com /2009/05/17/opinion/17exum.html. Also cited in Chamayou, *A Theory of the Drone*, 65.

17. Chamayou, *A Theory of the Drone*, 62.

18. Ibid., 12.

19. Kilcullen and Exum, "Death from Above, Outrage Down Below."

20. US Director of National Intelligence, "Summary of Information Regarding US Counterterrorism Strikes Outside Areas of Active Hostilities," https://content .govdelivery.com/attachments/USODNI/2016/07/01/file_attachments/579487/ DNI%2BRelease%2Bon%2BCT%2BStrikes%2BOutside%2BAreas%2Bof%2BAc-tive%2BHostilities_FINAL.PDF; Office of the Press Secretary, "Executive Order on the US Policy on Pre & Post-Strike Measures," The White House, Statements and Releases, July 1, 2016, https://www.whitehouse.gov/the-press-office/2016/07 /01/fact-sheet-executive-order-us-policy-pre-post-strike-measures-address; and Charlie Savage and Scott Shane, "US Reveals Death Toll From Airstrikes Outside War Zones," *New York Times*, July 1, 2016, http://www.nytimes.com/2016/07/02/ world/us-reveals-death-toll-from-airstrikes-outside-of-war-zones.html.

21. Savage and Shane, "US Reveals Death Toll."

22. Jack Serle, "Obama Drone Casualty Numbers a Fraction of Those Recorded by the Bureau Comments," Bureau of Investigative Journalism, July 1, 2016, https://www.thebureauinvestigates.com/2016/07/01/obama-drone -casualty-numbers-fraction-recorded-bureau/; Savage and Shane, "US Reveals Death Toll" and Greg Miller, "Why the White House Claims on Drone Casualties Remain in Doubt," *Washington Post*, July 1, 2016, https://www .washingtonpost.com/world/national-security/why-the-white-house-claims-on -drone-casualties-remain-in-doubt/.

23. "Out of the Shadows: Recommendations to Advance Transparency in the Use of Lethal Force," Columbia Law School Human Rights Clinic and Sana'a Center for Strategic Studies, June 2017, https://www.outoftheshadowsreport .com/#new-page; and Hussain, "US Has Only Acknowledged a Fifth of Its Lethal Strikes."

24. "Strikes in Afghanistan," the Bureau of Investigative Journalism, https:// www.thebureauinvestigates.com/projects/drone-war/charts?show_casualties =1&show_injuries=1&show_strikes=1&location=afghanistan&from=2015-1 -1&to=now.

25. Kilcullen and Exum, "Death from Above, Outrage Down Below."

26. Henry Barnes, "'The PTSD Stems from This Dirty Work': New Film Documents Regretful Drone Pilots," *Guardian*, February 15, 2016, https://www.the guardian.com/film/2016/feb/15/sonia-kennebeck-us-air-force-drone-war-home -roost. Hugh Gusterson examines the questions of proximity and distance in remote killings in his book, *Drone: Remote Control Warfare* (Cambridge, MA: MIT Press, 2016).

27. Eric Fair, "An Interrogator's Nightmare," *Washington Post*, February 9, 2007, http://www.washingtonpost.com/wp-dyn/content/article/2007/02/08/AR2007020801680.html; and Eric Fair, *Consequence: A Memoir* (New York: Henry Holt and Company, 2016).

28. Eric Fair, "Owning Up to Torture," *New York Times*, March 19, 2016, http://www.nytimes.com/2016/03/20/opinion/sunday/owning-up-to-torture.html.

29. For a few, see Eric Fair on *Democracy Now*, https://youtu.be/2oGh93UnxQg and https://youtu.be/VRQzf2QcidA, or the drone operators on *Democracy Now*, https://youtu.be/S6sqUJaxMdM and https://youtu.be/ArlvkgvfvgA.

30. Chamayou, *A Theory of the Drone*, 16, 15, and 177.

31. Theodor Adorno, *Minima Moralia: Reflections on a Damaged Life* (1944; repr. London: Verso, 2005); discussed also in Chamayou, *A Theory of the Drone*, 205.

32. See Chris Woods and Jack Serle, "Hostage Deaths Mean 38 Westerners Killed by US Drone Strikes, Bureau Investigation Reveals," Bureau of Investigative Journalism, April 23, 2015, https://www.thebureauinvestigates.com/2015/04/23/hostage-deaths-mean-38-westerners-killed-us-drone-strikes/.

5. WINNING HEARTS AND MINDS

1. Trinquier, *Modern Warfare*, 105; and FM, 35.

2. Rosa Brooks, *How Everything Became War and the Military Became Everything: Tales from the Pentagon* (New York: Simon & Schuster, 2016), 344, 341, and 14.

3. See generally chap. 2 in Mathias, *Galula in Algeria*, which details what Galula actually did in Djebel Aïssa Mimoun, Algeria.

4. FM, 54–55.

5. FM, 98; and see also Sitaraman, *The Counterinsurgent's Constitution*, 11 and 38. "Economically, counterinsurgents seek a stable environment that fosters reconstruction and development projects. Socially, counterinsurgents provide essential services, like water, sewage, and trash, and they represent local religious and cultural customs" (Sitaraman, 11).

6. Peter Baker, "Trump Chooses H. R. McMaster as National Security Adviser," *New York Times*, February 20, 2017, https://www.nytimes.com/2017/02/20/us/politics/mcmaster-national-security-adviser-trump.html; see also FM, 375; and "Clear-Hold-Build in Tal Afar, 2005–2006: Office of the Assistant Secretary of Defense (Public Affairs)," news briefing with Col. H. R. McMaster, January 27, 2006.

7. FM, 183–184.

8. Galula, *Counterinsurgency Warfare*, 78.

9. Quoted in Broadwell, *All In*, 59 and 61–62.

10. Broadwell, *All In*, 62.

11. Matthieu Aikins, "The Bidding War," *New Yorker*, March 7, 2016, http://www.newyorker.com/magazine/2016/03/07/the-man-who-made-millions-off

-the-afghan-war; and Alissa J. Rubin, "Afghan Commander Issues Rules on Contractors," *New York Times*, September 12, 2010, http://www.nytimes.com /2010/09/13/world/13petraeus.html.

12. Aikins, "The Bidding War."

13. Ibid.

14. Ibid.

15. Ibid.; Broadwell, *All In*, 77–79; and Rubin, "Afghan Commander Issues Rules on Contractors."

16. Chaliand, *Guerrilla Strategies*, 29; Marnia Lazreg, *Torture and the Twilight of Empire*, 58. In this regard, it is interesting to note that after his command in Algeria, David Galula spent several years working on radio counterpropaganda through the "Psychological Action Branch" of the French Ministry of Defense. See chap. 5 in Mathias, *Galula in Algeria*.

17. Kimberly Dozier, "Anti-ISIS-Propaganda Czar's Ninja War Plan: We Were Never Here," *The Daily Beast*, March 15, 2016, http://www.thedailybeast .com/articles/2016/03/15/obama-s-new-anti-isis-czar-wants-to-use-algorithms -to-target-jihadis.html.

18. For further commentary on Target's ability to digitally identify newly pregnant women, see Harcourt, *Exposed*, 124, 194, and 246; and see also Dozier, "Anti-ISIS-Propaganda Czar's Ninja War Plan."

19. Dozier, "Anti-ISIS-Propaganda Czar's Ninja War Plan."

20. Ibid.

21. Ibid.

22. Ibid.

23. Galula, *Pacification in Algeria*, 102.

24. Dozier, "Anti-ISIS-Propaganda Czar's Ninja War Plan."

25. See Aussaresses, *Services Spéciaux*; and Aussaresses, *The Battle of the Casbah*.

26. General Massu, *The Real Battle of Algiers*, quoted in Kaufman, "The World: Film Studies."

6. GOVERNING THROUGH TERROR

1. Trinquier, *Modern Warfare*, 113.

2. The idea of governing through terror that I develop in this chapter is indebted to Foucault's writings on governmentality, as well as Ian Hacking's, and to Jonathan Simon's brilliant book about governing techniques in the war on crime, *Governing Through Crime* (New York: Oxford University Press, 2006).

3. Alleg, *The Question*, 38, 41, and 47.

4. Page duBois, *Torture and Truth* (New York: Routledge, 1991), 152 and 7.

5. Ibid., 64 and 65.

6. Ibid., 35.

7. Not that the Visigoths did not use torture. They too had rules and norms surrounding the use of torture—perhaps even more "responsibilizing" rules

and norms, regulations that imposed greater responsibility on the person who was using torture. See Robert Burns's summary of Visigothic regulations, of particular interest here, in *Las Siete Partidas*, ed. Robert I. Burns, trans. Samuel Parsons Scott (Philadelphia: University of Pennsylvania Press, 2000) (hereafter "LSP"), 1462; and see also Jesús R. Velasco, *Dead Voice* (Philadelphia: University of Pennsylvania Press, forthcoming).

8. LSP, 1459, 650, and 1459–1460. The liability warnings are particularly interesting. As Homza writes, "Inquisitors explicitly warned defendants that any injuries they suffered during torture would be their own fault" (Homza, *The Spanish Inquisition*, xxv). We read this in every case of torture. So, for instance, again in the case of Marina González tried in Toledo in 1494, the inquisitors "said that if during the torture some evil, damage, wound, or death occurred to her, it would be her fault and not theirs" (Homza, *The Spanish Inquisition*, 45). Or, in the case of María González in Toledo in 1513, the inquisitors emphasized that "if she should receive death, a wound, or the loss of some limb during the torture, it would be her own fault" (Homza, *The Spanish Inquisition*, 55). By contrast, responsibility seemed to fall on the inquisitor in the *Partidas*.

9. Homza, *The Spanish Inquisition*, xiii–xiv and 64–79.

10. Ibid., xiv; and LSP, 1462n.

11. Emmanuel Le Roy Ladurie, *Montaillou: The Promised Land of Error* (New York: Vintage Books, 1978), xiv and xv.

12. See, generally, Karen J. Greenberg, *Rogue Justice: The Making of the Security State* (New York: Crown Publishers, 2016), 174–182.

13. Bob v. State, 32 Ala. 560, 562 (1858).

14. Mose v. State, 36 Ala. 211, 226 (1860).

15. State v. Clarissa, 11 Ala. 57 (1847), see pp. 61 and 61–62.

16. Ibid., 62.

17. As the Alabama Supreme Court explained, the slaveholder had an "interest to prevent a conviction, the consequence of which would be, the certain loss of one half his value, and the possible loss of his entire value." The State v. Marshall, 8 Ala. 302, 307 (1845).

18. The jailor, McGehee, told the slave, Bob, while he was detained in the county jail: "Bob you are a fool; you had better confess your guilt; everybody around here believes you are guilty; and you ought to know that it would be better for you to confess, and for your master to have your value in his pocket, than for you to have your neck broke, and he have no money for you." Bob v. State, 32 Ala. 560, 562–563 (June 1858).

19. Flag of the Union, December 7, 1842.

20. See generally Bernard E. Harcourt, "Imagery and Adjudication in the Criminal Law: The Relationship Between Images of Criminal Defendants and Ideologies of Criminal Law in Southern Antebellum and Modern Appellate Decisions," *Brooklyn Law Review* 61 (1995): 1206–214.

21. Feodor Dostoevsky, "The Grand Inquisitor," trans. Helena Blavatsky (1881; repr. Project Gutenberg, 2005), https://www.gutenberg.org/files/8578/8578-h/8578-h.htm.

22. Ashley Parker and Maggie Haberman, "Donald Trump, After Difficult Stretch, Shows a Softer Side," *New York Times*, April 20, 2016, http://www.nytimes.com/2016/04/21/us/politics/donald-trump-interview.html; Alex Myers, "Donald Trump Compares Winning Presidential Primaries to Winning Club Championships," *GolfDigest*, March 6, 2016, http://www.golfdigest.com/story/donald-trump-compares-winning-presidential-primaries-to-winning-club-championships; and Ian Schwartz, "Trump: 'We Will Have So Much Winning If I Get Elected That You May Get Bored with Winning,'" *RealClear-Politics*, September 9, 2015, http://www.realclearpolitics.com/video/2015/09/09/trump_we_will_have_so_much_winning_if_i_get_elected_that_you_may_get_bored_with_winning.html.

23. Richard C. Paddock, "Becoming Duterte: The Making of a Philippine Strongman," *New York Times*, March 21, 2017, https://www.nytimes.com/2017/03/21/world/asia/rodrigo-duterte-philippines-president-strongman.html.

24. Ibid.

25. Alleg, *The Question*, 81–82.

26. Ibid., 82.

27. Marnia Lazreg, "Women: Between Torture and Military Feminism," *Torture and the Twilight of Empire*, 145–169.

28. Alleg, *The Question*, 68 and 85.

29. Ibid., 93.

30. Ibid.

31. Jean-Paul Sartre, preface to *The Question*, by Henri Alleg, xxxi and xliii.

32. Alleg, *The Question*, 96.

33. Ibid. (emphasis added).

34. Sartre, preface to *The Question*, xliii.

35. Lazreg, *Torture and the Twilight of Empire*, 155.

36. Ibid., 268.

37. James Baldwin, "Here Be Dragons or Freaks and the American Ideal of Manhood" (1985), reprinted in Rudolph P. Byrd and Beverly Guy-Sheftall, eds., *Traps: African American Men on Gender and Sexuality* (Bloomington: Indiana University Press, 2001), 212.

38. Ibid., 208.

39. Jean-Paul Sartre, preface to *The Wretched of the Earth*, by Franz Fanon, trans. Richard Philcox (New York: Grove Press, 2004), 36.

40. Cf. Moustafa Bayoumi, *This Muslim American Life: Dispatches from the War on Terror* (New York: New York University Press, 2015), which traces the history of the racialization of Islam since the late nineteenth century in America.

41. Agamben, *Homo Sacer*, 114 and 154.

42. Ibid. 184–185 and 185.

43. Ibid., 8.

44. This is not to deny, in any way, the rich human lives that resist this bare life. While Agamben is surely right that the camp functions to dehumanize, it is important for us never to stop seeing and writing about the complexity of the lived experience and will to life in these situations. When we speak of "bare life," we almost inhabit the worldview of the Nazi leadership or the prison warden. But the concept of "bare life" always does injustice to the humanity of the victim. That may be its function, though ours is to resist. As an ethical matter, it is urgent that we resist the nudity of bare life. In other words, it is essential never to treat life ever as mere existence and instead, to always seek to find, in that nudity, the complexity of life. See, e.g., Banu Bargu, *Starve and Immolate: The Politics of Human Weapons* (New York: Columbia University Press, 2014).

45. Adriana Cavarero, *Horrorism: Naming Contemporary Violence* (New York: Columbia University Press, 2009). With more time and space, it would of course be crucial to develop the contributions of, among others, Allen Feldman, *Archives of the Insensible: Of War, Photopolitics, and Dead Memory* (Chicago: University of Chicago Press, 2015); Achille Mbembe, "Necropolitics," *Public Culture* 15 (2003): 11–40; Orlando Patterson, *Slavery and Social Death: A Comparative Study* (Cambridge, MA: Harvard University Press, 1982); Elaine Scarry, *The Body in Pain: The Making and Unmaking of the World* (New York: Oxford University Press, 1987); and Alexander G. Weheliye, *Habeas Viscus: Racializing Assemblages, Biopolitics, and Black Feminist Theories of the Human* (Durham, NC: Duke University Press, 2014), who have all contributed importantly to these debates.

46. See Michel Foucault, *Théories et institutions pénales. Cours au Collège de France. 1971– 1972* (Paris: Gallimard/Le Seuil, 2015).

47. Heather Ann Thompson, *Blood in the Water: The Attica Prison Uprising of 1971 and Its Legacy* (New York: Pantheon Books, 2016).

48. Jean-Paul Sartre, *Critique of Dialectical Reason*, trans. Alan Sheridan-Smith (London: Verso, 1991), 43; see also Sartre, preface to *The Wretched of the Earth*; and Wolin, *The Wind from the East*.

49. Dostoevsky, "The Grand Inquisitor."

PART III: THE DOMESTICATION OF COUNTERINSURGENCY

1. For background on Anwar al-Awlaki, see Scott Shane, "The Lessons of Anwar al-Awlaki," *New York Times*, August 27, 2015, http://www.nytimes.com /2015/08/30/magazine/the-lessons-of-anwar-al-awlaki.html; Adam Taylor, "The US Keeps Killing Americans in Drone Strikes, Mostly by Accident," *Washington Post*, April 23, 2015, https://www.washingtonpost.com/news/ worldviews/wp/2015/04/23/the-u-s-keeps-killing-americans-in-drone-strikes -mostly-by-accident/; and Michael Boyle and Hina Shamsi, "Killing Americans

Abroad: Is the Obama Administration Justified?", Al Jazeera America, June 24, 2014, http://america.aljazeera.com/watch/shows/inside-story/articles/2014/6/24 /drones-memo-releasewastheobamaadministrationjustified.html.

2. Memorandum from David J. Barron to the attorney general, US Department of Justice, July 16, 2010, https://www.aclu.org/sites/default/files/assets /2014-06-23_barron-memorandum.pdf; and Spencer Ackerman, "US Cited Controversial Law in Decision to Kill American Citizen by Drone," *Guardian*, June 23, 2014, http://www.theguardian.com/world/2014/jun/23/us-justification -drone-killing-american-citizen-awlaki.

3. Jonathan Masters, "Targeted Killings," Council of Foreign Relations, updated May 23, 2013, http://www.cfr.org/counterterrorism/targeted-killings/ p9627. The ACLU filed two lawsuits challenging the drone killings of al-Awlaki. The first was dismissed because the federal district court held that the plaintiff lacked standing and the case raised political questions. The second was dismissed because the federal district court held that there was no implied right of action for the plaintiff to bring a *Bivens* claim. See Al Aulaqi v. Panetta, Center for Constitutional Rights, June 29, 2015, https://ccrjustice.org/home/what-we -do/our-cases/al-aulaqi-v-panetta; and "Al-Aulaqi v. Panetta—Constitutional Challenge to Killings of Three US Citizens," ACLU, June 4, 2014, https://www .aclu.org/cases/al-aulaqi-v-panetta-constitutional-challenge-killing-three-us -citizens. The ACLU and the *New York Times* also filed suits to force the government to release documents containing the legal justifications for al-Awlaki's killing, resulting in the release of the July 16, 2010, memorandum. See Devlin Barrett and Siobhan Gorman, "US Memo Outlines Rationale for Drone Strikes on Citizens," *Wall Street Journal*, June 26, 2014, http://www.wsj.com/articles/u-s -can-kill-citizens-abroad-under-certain-circumstances-memo-says -1403542004. For reactions to rationale, see Ackerman, "US Cited Controversial Law"; and interview of David Sedney in Boyle and Shamsi, "Killing Americans Abroad: Is the Obama Administration Justified?," Al Jazeera America, June 24, 2014, http://america.aljazeera.com/watch/shows/inside-story/articles/2014/6/24 /drones-memo-releasewastheobamaadministrationjustified.html.

4. Masters, "Targeted Killings."

5. As per the Bureau of Investigative Journalism on April 23, 2015, see Woods and Serle, "Hostage Deaths Mean"; and Adam Taylor, "The US Keeps Killing Americans."

6. Adam Baron, "US Drone Strikes Came Despite Yemen's Hopes to Limit Them," April 24, 2014, http://www.mcclatchydc.com/news/nation-world/world /middle-east/article24766561.html; Taylor, "The US Keeps Killing Americans"; Craig Whitlock et al., "Obama Apologizes for Attack That Killed Two Hostages," *Washington Post*, April 23, 2015, https://www.washingtonpost.com/ world/national-security/us-operation-kills-al-qaeda-hostages-including -american/2015/04/23/8e9fcaba-e9bd-11e4-aae1-d642717d8afa_story.html; and Mark Mazzetti, "Killing of Americans Deepens Debate Over Use of Drone

Strikes Abroad," *New York Times*, April 23, 2015, http://www.nytimes.com/2015 /04/24/world/asia/killing-of-americans-deepens-debate-over-proper-use-of -drone-strikes.html.

7. Sewell Chan and Kimiko de Freytas-Tamura, "Pentagon Says 'Jihadi John' Was Probably Killed in Airstrike," *New York Times*, November 13, 2015, http:// www.nytimes.com/2015/11/14/world/europe/jihadi-john-mohammed-emwazi -david-cameron-statement.html; Adam Goldman et al., "US Strike Believed to Have Killed 'Jihadi John,' Islamic State Executioner," *Washington Post*, November 13, 2015, https://www.washingtonpost.com/world/national-security/us -drone-strike-targeted-jihadi-john-the-briton-linked-to-hostage-beheadings /2015/11/13/8d58595c-89df-11e5-be39-0034bb576eee_story.html; and Prime Minister David Cameron, as quoted in Chan and de Freytas-Tamura, "Pentagon Says."

8. Nash Jenkins, "German Rapper Who Joined ISIS Killed in US Air Strike in Syria," *Time*, October 30, 2015, http://time.com/4093945/denis-cuspert-deso -dogg-isis/; Christine Hauser, "Pentagon Says Deso Dogg, Ex-Rapper and ISIS Recruiter, Survived Airstrike After All," *New York Times*, August 3, 2016, http:// www.nytimes.com/2016/08/04/world/pentagon-says-isis-recruiter-survived -airstrike-in-2015-after-all.html; and Terrorist Designation of Denis Cuspert, US Department of State, February 9, 2015, https://www.state.gov/j/ct/rls/other/ des/266538.htm.

9. See Woods and Serle, "Hostage Deaths Mean."

7. COUNTERINSURGENCY COMES HOME

1. Sewell Chan, "Shootings in Dallas, Minnesota and Baton Rouge: What We Know," *New York Times*, July 8, 2016, http://www.nytimes.com/2016/07/09/us/ dallas-attacks-what-we-know-baton-rouge-minnesota.html; and Henry Fountain and Michael S. Schmidt, "'Bomb Robot' Takes Down Dallas Gunman, but Raises Enforcement Questions," *New York Times*, July 8, 2016, http://www .nytimes.com/2016/07/09/science/dallas-bomb-robot.html.

2. Noah Feldman, "Crime Scenes and Weapons of War," *Bloomberg View*, July 11, 2016, http://www.bloomberg.com/view/articles/2016-07-11/crime -scenes-and-weapons-of-war.

3. Ibid.

4. One can get a good sense of this by reading the contributions to *Life During Wartime: Resisting Counterinsurgency*, eds. Kristian Williams, Will Munger, and Lara Messersmith-Glavin (Oakland, CA: AK Press, 2013), which addresses the domestication of counterinsurgency.

5. Niraj Chokshi, "Militarized Police in Ferguson Unsettles Some; Pentagon Gives Cities Equipment," *Washington Post*, August 14, 2014, https://www .washingtonpost.com/politics/militarized-police-in-ferguson-unsettles-some -pentagon-gives-cities-equipment/2014/08/14/4651f670-2401-11e4-86ca-6f03cbd 15c1a_story.html.

6. Matt Apuzzo, "War Gear Flows to Police Departments," *New York Times*, June 8, 2014, https://www.nytimes.com/2014/06/09/us/war-gear-flows-to-police -departments.html; "MRAPs And Bayonets: What We Know About The Penta- gon's 1033 Program," NPR, September 2, 2014, www.npr.org/2014/09/02/342494225 /mraps-and-bayonets-what-we-know-about-the-pentagons-1033-program; and Shane Bauer, "The Making of the Warrior Cop," *Mother Jones*, October 2014, http://www.motherjones.com/politics/2014/10/swat-warrior-cops-police -militarization-urban-shield.

7. "Obama Administration Military Surplus Review," *Congressional Digest* 94, no. 2 (February 2015): 4. MAS Ultra—School Edition, EBSCOhost, accessed May 12, 2017.

8. Radley Balko, *Rise of the Warrior Cop: The Militarization of America's Police Forces* (New York: Public Affairs, 2013), 333.

9. Chokshi, "Militarized Police."

10. Alex Horton, "In Iraq, I Raided Insurgents. In Virginia, the Police Raided Me," *Washington Post*, July 24, 2015, https://www.washingtonpost.com/ opinions/in-iraq-i-raided-insurgents-in-virginia-the-police-raided-me/2015/07 /24/2e114e54-2b02-11e5-bd33-395c05608059_story.html.

11. See Urbandictionary.com, top definition of *swatting*.

12. Jason Fagone, "The Serial Swatter: Internet Trolls Have Learned to Ex- ploit Our Over-Militarized Police," *New York Times*, November 24, 2015, https://www.nytimes.com/2015/11/29/magazine/the-serial-swatter.html.

13. NPR, "North Dakota Legalizes Armed Police Drones," August 27, 2015, http://www.npr.org/sections/thetwo-way/2015/08/27/435301160/north-dakota -legalizes-armed-police-drones; and Police Foundation, "New Publication— Community Policing & Unmanned Aircraft Systems (UAS): Guidelines to En- hance Community Trust," https://www.policefoundation.org/new-publication -community-policing-unmanned-aircraft-systems-uas-guidelines-to-enhance -community-trust/.

14. Redditt Hudson, "I'm a Black Ex-Cop, and This Is the Real Truth About Race and Policing," *Vox*, July 7, 2016, http://www.vox.com/2015/5/28/8661977/ race-police-officer.

15. Jack Maple and Chris Mitchell, *The Crime Fighter: Putting the Bad Guys Out of Business* (New York: Doubleday, 1999), 31, 7.

16. J. Edgar Hoover memo, August 25, 1967, quoted in Bloom and Martin, *Black Against Empire*, 201. Although the "COIN" in the neologism COINTEL- PRO was not literally intended to mean "counterinsurgency," the family resem- blance was striking. For a discussion of some of the similarities, see Walidah Imarisha and Kristian Williams, "COINTELPRO TO COIN: Claude Marks Interviewed," in *Life During Wartime*, 27–43.

17. Hoover expressly viewed the Panthers as insurgents. He perceived them through the lens of the armed anticolonial revolutionary movements. And in fact, some members of the Panthers were in fact Maoist and did support

revolutionary liberation movements in Africa and Asia. When Eldridge Cleaver fled the United States to Algeria in 1968 and inaugurated the international section of the Black Panther Party, Cleaver would align the international section with the liberation movements in Algeria, North Korea, North Vietnam, and China. But what matters here is not so much their politics, as the fact that Hoover *perceived* the Panthers as insurgents—identifying them with the liberation movements around the globe. In fact, Hoover viewed the Panthers as, in his own words, "the greatest threat to the internal security of the country." Bloom and Martin, *Black Against Empire*, 3; and Wolin, *The Wind from the East*, 14.

18. J. Edgar Hoover memo, March 1968, quoted in Bloom and Martin, *Black Against Empire*, 202. It was particularly important to the FBI to discredit the Panthers, given the popularity of the Panthers' social programs, such as the Free Breakfast for Children program—programs intended to serve the communities and inspired, in part, by Maoist ideals and strategies.

19. Frank Trippett, "It Looks Just Like a War Zone," *Time*, June 24, 2001, http://content.time.com/time/magazine/article/0,9171,141842,00.html.

20. Charles F. Sabel and William H. Simon, "The Duty of Responsible Administration and the Problem of Police Accountability" (working paper in author's possession, September 22, 2015).

21. Bernard E. Harcourt, *Illusion of Order: The False Promise of Broken-Windows Policing* (Boston: Harvard University Press, 2001).

22. Ibid.; Sabel and Simon, "The Duty," 27–28.

23. Maple and Mitchell, *The Crime Fighter*, 31.

24. Sabel and Simon, "The Duty," 28.

25. For all these references, see Maple and Mitchell, *The Crime Fighter*, 31, 79, 135–138, 144, 178, 222, and 242.

26. Ibid., 31.

27. Sabel and Simon, "The Duty," 33, 36, and 40. Problem-oriented policing is closely associated with the Wisconsin law professor Herman Goldstein, who spelled out the principles of his approach in a book, *Problem-Oriented Policing* (New York: McGraw Hill, 1990).

28. Sabel and Simon, "The Duty," 41.

29. Heather Mac Donald, "The New Nationwide Crime Wave," *Wall Street Journal*, May 29, 2015, http://www.wsj.com/articles/the-new-nationwide-crime-wave-1432938425.

30. *Guardian*, https://www.theguardian.com/us-news/ng-interactive/2015/jun/01/the-counted-police-killings-us-database; and *Washington Post*, https://www.washingtonpost.com/graphics/national/police-shootings-2016/.

31. Elizabeth Hinton, *From the War on Poverty to the War on Crime: The Making of Mass Incarceration in America* (Cambridge, MA: Harvard University Press, 2016).

32. National Weed and Seed Program, US Department of Justice, https:// www.ojjdp.gov/pubs/gun_violence/sect08-e.html.

8. SURVEILLING AMERICANS

1. FM, 79.

2. Galula, *Pacification in Algeria*, 72.

3. Apuzzo and Goldman, "With CIA Help"; "Highlights of AP's Pulitzer Prize–winning probe into NYPD intelligence operations," Associated Press (with links to stories and documents), https://www.ap.org/about/awards-and -recognition/highlights-of-aps-pulitzer-prize-winning-probe-into-nypd -intelligence-operations; and Ryan Devereaux, "Judge Who Approved Expand-ing NYPD Surveillance of Muslims Now Wants More Oversight," *The Intercept*, November 7, 2016, https://theintercept.com/2016/11/07/judge-who-approved -expanding-nypd-surveillance-of-muslims-now-wants-more-oversight.

4. "Target of Surveillance," https://www.ap.org/about/awards-and -recognition/highlights-of-aps-pulitzer-prize-winning-probe-into-nypd -intelligence-operations.

5. "Nov. 22, 2006 NYPD Weekly MSA Report," https://www.ap.org/about/ awards-and-recognition/highlights-of-aps-pulitzer-prize-winning-probe-into -nypd-intelligence-operations.

6. "April 25, 2008 Deputy Commissioner's Briefing," https://www.ap.org/ about/awards-and-recognition/highlights-of-aps-pulitzer-prize-winning -probe-into-nypd-intelligence-operations.

7. "April 25, 2008 Deputy Commissioner's Briefing," https://www.ap.org/ about/awards-and-recognition/highlights-of-aps-pulitzer-prize-winning -probe-into-nypd-intelligence-operations.

8. "Sept. 25, 2007 Newark, N.J. Demographics Report," 48 and 50, https:// www.ap.org/about/awards-and-recognition/highlights-of-aps-pulitzer-prize -winning-probe-into-nypd-intelligence-operations.

9. Apuzzo and Goldman, "With CIA Help."

10. DOI's Inspector General for NYPD, "An Investigation."

11. See Handschu v. NYPD, case no. 1:71-cv-02203-CSH-SCS, "Ruling on Proposed Settlement Agreement," document 465 filed October 28, 2016 (opin-ion tracing history of *Handschu* and *Raza* litigation), https://www.aclu.org/legal -document/raza-v-new-york-handschu-court-ruling-proposed-revisions -handschu-guidelines; and "Raza v. City of New York—Legal Challenge to NYPD Muslim Surveillance Program," ACLU, March 6, 2017, https://www.aclu .org/cases/raza-v-city-new-york-legal-challenge-nypd-muslim-surveillance -program.

12. See Mark Hensch, "Trump Won't Rule Out Database, Special ID for Mus-lims in US," *The Hill*, November 19, 2015, http://thehill.com/blogs/ballot-box/ presidential-races/260727-trump-wont-rule-out-database-special-id-for

-muslims; and Dean Obeidallah, "Donald Trump's Horrifying Words About Muslims," CNN, November 21, 2015, http://www.cnn.com/2015/11/20/opinions /obeidallah-trump-anti-muslim/.

13. Hensch, "Trump Won't Rule."

14. "The US Attorney's Letter," CNN, November 27, 2001, http://www.cnn .com/2001/US/11/27/inv.questioning.letters/; see generally "Hundreds in Michigan Asked to Submit to 'Terror Questioning,'" CNN, November 28, 2001, http://edition.cnn.com/2001/US/11/27/inv.michigan.interviews/index.html; Mitch Frank, "Feds and Cops at Odds over Terror Investigation," *Time*, November 29, 2001, http://content.time.com/time/nation/article/0,8599,186383,00 .html; and Jodi Wilgorennov, "A Nation Challenged: The Interviews; Michigan 'Invites' Men From Mideast to Be Interviewed," *New York Times*, November 27, 2001, http://www.nytimes.com/2001/11/27/us/nation-challenged-interviews -michigan-invites-men-mideast-be-interviewed.html.

15. Julia Angwin et al., "AT&T Helped US Spy on Internet on a Vast Scale," *New York Times*, August 15, 2015, http://www.nytimes.com/2015/08/16/us/ politics/att-helped-nsa-spy-on-an-array-of-internet-traffic.html.

16. Statement of President Obama on the USA FREEDOM Act, https://www .whitehouse.gov/the-press-office/2015/06/02/statement-president-usa-freedom-act.

17. Alan Yuhas, "NSA Reform: USA FREEDOM Act Passes First Surveillance Reform in Decade—As It Happened," *Guardian*, June 2, 2015, http://www .theguardian.com/us-news/live/2015/jun/02/senate-nsa-surveillance-usa -freedom-act-congress-live.

18. Mark Hosenball and Patricia Zengerle, "US Lawmakers Warn Proposed Changes Could Doom Spy Bill," Reuters, June 1, 2015, http://www.reuters.com/ article/2015/06/02/usa-security-surveillance-congress-idUSL1N0YN23X20150602.

19. The President's Review Group on Intelligence and Communications Technologies et al., *The NSA Report: Liberty and Security in a Changing World* (Princeton, NJ: Princeton University Press, 2014), 118 and 119n118, report available at https://obamawhitehouse.archives.gov/blog/2013/12/18/liberty-and -security-changing-world.

20. Quoted in David Cole, "Can the NSA Be Controlled?," *New York Review of Books*, June 19, 2014, 16.

9. TARGETING AMERICANS

1. Thomas C. Greene, "Database Snafu puts US Senator on Terror Watch List," *The Register*, August 19, 2004, http://www.theregister.co.uk/2004/08/19/ senator_on_terror_watch; Sara Kehaulani Goo, "Faulty 'No-Fly' System Detailed," *Washington Post*, October 9, 2004, http://www.washingtonpost.com/wp -dyn/articles/A18735-2004Oct8.html; and "In First, Government Officially Tells ACLU Clients Their No Fly List Status," ACLU, October 10, 2014, https://www .aclu.org/news/first-government-officially-tells-aclu-clients-their-no-fly-list

-status?redirect=national-security/first-government-officially-tells-aclu-clients
-their-no-fly-list-status.

2. Jeremy Scahill and Ryan Devereaux, "The Secret Government Rulebook
For Labeling You a Terrorist," *The Intercept*, July 23, 2014, https://theintercept
.com/2014/07/23/blacklisted/; Steve Kroft, "Unlikely Terrorists On No Fly List,"
CBS, October 8, 2006, http://www.cbsnews.com/news/unlikely-terrorists-on
-no-fly-list/; US Department of Justice Office of the Inspector General Audit
Division, "Follow-up Audit of the Terrorist Screening Center," September 2007,
https://oig.justice.gov/reports/FBI/a0741/final.pdf; Jamie Tarabay, "No-Fly List:
FBI Says It's Smaller Than You Think," NPR, Morning Edition, January 26,
2011, http://www.npr.org/2011/01/26/133187841/the-no-fly-list-fbi-says-its
-smaller-than-you-think; Jeremy Scahill and Ryan Devereaux, "Barack Obama's
Secret Terrorist-Tracking System, by the Numbers," *The Intercept*, August 5,
2014, https://theintercept.com/2014/08/05/watch-commander/; Michelle Ye
Hee Lee, "Democrats' Misleading Claims about Closing the No-Fly List 'Loop-
hole,'" *Washington Post*, December 11, 2015, https://www.washingtonpost.com
/news/fact-checker/wp/2015/12/11/democrats-misleading-claims-about
-closing-the-no-fly-list-loophole/; and Stephen Dinan, "FBI No-Fly List Revealed: 81,000 Names, but Fewer than 1,000 Are Americans," *The Washington
Times*, June 20, 2016, http://www.washingtontimes.com/news/2016/jun/20/fbi
-no-fly-list-revealed-81k-names-fewer-1k-us/. In addition, over six thousand
United States citizens or permanent residents are on a separate Terrorist Watch
List.

3. Jennifer Gonnerman, "Fighting for the Immigrants of Little Pakistan,"
New Yorker, June 25, 2017, http://www.newyorker.com/magazine/2017/06/26/
fighting-for-the-immigrants-of-little-pakistan; Ziglar v. Abbasi, 582 U.S. __
(United States Supreme Court, June 19, 2017), https://www.supremecourt.gov/
opinions/16pdf/15-1358_6khn.pdf (detailing allegations by 84 detainees of solitary confinement, strip searches, sleep deprivation, and physical and verbal
abuse, including wall slamming, broken bones, sexual humiliation, and other
physical and mental abuse, see slip opinion at p.4).

4. Gonnerman, "Fighting for the Immigrants of Little Pakistan"; Maia Jachi-
mowicz and Ramah McKay, "'Special Registration' Program," *Migration Information Source*, April 1, 2003, http://www.migrationpolicy.org/article/special
-registration-program#2a.

5. Chicago attorney Thomas Durkin has been litigating this issue strenu-
ously in the Daoud case. See generally U.S. v. Daoud Seventh Circuit Opinion,
755 F.3d 479 (7th Cir. 2014); Patrick Toomey and Brett Max Kaufman, "The
Notice Paradox: Secret Surveillance, Criminal Defendants, & the Right to Notice," *Santa Clara Law Review* 54 (2015): 844–900; and William C. Banks, "Pro-
grammatic Surveillance and FISA: Needles in Haystacks," *Texas Law Review* 88
(2010): 1633–667.

6. Christopher Ingraham, "Republican Lawmakers Introduce Bills to Curb Protesting in at Least 18 States," *Washington Post*, February 24, 2017, https://www.washingtonpost.com/news/wonk/wp/2017/02/24/republican-lawmakers -introduce-bills-to-curb-protesting-in-at-least-17-states/.

7. Evan Osnos, "The Imam's Curse: A Family Accused of Financing Terrorists," *New Yorker*, September 21, 2015, 50.

8. Ibid., 52.

9. Ibid., 52 and 56.

10. Ibid., 52.

11. Ibid., 53 and 56.

12. Ibid., 54.

13. Ibid., 55.

14. Ibid., 58 and 56.

15. Manny Fernandez and Christine Hausersept, "Handcuffed for Making Clock, Ahmed Mohamed, 14, Wins Time With Obama," *New York Times*, September 16, 2015, http://www.nytimes.com/2015/09/17/us/texas-student-is -under-police-investigation-for-building-a-clock.html; Matthew Teague, "Ahmed Mohamed Is Tired, Excited to Meet Obama—and Wants His Clock Back," *Guardian*, September 17, 2015, http://www.theguardian.com/us-news /2015/sep/17/ahmed-mohamed-is-tired-excited-to-meet-obama-and-wants-his -clock-back; Sebastian Murdock, "Police Knew Ahmed Didn't Have A Bomb, Arrested the Teen Anyway," *Huffington Post*, September 18, 2015, http://www .huffingtonpost.com/entry/ahmed-mohamed-police-not-bomb _55fc4510e4b08820d9187013; and Joanna Walters, "Texas Teen Arrested Over Homemade Clock Gets It Back Days Before Leaving US in New York," *Guardian*, October 24, 2015, http://www.theguardian.com/us-news/2015/oct/24/texas -teen-ahmed-mohamed-gets-homemade-clock-back.

16. Lauren Gambino, "Ahmed Mohamed Meets Sudanese President with Whom Father Had Rivalry," *Guardian*, October 16, 2015, http://www .theguardian.com/world/2015/oct/16/ahmed-mohamed-sudan-president-omar -al-bashir-texas-clock.

17. MSNBC Live interview, available at Murdock, "Police Knew Ahmed."

18. Jeffrey Fagan and Bernard Harcourt, "Fact Sheet in Richmond County (Staten Island) Grand Jury in Eric Garner Homicide," http://www.law.columbia .edu/social-justice/forum-on-police-accountability/facts/faqs-eric-garner; Sandhya Somashekhar and Kimbriell Kelly, "Was Michael Brown Surrendering or Advancing to Attack Officer Darren Wilson?," *Washington Post*, November 29, 2014, https://www.washingtonpost.com/politics/2014/11/29/b99ef7a8-75d3-11e4 -a755-e32227229e7b_story.html; Department of Justice, *Department of Justice Report Regarding the Criminal Investigation into the Shooting Death of Michael Brown by Ferguson, Missouri Police Officer Darren Wilson*, March 4, 2015, https://www.justice.gov/opa/pr/justice-department-announces-findings-two

-civil-rights-investigations-ferguson-missouri; Jeremy Gorner et al., "Most of Chicago Police Force Ordered into Uniform As City Prepares for Video Release," *Chicago Tribune,* November 24, 2015, http://www.chicagotribune.com/news/ local/breaking/ct-chicago-police-laquan-mcdonald-shooting-video-release -20151123-story.html; and Dan Good, "Chicago Police Officer Jason Van Dyke Emptied His Pistol and Reloaded As Teen Laquan McDonald Lay on Ground During Barrage; Cop Charged with Murder for Firing 16 times," *New York Daily News,* November 24, 2015, http://www.nydailynews.com/news/national/shot -laquan-mcdonald-emotionless-court-arrival-article-1.2445077.

19. Chris Hayes, *A Colony in a Nation* (New York: W.W. Norton & Company, 2017), 67.

20. Niraj Chokshi, "Militarized Police in Ferguson Unsettles Some" (see especially video "What Weapons Are Police Using in Ferguson?": https://www .washingtonpost.com/politics/militarized-police-in-ferguson-unsettles-some -pentagon-gives-cities-equipment/2014/08/14/4651f670-2401-11e4-86ca -6f03cbd15c1a_story.html?utm_term=.985b860733da); Paul D. Shinkman, "Ferguson and the Militarization of Police: Camo-Clad Snipers Trained on Michael Brown Protesters Elicits Concern from Americans, Including Iraq, Afghanistan Vets," *US News & World Report,* August 14, 2014, https://www .usnews.com/news/articles/2014/08/14/ferguson-and-the-shocking-nature-of -us-police-militarization; and for descriptions of these weapons and their dissemination in police forces around the country, see Apuzzo, "War Gear Flows to Police Departments."

21. Hayes, *A Colony in a Nation,* 69.

22. Ibid., 83.

23. Ibid., 31 and 76.

24. Section 3(c) of Executive Order 13769 states that "the immigrant and nonimmigrant entry into the United States of aliens from countries referred to in section 217(a)(12) of the INA, 8 U.S.C. 1187(a)(12), would be detrimental to the interests of the United States," and it therefore "suspend[s] entry into the United States, as immigrants and nonimmigrants, of such persons for 90 days from the date of this order." The seven countries that fit the criteria in 8 U.S.C. § 1187(a)(12) include Iraq, Iran, Libya, Somalia, Sudan, Syria, and Yemen. See also State of Washington v. Donald J. Trump et al., No. 17-35105, Order on Motion for Stay of an Order (9th Cir. February 9, 2017), slip opinion at 3-5.

25. Jennifer Gonnerman, "A Syrian Doctor with a Visa Is Suing the Trump Administration," *New Yorker,* February 1, 2017, http://www.newyorker.com/news /news-desk/a-syrian-doctor-with-a-visa-is-suing-the-trump-administration. Thomas Durkin, Robin Waters, and I represented Dr. Al Homssi. After filing a federal lawsuit, Dr. Al Homssi was allowed to reenter the country. See Jennifer Gonnerman, "A Syrian Doctor Returns to Illinois," *New Yorker,* February 2, 2017, http://www.newyorker.com/news/news-desk/a-syrian-doctor-returns-to-illinois.

26. Glenn Kessler, "The Number of People Affected by Trump's Travel Ban: About 90,000," *Washington Post*, January 30, 2017, https://www.washingtonpost .com/news/fact-checker/wp/2017/01/30/the-number-of-people-affected-by -trumps-travel-ban-about-90000/?utm_term=.a5924c5718b4.

27. "Donald J. Trump Statement on Preventing Muslim Immigration," December 7, 2015, formerly online at https://www.donaldjtrump.com/press -releases/donald-j.-trump-statement-on-preventing-muslim-immigration; and Christine Wang, "Trump Website Takes Down Muslim Ban Statement After Reporter Grills Spicer in Briefing," CNBC, May 8, 2017, http://www.cnbc.com /2017/05/08/trump-website-takes-down-muslim-ban-statement-after-reporter -grills-spicer-in-briefing.html.

28. Exhibits 2 and 3 to the complaint filed by the State of Washington in State of Washington v. Donald Trump et al., Civ. Action # 2:17-cv-00141, Complaint for Declaratory and Injunctive Relief filed on January 30, 2017; and Elina Saxena, "Highlights from the 6th GOP Presidential Debate," *Lawfare*, January 15, 2016, https://www.lawfareblog.com/highlights-6th-gop-presidential -debate.

29. Haeyoun Park, "Millions Could Be Blocked From Entering the US Depending on How Trump Would Enforce a Ban on Muslim Immigration," *New York Times*, December 22, 2016, https://www.nytimes.com/interactive/2016/07 /22/us/politics/trump-immigration-ban-how-could-it-work.html; Greg Sargent, "Is This a 'Muslim Ban'? Look at the History—and at Trump's Own Words," *Washington Post*, January 31, 2017, https://www.washingtonpost.com /blogs/plum-line/wp/2017/01/31/is-this-a-muslim-ban-look-at-the-history-and -at-trumps-own-words; Exhibit 4 to complaint filed by the State of Washington in State of Washington v. Donald Trump et al., Civ. Action # 2:17-cv-00141.

30. See Exhibit 5 to complaint filed by the State of Washington in State of Washington v. Donald Trump et al., Civ. Action # 2:17-cv-00141, video at https://www.c-span.org/video/?4139771/donald-trump-delivers-foreign-policy -address, remarks at 50:46.

31. Tim Brown, "President Trump: We're Going to Help Persecuted Christians," *Washington Standard*, January 28, 2017, http://thewashingtonstandard .com/president-trump-going-help-persecuted-christians/.

32. See complaint at https://www.cairflorida.org/newsroom/press-releases /769-cair-complaint-for-injunctive-and-declaratory-relief-and-jury-demand -challenging-trump-s-executive-orders.html.

33. Mark Berman, "Donald Trump Says Muslims Should Report Suspicious Activity. The FBI Says They Already Do," *Washington Post*, October 9, 2016, https://www.washingtonpost.com/politics/2016/live-updates/general-election/ real-time-fact-checking-and-analysis-of-the-2nd-2016-presidential-debate/ donald-trump-says-muslims-should-report-suspicious-activity-the-fbi-says -they-already-do/?utm_term=.bc6266442833; Mark Hensch, "Trump Won't

Rule Out Database, Special ID for Muslims in US," *The Hill*, November 19, 2015, http://thehill.com/blogs/ballot-box/presidential-races/260727-trump-wont -rule-out-database-special-id-for-muslims; and Dean Obeidallah, "Donald Trump's Horrifying Words About Muslims," *CNN*, November 21, 2015, http:// www.cnn.com/2015/11/20/opinions/obeidallah-trump-anti-muslim/.

34. Trump v. Hawai'i, 582 U.S. __, Order in Pending Case No. 16-1540 (US July 19, 2017), https://www.supremecourt.gov/orders/courtorders/071917zr_o7jp.pdf.

35. Chamayou discusses this very astutely from pages 67 to 72 of his book *A Theory of the Drone*. See also Sitaraman, *The Counterinsurgent's Constitution*, 32–34.

36. Chamayou, *A Theory of the Drone*, 68.

37. Ibid.

10. DISTRACTING AMERICANS

1. Andrew J. Bacevich, "He Told Us to Go Shopping. Now the Bill Is Due," *Washington Post*, October 5, 2008, http://www.washingtonpost.com/wp-dyn/ content/article/2008/10/03/AR2008100301977.html.

2. "President Bush's News Conference," *New York Times*, December 20, 2006, http://www.nytimes.com/2006/12/20/washington/20text-bush.html.

3. Andrew Sullivan, "I Used to Be a Human Being," *New York* magazine, September 18, 2016, http://nymag.com/selectall/2016/09/andrew-sullivan -technology-almost-killed-me.html.

4. Evgeny Morozov, *The Net Delusion: The Dark Side of Internet Freedom* (New York: PublicAffairs, 2012).

5. Joseph Lawless has written a remarkable text on the dating application Grindr in relation to questions of torture and confession. See Joseph Lawless, "The Viral Inquisition of the HIV-Positive Body: Theorizing the Technologies of Torture and Confession on Grindr," http://columbia.academia.edu/ JosephLawless.

6. Sullivan, "I Used to Be a Human Being."

7. Ibid.; Sally Andrews et al., "Beyond Self-Report: Tools to Compare Estimated and Real-World Smartphone Use," *PLOS ONE*, October 28, 2015, https:// doi.org/10.1371/journal.pone.0139004; and Carolyn Gregoire, "You Probably Use Your Smartphone Way More Than You Think. Many Young Adults Spend a Third of Their Waking Lives on Their Device," *Huffington Post*, November 2, 2015, http://www.huffingtonpost.com/entry/smartphone-usage-estimates_us _5637687de4b063179912dc96 .

8. Bernard E. Harcourt, "The Invisibility of the Prison in Democratic Theory: A Problem of 'Virtual Democracy,'" *The Good Society* 23, no. 1 (2014): 6–16; and Harcourt, *Exposed*, 253–261.

9. Stephen Battaglio, "First Clinton-Trump Matchup Breaks Presidential Debate Record with 84 Million TV Viewers," *Los Angeles Times*, September 27,

2016, http://www.latimes.com/entertainment/envelope/cotown/la-et-ct-debate-ratings-20160927-snap-story.html.

10. Van Jones, "Trump: The Social Media President?," CNN, October 26, 2015, http://www.cnn.com/2015/10/26/opinions/jones-trump-social-media/.

11. Nick Gass, "Trump Wins Night on Search and Social," *Politico*, January 29, 2016, http://www.politico.com/blogs/live-from-des-moines/2016/01/donald-trump-social-search-engine-218391#ixzz41Zf7yD2d.

12. Kimberly Alters, "Donald Trump's Social Media Strategy? 'Be Associated with Interesting Quotes,'" *The Week*, February 28, 2016, http://theweek.com/speedreads/609090/donald-trumps-social-media-strategy-associated-interesting-quotes.

13. Van Jones, "Trump: The Social Media President?"

14. Taylor Weatherby, "'Damn Daniel' Star Recreates His Viral Video with Ellen DeGeneres—Watch," *Hollywood Life*, February 23, 2016, http://hollywoodlife.com/2016/02/23/damn-daniel-ellen-degeneres-interview-viral-video/.

15. "Damn Daniel" official video, https://youtu.be/tvk89PQHDIM.

16. Taylor Weatherby, "'Damn Daniel': Rappers Create Epic Song After Video Goes Viral—Listen," *Hollywood Life*, February 21, 2016, http://hollywoodlife.com/2016/02/21/damn-daniel-song-rap-viral-video-listen/; and "Damn Daniel! RAP SONG! Little Feat. Teej & LeBlanc (ORIGINAL)," https://www.youtube.com/watch?v=CjlUVvGGE5A.

17. "Suhmeduh—Damn Daniel Trap Remix (Official)," https://www.youtube.com/watch?v=gP2ejq9Qp6o#t=43.

18. Alyssa Montemurro, "Justin Bieber & 6 Other Celebs Rocking the White Vans Like 'Damn, Daniel,'" *Hollywood Life*, February 26, 2016, http://hollywoodlife.com/2016/02/26/celebrities-wearing-white-vans-damn-daniel-shoes-pics/.

19. Katie Rogers, "We Should Probably Have a Conversation About 'Damn, Daniel,'" *New York Times*, February 25, 2016, http://www.nytimes.com/2016/02/26/style/damn-daniel-video-vans.html.

20. Beth Shilliday, "Damn Daniel Petrified He Might Get 'Swatted' Like Joshua Holz After Newfound Fame," *Hollywood Life*, February 26, 2016, http://hollywoodlife.com/2016/02/26/damn-daniel-swatting-viral-video-teen-afraid/.

21. "Damn Daniel! RAP SONG! Little Feat. Teej & LeBlanc (ORIGINAL)."

22. Trinquier, *Modern Warfare*, 24 and 25.

23. Paret, *French Revolutionary Warfare*, 5.

24. Paret and Shy, *Guerrillas in the 1960's*, 19.

25. Greenberg and Dratel, eds., *The Torture Papers*, 134 (Memo 11, dated February 7, 2002).

11. THE COUNTERREVOLUTION IS BORN

1. It is The Counterrevolution, and not the revolution, this time around, that seems to have been "inwardly working ever forward," to borrow Hegel's words;

and, defying Marx's prediction, it is the advent of The Counterrevolution that might prompt us to respond, this time perplexedly, "Well grubbed, old mole!" History has perhaps reversed itself, or we are one step closer to the next stage— or, as I suggest in conclusion, we face an endless struggle against recurring forms of tyranny. G.W.F. Hegel, *Lectures on the History of Philosophy* vol. 3, trans. E. S. Haldane and Frances H. Simson (New York: The Humanities Press, 1974), 547; Karl Marx, *The Eighteenth Brumaire of Louis Bonaparte*, in *The Marx-Engels Reader*, 2nd ed., ed. Robert C. Tucker (New York: W.W. Norton & Company, 1978), 606; cf. William Shakespeare, *Hamlet*, ed. Sylvan Barnet, 2nd rev. ed. (New York: Signet Classics, 1998), act 1, scene 5, p. 33.

2. Sharon Lafraniere, Sarah Cohen, and Richard A. Oppel Jr., "How Often Do Mass Shootings Occur? On Average, Every Day, Records Show," *New York Times*, December 2, 2015, https://www.nytimes.com/2015/12/03/us/how-often -do-mass-shootings-occur-on-average-every-day-records-show.html; Sharon Lafraniere, Daniela Porat, and Agustin Armendariz, "A Drumbeat of Multiple Shootings, but America Isn't Listening," *New York Times*, May 22, 2016, https:// www.nytimes.com/2016/05/23/us/americas-overlooked-gun-violence.html.

3. Richard Stengel, "Why Saying 'Radical Islamic Terrorism' Isn't Enough," *New York Times*, February 13, 2017, https://www.nytimes.com/2017/02/13/ opinion/why-saying-radical-islamic-terrorism-isnt-enough.html.

4. Tim Arango, "Iran Dominates in Iraq After US 'Handed the Country Over,'" *New York Times*, July 15, 2017, https://www.nytimes.com/2017/07/15/ world/middleeast/iran-iraq-iranian-power.html; David Leigh, "Iraq War Logs Reveal 15,000 Previously Unlisted Civilian Deaths—Leaked Pentagon Files Contain Records of More than 100,000 Fatalities Including 66,000 Civilians," *Guardian*, October 22, 2010, https://www.theguardian.com/world/2010/oct/22 /true-civilian-body-count-iraq; and Gilbert Burnham et. al, "Mortality After the 2003 Invasion of Iraq: A Cross-sectional Cluster Sample Survey," *The Lancet*, October 11, 2006, https://web.archive.org/web/20150907130701/http:// brusselstribunal.org/pdf/lancet111006.pdf.

5. They even create domestic terrorists through aggressive sting operations that invent and make possible plots that would never have arose; as the federal judge in the "Newburgh Four" case writes, a case involving four Muslim men in upstate New York, the FBI "came up with the crime, provided the means, and removed all relevant obstacles," and thereby entrapped someone "whose buffoonery is positively Shakespearean in scope." David K. Shipler, "Terrorist Plots, Hatched by the F.B.I.," *New York Times*, April 28, 2012, http://www.nytimes .com/2012/04/29/opinion/sunday/terrorist-plots-helped-along-by-the-fbi.html; and Human Rights Watch and Columbia Law School's Human Rights Institute, "Illusion of Justice: Human Rights Abuses in US Terrorism Prosecutions," July 21, 2014, https://www.hrw.org/report/2014/07/21/illusion-justice/human-rights -abuses-us-terrorism-prosecutions.

6. Stengel, "Why Saying 'Radical Islamic Terrorism' Isn't Enough."

7. See FM, xv–xvi; and Broadwell, *All In,* 351. As Paula Broadwell writes in her official biography of Petraeus, "Petraeus and Mattis teamed up to draft the new *Counterinsurgency Field Manual* in 2006." On the social network of soldier-scholars, see Laleh Khalili, "The New (and Old) Classics of Counterinsurgency," *Middle East Report* 255 (2010), http://www.merip.org/mer/mer255/khalili.html.

8. Peter Baker, "Trump Chooses H. R. McMaster as National Security Adviser," *New York Times*, February 20, 2017, https://www.nytimes.com/2017/02/20/us/politics/mcmaster-national-security-adviser-trump.html.

9. "H. R. McMaster: 5 Fast Facts You Need to Know," *Heavy*, February 20, 2017, http://heavy.com/news/2017/02/h-r-mcmaster-donald-trump-national-security-adviser-wife-career-bio-age-who-is-books-flynn/.

10. "President Trump's Taxpayer First Budget," The White House, https://www.whitehouse.gov/taxpayers-first; Binyamin Appelbaum and Alan Rappeport, "Trump's First Budget Works Only if Wishes Come True," *New York Times*, May 22, 2017, https://www.nytimes.com/2017/05/22/us/politics/budget-spending-federal-deficit.html; Gregor Aisch and Alicia Parlapiano, "How Trump's Budget Would Affect Every Part of Government," *New York Times*, May 23, 2017, https://www.nytimes.com/interactive/2017/05/23/us/politics/trump-budget-details.html?q=refugee%20programs; Erica L. Greenmay, "Trump's Budget, Breaking Tradition, Seeks Cuts to Service Programs," *New York Times*, May 25, 2017, https://www.nytimes.com/2017/05/25/us/politics/trump-budget-americorps-peace-corps-service.html; and Zachary Cohen, "Trump Proposes $54 Billion Defense Spending Hike," CNN, March 16, 2017, http://www.cnn.com/2017/03/16/politics/donald-trump-defense-budget-blueprint/index.html.

11. Arlette Saenz, "President Trump tells ABC News' David Muir He 'Absolutely' Thinks Waterboarding Works," *ABC News*, January 25, 2017, http://abcnews.go.com/Politics/president-trump-tells-abc-news-david-muir-absolutely/story?id=45045055; Republican presidential debate, *ABC News*, https://www.youtube.com/watch?v=Upnc_y1cKEk; Charlie Atkin, "Donald Trump Quotes: The 10 Scariest Things the Presumptive Republican Nominee Has Ever Said," *Independent,* May 6, 2016, http://www.independent.co.uk/us/donald-trump-quotes-the-10-scariest-things-the-presumptive-republican-nominee-has-ever-said-a7015236.html; and Charlie Savage, "Obama Policies Give Successor a Path to Vast Security Powers," *New York Times*, November 14, 2016, A1, https://www.nytimes.com/2016/11/14/us/politics/harsher-security-tactics-obama-left-door-ajar-and-donald-trump-is-knocking.html.

12. Donald J. Trump, "Flashback: I Will Do Whatever It Takes, Trump Says," *USA Today*, February 15, 2016, http://www.usatoday.com/story/opinion/2016/02/15/donald-trump-torture-enhanced-interrogation-techniques-editorials-debates/80418458/.

13. Berman, "Donald Trump Says Muslims,"; "Donald Trump's Muslim Ban Is Back Up on His Website," *AOL News*, November 11, 2016, https://www.aol

.com/article/news/2016/11/11/donald-trump-s-muslim-ban-is-back-up-on-his
-website/21604038/; Michelle Ye Hee Lee, "Donald Trump's False Comments
Connecting Mexican Immigrants and Crime," *Washington Post*, July 8, 2015,
https://www.washingtonpost.com/news/fact-checker/wp/2015/07/08/donald
-trumps-false-comments-connecting-mexican-immigrants-and-crime/?utm
_term=.815e72ec4e59; and Savage, "Obama Policies Give Successor a Path to
Vast Security Powers."

14. Hensch, "Trump Won't Rule Out Database."

15. David A. Fahrehhold, "Trump Recorded Having Extremely Lewd Conversation About Women in 2005," *Washington Post*, October 7, 2016, https://
www.washingtonpost.com/politics/trump-recorded-having-extremely-lewd
-conversation-about-women-in-2005/2016/10/07/3b9ce776-8cb4-11e6-bf8a
-3d26847eeed4_story.html; and Matt Baume, "The Top Ten Worst Comments
Donald Trump Has Made About LGBTQ people," *LGBTQ Nation*, February 4,
2016, https://www.lgbtqnation.com/2016/02/the-top-ten-worst-comments
-donald-trump-has-made-about-lgbtq-people/.

16. Nonprofit VOTE and US Elections Project, "America Goes to the Polls: A
Report on Voter Turnout, 2016 Presidential Elections," http://www.nonprofitvote
.org/america-goes-to-the-polls-2016/; "Presidential Results," CNN, "Election
2016," http://www.cnn.com/election/results/president.

17. Hannah Arendt, *The Origins of Totalitarianism* (New York: Harcourt,
Brace & World, 1966), vii (emphasis added).

18. Samuel Moyn, "Why the War on Terror May Never End," *New York
Times Book Review*, June 24, 2016, http://www.nytimes.com/2016/06/26/books
/review/spiral-by-mark-danner.html.

12. A STATE OF LEGALITY

1. Proclamation 7463—Declaration of National Emergency by Reason of
Certain Terrorist Attacks, September 14, 2001; see also Executive Order 13223
of September 14, 2001, "Ordering the Ready Reserve of the Armed Forces to
Active Duty and Delegating Certain Authorities to the Secretary of Defense and
the Secretary of Transportation"; and Greenberg and Dratel, eds., *The Torture
Papers*, 25 (Military Order of November 13, 2001).

2. Greenberg and Dratel, eds., *The Torture Papers*, 134 (Memo 11, dated February 7, 2002).

3. Oona Hathaway and Scott Shapiro, "Schmitt at Nuremberg," in *The Worst
Crime of All: The Paris Peace Pact and the Beginning of the End of War* (working
paper in author's possession, September 16, 2015), 12–13 and 22.

4. Hathaway and Shapiro, 22, quoting from *Third Reich Sourcebook*, 64.

5. Carl Schmitt, *Political Theology: Four Chapters on the Concept of Sover-
eignty*, trans. George Schwab (Chicago: University of Chicago Press, 2006), 5.

6. Carl Schmitt, *The Concept of the Political*, trans. George Schwab (1932;
repr. Chicago: University of Chicago Press, 2007); and Carl Schmitt, *Dictatorship* (1921; repr. Polity Press, 2013).

7. Hathaway and Shapiro, 19, quoting from Bernd Rüthers, "On the Brink of Dictatorship—Hans Kelsen and Carl Schmitt at Cologne 1933," in *Hans Kelsen and Carl Schmitt: A Juxtaposition*, eds. Dan Diner and Michael Stolleis (Gerlingen: Bleicher, 1999).

8. Giorgio Agamben, *State of Exception*, trans. Kevin Attell (Chicago: University of Chicago Press, 2005), 2, 20, 87, and 23.

9. Ibid., 86 and 4.

10. Michael Hardt and Antonio Negri, *Multitude* (London: Hamish Hamilton, 2005), 7. Hardt and Negri had already used the concept in *Empire*, describing the "right to intervention" as stemming from "a permanent state of emergency and exception justified by the appeal to essential values of justice." Michael Hardt and Antonio Negri, *Empire* (Cambridge: Harvard University Press, 2000), 18.

11. Judith Butler, "Guantánamo Limbo," *The Nation*, March 14, 2002, https://www.thenation.com/article/Guantánamo-limbo/; see also Judith Butler, *Precarious Life: The Powers of Mourning and Violence* (London: Verso, 2004).

12. Slavoj Žižek, "Are We In a War? Do We Have an Enemy?," *London Review of Books*, May 23, 2002, 3–6, http://www.lrb.co.uk/v24/n10/slavoj-zizek/are-we-in-a-war-do-we-have-an-enemy.

13. Thomas Anthony Durkin, "Permanent States of Exception: A Two-Tiered System of Criminal Justice Courtesy of the Double Government Wars on Crime, Drugs & Terror," *Valparaiso University Law Review* 50 (2016): 419–492, http://scholar.valpo.edu/vulr/vol50/iss2/3; and Kim Lane Scheppele, "Law in a Time of Emergency: States of Exception and the Temptations of 9/11," *University of Pennsylvania Journal of Constitutional Law* 6 (2004): 1001–1083, http://papers.ssrn.com/sol3/papers.cfm?abstract_id=611884.

14. Eric Posner and Adrian Vermeule, "Should Coercive Interrogation Be Legal?," *Michigan Law Review* 104 (2006): 671–707; Eric Posner and Adrian Vermeule, "Demystifying Schmitt," in *The Oxford Handbook of Carl Schmitt*, eds. Jens Meierhenrich and Oliver Simons (New York: Oxford University Press, 2017); John Yoo, *War by Other Means: An Insider's Account on the War on Terror* (New York: Atlantic Monthly Press, 2006); and see generally Yoo memos in Greenberg and Dratel, eds., *The Torture Papers*.

15. Bruce Ackerman, "The Emergency Constitution," *Yale Law Journal* 113 (2004): 1030, 1037, and 1044, http://www.yalelawjournal.org/essay/the-emergency-constitution. For an in-depth discussion of the exception in American constitutionalism, see Thomas P. Crocker's book manuscript, *Overcoming Necessity: Emergency, Constraint, and the Meanings of American Constitutionalism*.

16. Fareed Zakaria, "End the War on Terror and Save Billions," *Washington Post*, December 6, 2012, https://www.washingtonpost.com/opinions/fareed-zakaria-end-the-war-on-terror-and-save-billions/2012/12/06/a468db2a-3fc4-11e2-ae43-cf491b837f7b_story.html.

17. Scott Horton, "State of Exception: Bush's War on the Rule of Law," *Harper's Magazine*, July 2007, http://users.clas.ufl.edu/burt/Renaissancetragedy/

Harpers.pdf; see also Scott Horton, "Benjamin—History and the State of Exception," *Harper's Magazine*, May 14, 2010, http://harpers.org/blog/2010/05/benjamin-history-and-the-state-of-exception/.

18. See also Mark Danner, "After September 11: Our State of Exception," *London Review of Books*, October 13, 2011, http://www.nybooks.com/articles/archives/2011/oct/13/after-september-11-our-state-exception/; and David C. Unger, *The Emergency State: America's Pursuit of Absolute Security at All Costs* (New York: Penguin Books, 2013). Unger argues that presidents since World War II have inflated external threats in order to justify the creation of an "emergency state," which not only expands the powers of the executive branch and erodes civil liberties, but is also ineffective at protecting the nation.

19. The relationship between democracy and war, though, is complex, and for a nuanced discussion that explores the role of collective decision-making in rendering violence legitimate, see Christopher Kutz, *On War and Democracy* (Princeton: Princeton University Press, 2016).

20. Galula, *Counter-insurgency Warfare*, 56. I am by no means the first or only one to resist the framework of the state of exception. The historian Samuel Moyn also rejects the notion of exception, arguing that what we face today is a more restrained and humane war without end—we face what Moyn refers to as "a new form of humane warfare simultaneously without boundaries in time and space." Samuel Moyn, "Why the War on Terror May Never End," *New York Times Book Review*, June 24, 2016, http://www.nytimes.com/2016/06/26/books/review/spiral-by-mark-danner.html. Fleur Johns vehemently rejects the understanding of Guantánamo Bay as a domain of sovereign exception, arguing instead that Guantánamo is "an instance of the norm struggling to overtake the exception." (Fleur Johns, "Guantánamo Bay and the Annihilation of the Exception," *European Journal of International Law* 16, no. 4 (2005): 614–615, http://www.ejil.org/pdfs/16/4/311.pdf. Naser Hussain, in the pages of *Critical Inquiry*, contends that, rather than unique or exceptional, "many of the mechanisms and justifications we find there are continuous and consonant with a range of regular law and daily disciplinary state practices, in particular, the domains of immigration and domestic incarcerations—the difference being one more of degree than kind." (Naser Hussain, "Beyond Norm and Exception: Guantánamo," *Critical Inquiry* (2007), http://www.jstor.org/stable/10.1086/521567). Others as well criticize the turn to exception as an explanatory mechanism. See, for example, Venator Santiago, "From the Insular Cases to Camp X-Ray: Agamben State of Exception and United States Territorial Law," *Studies in Law, Politics, and Society* 15, no. 5 (a critical account of Agamben's use of the state of exception, especially in the United States). But none, to the best of my knowledge, have proposed the framework of counterinsurgency warfare.

21. Michel Foucault, *The Punitive Society: Lectures at the Collège de France, 1972–1973*, ed. Bernard E. Harcourt (New York: Palgrave, 2015), 144; and see generally the discussion of illegalisms in the "Course Context," in Ibid., 281–293.

22. Ibid., 156, 146, and 149.

23. For a similar argument in the context of the death penalty, see Cass R. Sunstein and Adrian Vermeule, "Is Capital Punishment Morally Required? Acts, Omissions, and Life-Life Tradeoffs," *Stanford Law Review* 58, no. 3 (April 2010): 703.

24. Quoted in Greenberg, *Rogue Justice*, 221.

25. Robert M. Cover, *Justice Accused: Antislavery and the Judicial Process* (New Haven: Yale University Press, 1984).

26. Robert Weisberg, "De-regulating Death," *Supreme Court Review* (1983): 305–395.

27. Senate Report, 19.

28. Greenberg, *Rogue Justice*, 252, 266, and 7.

29. National Defense Authorization Act (NDAA), quoted in Ibid., 206.

30. Greenberg, *Rogue Justice*, 206.

31. See Wadie E. Said, *Crimes of Terror: The Legal and Political Implications of Federal Terrorism Prosecutions* (New York: Oxford University Press, 2015); and Jameel Jaffer, introduction to *The Drone Memos: Targeted Killing, Secrecy, and the Law*, ed. Jameel Jaffer (New York: The New Press, 2016). For a fascinating critical theory and historical engagement with the notion of the rule of law, see Keally McBride, *Mr. Mothercountry: The Man Who Made the Rule of Law* (New York: Oxford, 2016).

32. Eric Holder, quoted in Greenberg, *Rogue Justice*, 206.

33. The American Constitution Society workshop, "Charlie Savage on the National Security State," Thursday, November 12, 2015, Jerome Greene Hall 102A, Columbia University.

34. Greenberg, "From Fear to Torture," xvii–xx, at xvii.

35. Memo to Commander, Joint Task Force 170 at Guantánamo Bay, October 11, 2002, signed by Diane E. Beaver, in Greenberg and Dratel, eds. *The Torture Papers*, 229.

36. Sitaraman, *The Counterinsurgent's Constitution*, 240.

37. Michel Foucault, *Abnormal: Lectures at the Collège de France, 1974–1975*, eds. Valerio Marchetti and Antonella Salomoni (London and New York: Verso, 2004), 117 and 129; Michel Foucault, "About the Concept of the 'Dangerous Individual' in 19th Century Legal Psychiatry," *International Journal of Law and Psychiatry* 1 (1978): 1–18.

13. A NEW SYSTEM

1. Bruce L. R. Smith, *The RAND Corporation: Case Study of a Nonprofit Advisory Corporation* (Cambridge: Harvard University Press, 1966), 6–7.

2. In the United Kingdom, where OR largely originated, it was called "operational research." This definition is from the Operational Research Society of Great Britain, *Operational Research Quarterly* 13, no. 3 (1962): 2822, http://www .wata.cc/forums/uploaded/136_1167433681.pdf. For a history of Operations

Research, see Maurice W. Kirby, *Operational Research in War and Peace: The British Experience from the 1930s to 1970* (London: Imperial College Press 2003); and S. M. Amadae, *Rationalizing Capitalist Democracy: The Cold War Origins of Rational Choice Liberalism* (Chicago: University of Chicago Press, 2003).

3. *Operational Research Quarterly* 13, no. 3 (1962): 282.

4. Edward S. Quade, *Systems Analysis Techniques for Planning-Programming-Budgeting* (Santa Monica: RAND Corporation, 1966), 3.

5. Smith, *The RAND Corporation*, 8.

6. Quade, *Systems Analysis Techniques*, 9.

7. Ibid., 10–11.

8. Ibid., 28.

9. On McNamara, see Deborah Shapley, *Promise and Power: The Life and Times of Robert McNamara* (Boston: Little, Brown and Company, 1993); John A. Byrne, *The Whiz Kids: Ten Founding Fathers of American Business—and the Legacy They Left Us* (New York: Doubleday, 1993); and H. R. McMaster, *Dereliction of Duty: Lyndon Johnson, Robert McNamara, the Joint Chiefs of Staff, and the Lies that Led to Vietnam* (New York: Harper Collins, 1997). I sketched some of this history in my previous book *Exposed*, 153–156, and there are excellent histories of the birth of systems analysis, see especially Amadae, *Rationalizing Capitalist Democracy.*

10. Quade, *Systems Analysis Techniques*, 2.

11. United States General Accounting Office, *Survey of Progress in Implementing the Planning-Programming-Budgeting System in Executive Agencies; Report to the Congress* (Washington, DC, 1969), 4.

12. Quade, *Systems Analysis Techniques*, 2.

13. James R. Schlesinger, "Quantitative Analysis and National Security," *World Politics* 15, no. 2 (1963): 295–316, at 314.

14. See generally, W. Kip Viscusi and Joseph E. Aldy, "The Value of a Statistical Life: A Critical Review of Market Estimates throughout the World," NBER (working paper no. 9487, February 2003), 54–56, www.nber.org/papers/w9487 .pdf.

15. See President Carter's executive order E.O. 12044 (tasking all executive agencies with the duty to conduct economic impact studies of all major government regulations); President Reagan's executive order E.O. 12291 (assigning the responsibility to the Office of Management and Budget); and President Bill Clinton's 1996 executive order E.O. 12866 (on the "Economic Analysis of Federal Regulations").

16. The President's Review Group on Intelligence and Communications Technologies et al., *The NSA Report: Liberty and Security in A Changing World* (Princeton: Princeton University Press, 2014), 50–53, https://obamawhitehouse .archives.gov/blog/2013/12/18/liberty-and-security-changing-world.

17. Paret and Shy, *Guerrillas in the 1960's*, 3.

18. Marlowe, *David Galula*, 12.

19. Paret and Shy, *Guerrillas in the 1960's*, 3–4 and 4n3; Marlowe, *David Galula*, 13; and see generally Kristian Williams, introduction to *Life During Wartime: Resisting Counterinsurgency*, eds. Kristian Williams, Will Munger, and Lara Messersmith-Glavin (Oakland, CA: AK Press, 2013).

20. It is important to emphasize here—and it is somewhat remarkable—that Galula's seminal book, *Pacification in Algeria 1956–1958*, was originally published in English. In other words, it was originally published in translation, and only decades later published in its original French. This is true as well of his more theoretical treatise, *Counterinsurgency: Theory and Practice*. A French translation of *Counterinsurgency* appeared through the publishing house Economica in 2008; and a French translation of *Pacification in Algeria* was only published in 2016 by the publishing house Les Belles Lettres—which is mostly known for its ancient and classical texts, like the Loeb editions. That's rare and remarkable in the publishing business, and it reflects the influence of RAND and the extent to which RAND shaped the discourse on counterinsurgency.

21. See Marlowe, *David Galula*, 9.

22. Martin A. Lee and Bruce Shlain, *Acid Dreams: The CIA, LSD, and the Sixties Rebellion* (New York, Grove Press, Inc., 1985), 196–197.

23. Gompert and Gordon, *War by Other Means*, iii. The 2008 report created a number of other byproduct studies, including among others: *Byting Back—Regaining Information Superiority Against 21st-Century Insurgents: RAND Counterinsurgency Study*, vol. 1, by Martin C. Libicki et al.; *Counterinsurgency in Iraq (2003–2006): RAND Counterinsurgency Study*, vol. 2, by Bruce Pirnie and Edward O'Connell; *Heads We Win—The Cognitive Side of Counterinsurgency (COIN): RAND Counterinsurgency Study*, paper 1, by David C. Gompert; *Subversion and Insurgency: RAND Counterinsurgency Study*, paper 2, by William Rosenau; *Understanding Proto-Insurgencies: RAND Counterinsurgency Study*, paper 3, by Daniel Byman; *Money in the Bank—Lessons Learned from Past Counterinsurgency (COIN) Operations: RAND Counterinsurgency Study*, paper 4, by Angel Rabasa et al.; and *Rethinking Counterinsurgency—A British Perspective: RAND Counterinsurgency Study*, paper 5, by John Mackinlay and Alison al-Baddawy. See Gompert and Gordon, *War by Other Means*, vi–vii.

24. Gompert and Gordon, *War by Other Means*, vii.

25. There has also been a revolving door between the institutions: James Schlesinger, for instance, the former CIA director and secretary of defense, was a strategic analyst at the RAND Corporation, and Henry Rowen, who served as president of RAND, previously headed up the CIA's National Intelligence Command. Other lower-level agents and researchers would also go back and forth between the institutions. See generally Lee and Shlain, *Acid Dreams*, 197; and Valtin, "CIA, RAND Ties Muddy APA Torture 'Investigation,'" Daily Kos, June 7, 2015, http://www.dailykos.com/story/2015/06/07/1391345/-CIA-RAND-Ties

-Muddy-APA-Torture-Investigation ("Douglas Valentine in his book, *The Phoenix Project*, describes how top CIA Phoenix official, Robert "Blowtorch" Komer, left the Agency to work for RAND in 1970").

26. FM, 141–142.

27. FM, 142.

28. Ibid.

29. Cora Currier, "Blowing the Whistle on CIA Torture from Beyond the Grave," *The Intercept*, October 17, 2014, https://firstlook.org/theintercept/2014 /10/17/blowing-whistle-cia-torture-beyond-grave/; see also Scott Gerwehr, "Letter to the Editor: States of Readiness: Do New Threats Loom?; Stopping Terror," *New York Times*, October 1, 2001 ("The writer is a policy analyst specializing in deception and psychological operations at the RAND Corporation"), http:// www.nytimes.com/2001/10/01/opinion/l-states-of-readiness-do-new-threats -loom-stopping-terror-439100.html; Scott Gerwehr and Nina Hachigian, "In Iraq's Prisons, Try a Little Tenderness," *New York Times*, August 25, 2005, http:// www.nytimes.com/2005/08/25/opinion/in-iraqs-prisons-try-a-little-tenderness .html; Valtin, "CIA, RAND Ties"; "Shocking: 2003 CIA/APA 'Workshop' Plots New Torture Plans," *Invictus*, May 26, 2007, http://valtinsblog.blogspot.com /2007/05/shocking-2003-ciaapa-workshop-plots-new.html#.VYGMSUtq61w; and Tamsin Shaw, "The Psychologists Take Power," *New York Review of Books*, February 25, 2016, http://www.nybooks.com/articles/2016/02/25/the -psychologists-take-power/.

30. Valtin, "CIA, RAND Ties."

31. "Shocking: 2003 CIA/APA." The report and list of attendees of the 2003 workshop are available online here: https://www.documentcloud.org/documents /2065302-scienceofdeceptionworkshopreport.html.

32. Currier, "Blowing the Whistle on CIA Torture."

33. It is clear as well that RAND has had a significant role and its involvement in the systematic development of counterinsurgency theory continues to the present. Still today, RAND has an extensive list of current publications on counterinsurgency, which remains one of its important axes of research. See, for example, http://www.rand.org/pubs/monographs/MG595z5.html.

34. See, for example, Timothy Kudo, "How We Learned to Kill," *New York Times*, February 27, 2015: "Throughout the past century, military social systems and training evolved to make humans less reluctant to take a life"; "The madness of war is that while this system is in place to kill people, it may actually be necessary for the greater good"; "To fathom this system and accept its use for the greater good is to understand that we still live in a state of nature."

OCKHAM'S RAZOR, OR, RESISTING THE COUNTERREVOLUTION

1. William of Ockham, *Epistola ad fratres minores* in *Opera Politica*, vol. 3, 1–17, eds. Ralph Francis Bennett and Hilary Seton Offler (Manchester:

Manchester University Press, 1956), at p. 6; and see William of Ockham, *Court traité du pouvoir tyrannique*, trans. Jean-Fabien Spitz (Paris: Presses Universitaires de France, 1999), 4.

2. William of Ockham, *Breviloquium de principatu tyrannico,* in *Opera Politica*, vol. 4, 97–260, ed. Hilary Seton Offler (Oxford: Oxford University Press, 1997), bk. 1, chap. 4, p. 102 ("*Admonendi sunt subditi, ne plus quam expedit sint subiecti*"). Ockham is here quoting Pope Gregory. This is my translation. A more historically and theoretically faithful translation would be "subjects should be admonished not to be subjected more than is asked of them," with the Latin term *admonendi* rendered closer to the notion of forewarned, advised, instructed, and the Latin term *subiecti* rendered closer to the concept of subjectification. The latter is very close to the Foucaultian notion of *assujettissement*. However, in contemporary American English, the notion of subjectification is too rarified and the term admonished now too close to punishment. In addition, in the present political context, the meaning of *subiecti* comes close to the more forceful concept of subjugation; so to help readers understand the passage, I decided to strike a more modern balance. The Cambridge edition reads: "Subjects should be urged not to be more subject than is useful" (William of Ockham, *A Short Discourse on Tyrannical Government*, trans. John Kilcullen, ed. Arthur Stephen McGrade (Cambridge: Cambridge University Press, 1992), 9. The French edition translates the papal quotation as "*les sujets doivent être avertis de ne pas être assujettis plus qu'il n'est nécessaire*" (William of Ockham, *Court traité du pouvoir tyrannique*, trans. Jean-Fabien Spitz (Paris: Presses Universitaires de France, 1999), 102.

3. William of Ockham, bk. 2, chap. 3, p. 115, in *Breviloquium*; Ockham, *Court traité du pouvoir tyrannique*, 120–121; and Ockham, *A Short Discourse on Tyrannical Government*, 23–24.

4. Ockham, bk. 2, chap. 3, p. 114–115, in *Breviloquium*; Ockham, *Court traité du pouvoir tyrannique*, 119; and Ockham, *A Short Discourse on Tyrannical Government*, 22.

5. Michel Foucault, *Qu'est-ce que la critique?*, eds. Henri-Paul Fruchaud and Daniele Lorenzini (Paris: Vrin, 2015), 37; and Michel Foucault, *Théories et institutions pénales*, ed. Bernard E. Harcourt (Paris: Gallimard/Le Seuil, 2015).

6. Ockham, bk. 1, chap. 4, p. 102, in *Breviloquium* ("*subiectionem autem nimiam cavere non possunt, nisi sciant quam et quantam super eos praesidens habeat potestatem*"). A more literal and historical translation might be "subjects cannot be attentive to excessive subjection unless they know of what kind and to what extent the one who presides over them (*praesidens*, as in the one who is on top of them) exercises power over them." The use of *praesidens* here, related of course to the term *president*, is pregnant. For other translations, see Ockham, *Court traité du pouvoir tyrannique*, 102 ("*Or ils ne peuvent se défier de la sujétion excessive, à moins de savoir quelle est la nature et l'étendue du pouvoir que celui qui est à leur tête possède sur eux*"); and Ockham, *A Short Discourse on*

Tyrannical Government, 9 ("But they cannot be on guard against excessive subjection unless they know what and how much power their superior has over them").

7. See the Bureau of Investigative Journalism, "Drone Warfare"; and see also Pitch Interactive, "Out of Site, Out of Mind," http://drones.pitchinteractive.com/.

8. "Ce qu'il y a de plus scandaleux dans le scandale c'est qu'on s'y habitue." See Judith Surkis, "Ethics and Violence: Simone de Beauvoir, Djamila Boupacha, and the Algerian War," special issue, *French Politics, Culture & Society* 28, no. 2 (Summer 2010): 38–55, quote at 38.

9. Pierre Vidal-Naquet, *La Torture dans la République* (Paris: La Découverte/Maspero, 1975); Vidal-Naquet, *L'Affaire Audin* (Paris: Les Éditions de Minuit, 1958). In particular, Vidal-Naquet took on the cause of Marcel Audin, in reports and pamphlets denouncing what he would call his "assassination" (Vidal-Naquet, *L'Affaire Audin*, 100). Many years later, Aussaresses would confess to ordering the killing of Audin. See http://www.francetvinfo.fr/france/video-les-aveux-posthumes-du-general-aussaresses-on-a-tue-audin_500432.html.

10. See his famous article, "The Question," *L'Express*, January 15, 1955; cf. Stora, *Algeria 1830–2000*, 51.

11. Stora, *Algeria 1830–2000*, 50; and see generally, Jean Charles Jauffret, *Ces officiers qui ont dit non à la torture, Algéries 1954–1962* (Paris: Éditions Autrement, 2005).

INDEX

Abe, Shinzo, 189
"Abnormal" (Foucault), 231–232
Abu Ghraib, 72, 117, 118, 205
Acid Dreams (Lee and Shlain), 241
Ackerman, Bruce, 220
ACLU. *See* American Civil Liberties
    Union
active minorities, police as, 135–136
active minorities, surveillance of. *See*
    minorities, surveillance of
    active
Adorno, Theodor, 85
advertising, 160
    digital, 96–97, 153–154, 194
    domestication of
        counterinsurgency warfare
        and, 182, 187
    profiling, 191, 194
Afghanistan, 3, 10, 61, 81–82, 93–95,
    164
Africa, 20, 25, 27, 48
Africa, John, 138
African Americans, 12, 136–137, 203,
    253
    police and, 11, 132, 138, 142, 171
    targeting of, 13, 118, 146
Agamben, Giorgio, 75–76, 119,
    217–218, 221
Ahmed, Ali, 148
Aikins, Matthieu, 94

Al Qaeda, 126
Alabama Supreme Court, 109, 110
Alfonso X of Castile, 106–107
Alger républicain (newspaper), 43
Algeria, 25, 28, 45, 47, 79, 102, 117
    counterinsurgency warfare in, 20,
        24, 31, 46
    disappearances in, 41, 44
    torture in, 38–39, 40, 43, 48, 63
Alleg, Henri, 43, 103, 114–116
allegiance, of population, 8, 25,
    31–32, 37, 89
    See also population, winning
        hearts and minds of
Amazon, 95, 96, 97, 153, 154, 187
American Civil Liberties Union
    (ACLU), 59, 149, 254
American Muslims
    NYPD and, 4–5, 6, 147–151, 150
        (photo)
    targeting of, 11, 13, 14, 174–178
    See also Muslims
American Psychological Association,
    244
AmeriCorps, 29
Anderson, Tanisha, 171
Anemone, Louis, 139, 140
Angwin, Julia, 282
AOL, working with NSA, 4, 154
apathy, voting and, 188–189

Bernard E. Harcourt is the Isidor and Seville Sulzbacher Professor of Law and Professor of Political Science at Columbia University. The author of several books, including *The Illusion of Free Markets* and *Exposed*, he lives in New York City.